SPEAK FOR YOUR <u>SELF</u>

Julia Cummings-Wing

SPEAK FOR YOUR <u>SELF</u>
An Integrated Method of Voice and Speech Training

Nelson-Hall nh Chicago

Illustrations by Michael Wright Stockton.

LIBRARY OF CONGRESS CATALOGING IN PUBLICATION DATA

Cummings-Wing, Julia.
  Speak for your self.

  Includes index.
  1. Voice culture.   2. Speech.   I. Title   II. Title:
Speak for yourself.
PN4162.C78   1984   808.5   83-26862
ISBN 0-8304-1024-4 (cloth)
ISBN 0-88229-827-5 (paper)

Manufactured in the United States of America

10 9 8 7 6 5 4 3 2 1

The paper in this book is pH neutral (acid-free).

To
Mother and Laurie and Sheppard

Contents

Foreword

I HAVE BEEN A PROFESSIONAL actress for thirty-five years, and I have
never known how to breathe. Oh, breathe, as in sustaining life, yes, of
course, or I suppose I would not be writing this at all. But breathing, in
the sense of controlled vocal production in both my personal and professional lives, no, I never did that before meeting Dr. Julia C. Wing in
April of 1979. I was in the final rehearsal stage of a one-woman play,
Gertrude Stein Gertrude Stein Gertrude Stein, and petrified at the
thought of speaking without stop for two hours, much less acting *alone*
for that extensive time period. The *Stein* producer, Mary Ellyn Devery,
had heard of Dr. Wing's work at Temple University in Philadelphia and
had obtained her services for another show she was managing. She had
asked Dr. Wing to attend one of my run-throughs, so when an energetic
woman with sparkling eyes began speaking to me about the material, I
had a sneaking suspicion that this dynamo was *the* Dr. Wing. I urged her
to take notes on the second act, where I was having dreadful fatigue problems, tongue stumbles, and general vocal run-down. At the end of the
second act, Dr. Wing rushed up to me with pages of notes, suggestions,
and immediate first aid in the form of two breathing exercises. Since that
April, hardly a month goes by that I don't call Dr. Wing to question her
on a specific vocal problem; about every six months we have at least a
two-day session to reestablish correct vocal balance through breathing,
relaxation, and energization. It was a lucky day when my producer

thought to ask Dr. Wing to see my work, for three years later, after nearly seven hundred performances of this play, I have never missed a scheduled performance nor have I suffered any vocal problems.

Dr. Wing refers to the deep vocal muscles as "the power center," and she is that to those of us, professionals and students alike, who know how much she brings to her work — a deep understanding of what it is to present yourself to an audience, to struggle for that communication which actors, singers, speakers and teachers wish to achieve with groups of people. She knows what the nervous system can do to a person at such times and how necessary is the training to off-set the adrenalin and tension. She knows how focused energy can be the most relaxing (and at the same time, powerful) force in the world, helping you to ride over stumbling blocks and enabling you to communicate on any level, physical or psychic.

Dr. Wing is a teacher, a dedicated thinker who devotes her life to the highest degree of excellence. She would insist that you approach vocal work with a sense of how life-connected it is — not dull, boring "public speaking." She asks you to breathe to enhance your life, not just as a preparation for a speech before your local Kiwanis or gardening club, an opening night on Broadway, or a concert at Lincoln Center. She wants you to speak, to communicate. Let her help you find your own *power center*.

Pat Carroll

Preface

IN RECENT YEARS THERE HAS been a major shift in this country away from the "mumble-and-groan" stage speech that resulted from a gross misinterpretation of the Stanislavski method of actor training. This author is firmly in accord with the renewed enthusiasm for the use of intelligible speech by actors.

There has also been a tendency in much of the recent training and in several of the current popular texts in the field to separate the areas of voice and speech. This author does not hold that voice and speech are two separate areas of discipline.

The philosophy of this text supports the theory that the speaking voice is one unified event; that the area of voice and speech are inseparable and interdependent. In keeping with this philosophy, and with that of another recent trend in the use of holistic procedures in the fields of medicine and the development of human potential, this text also includes and integrates the study of the speaking voice with techniques of self-awareness, body and feeling life, relaxation and body energy, and mental energy and concentration.

Since the goal of all such training is the communication of meaning, the text also includes a section on word study — on the factors of allusion, figurative language, and imagery; on denotative, connotative, emotive, and cognitive meaning. Another section deals with the interpretative elements of phrasing and pauses, intonation and voice range, and the pitch, volume, and sound-duration factors of stressing key words.

Believing that, since speaking is a learned process, it can be relearned, we have attempted to establish an orderly procedure of structured units which build on each other and which lead to an integrated whole in the communication of intellectual and emotional meaning. Numerous diagrams and illustrations are included to assist the student in understanding both theoretical principles and practical exercises. Excerpts from play scripts are included for the workable application of word analysis and meaningful interpretation.

I am grateful to teachers, colleagues, and students along the way who have helped to formulate the principles of this book and who have helped to illuminate the effectiveness of their practical application.

·1·

INTRODUCTION:
Basic Considerations

THE SPEAKING VOICE IS AN extension of the self. It is the leading edge of individual identity—the audible expression of the personality. Vocal self-expression is an intricate, integrated behavior that can be destroyed by focusing too narrowly on small details, or improved slowly at best, but which can be readily changed by dwelling on large patterns of component parts. The speaking voice is best improved by treating mind, body, breathing, and "feeling" life as a unity and by letting work on one factor be reinforced, wherever possible, by integrating work on other factors. The speaking voice is not an aggregate of separate functions but an articulate whole which undergirds all analyses of separate functions. Separate functions derive their essential characteristics from the whole of which they are a part and can lose their identity when isolated from the whole. If we are to discover the ultimate mystery of the speaking voice, we must discover the pattern of the functions in relation to the whole.

To realize the dynamic speaking voice is to realize many elements simultaneously, and to ignore any of the elements decreases the effectiveness of an individual's potential for self-expression. There is no dynamic in a disembodied voice without feeling life and breath support, nor in a voice inhibited by excessive muscle tension, nor in a voice unfocused by the clarity of speech. The dynamic speaking voice involves many intricate factors and requires a combination of methods and integrated exercises to achieve. It is an expression of the body and the breath, of inner

1

thoughts and emotions, of all the aspects of behavior — instinct, perception, affection and memory, as well as the situation that calls forth the response. To get at the speaking voice we must get at the whole self; the dynamic speaking voice is a function of the entire organism.

Work to improve the speaking voice begins with self-awareness, and the best method of becoming aware of self is to stand outside and look objectively into one's own experience. Subjective observations limit, and generally distort, the facts and perceptions. The source of man's best achievements is his ability to see himself objectively and influence his own growth. As with Gestalt therapy, training in self-awareness emphasizes the importance of contacting one's immediate ongoing process here and now, since it is the tuning in to the immediate experience of what one is doing and feeling that is the control mechanism for change. It is the awareness of what we are actually doing and feeling when using the speaking voice that enables us to stop doing it and to direct our energies more effectively. To effect change means to be able to experience various parts of the body, to be able to recognize unnecessary tensions, to be aware of attitudes and feelings, and to be able to integrate all the working parts. Consciousness of self gives us the ability to see ourselves, to see ourselves as others see us, to see ourselves in relation to others and to better relate to them. The greater the awareness, the greater the self.

Along with increased self-awareness and the subsequent potential for change comes increased inner strength and self-control. Psychotherapist Rollo May has defined the self as the organizing function within the individual, and consciousness of self as that factor that actually expands our control of our lives by enabling us to realize our mistakes, understand our prejudices, make responsible decisions, and subsequently produce the capacity to be spontaneous and creative. For it is conscious awareness that can produce the rare insights that emerge from the subconscious and that give direction and meaning to our efforts.

Increased self-awareness means increased ability to live, to function, to change, and to grow. These functions take place within the self, as does the capacity for freedom to live, to function, to change, and to grow. And the greater the self-awareness, the greater the ability to acquire the wisdom to know how to live, to function, to change, and to grow.

Becoming aware of self also means becoming aware of the present moment — of the here-and-now. The more awareness one has of self, the more awareness one has of the present. The more awareness one has of self as the one who is acting in the present, the more awareness one has of the responsibility and the responsiveness to act. Much has been written on this subject and in relation to many different philosophies. The fundamental point to be made is that the here-and-now is the only reality we have. Most of us spend far too much time reflecting on the past and worrying about the future, and while we need to learn from the past and plan for the future it is both limiting and unreal to try to live in either of them. To try to live in the past or the future separates the self from reality and from the immediate awareness of the functioning of the self in the present that is the potential for growth. Living in the past or the future inhibits one's ability to confront present problems and responsibilities. Allowing the consciousness to dwell on "If only I had done this . . ." or "When the time comes . . ." is a subconscious dodge for doing nothing now. To be fully aware of responsibility and opportunity one must focus on the immediate present. To be fully alive one must be aware of one's presence in the present. Being fully alive to the self in the center of the present moment, which is in itself the dead center of reality, is an incredibly invigorating experience, and one that produces optimum understanding, energy, and the confidence to do what needs to be done.

Changes cannot be given to us by someone else. Changes have to be personally experienced and to experience change there must be a consciousness in which there is immediate perception. There is no immediate perception and change without total awareness in the immediate present. To effect a dynamic speaking voice one must develop moment-to-moment awareness and discipline of the thoughts, feelings, and actions that are involved.

Becoming aware of self means, first of all, becoming aware of the body. It has been said that it is not necessary to know the various materials and parts that go to make up a piano or a violin in order to play it. Possibly true. This statement has also been made regarding the speaking voice. This is not true. Some knowledge of the anatomy, physiology, and kinesthesia of the vocal and speech mechanism is essential to intelligent, effective usage. It is important to understand how rib and lung structure provide vocal energy, how the resonators provide vocal reinforcement and quality, and how the articulators provide focus and clarity of the spoken message. It is important to understand how proper body alignment frees the flow of breath, of energy, and of feeling life, and how the body and speaking voice reflect the psyche. And it is also important to understand how muscle tension can affect any or all of the above.

The ability to experience the speaking voice on the physical level is of central significance. The vocal self lives in the body and we must learn to deal with the body. We must be conscious of how we hold the body, how we move it, how it feels, and how it breathes. Keeping in close touch with the body is the means for self-adjustment of the speaking instrument. It also means increased perception and pleasure in its usage.

We must develop a positive body image. Far too many people hold a negative conception of the body and this has an adverse effect on the ability of the body to let go and to experience itself. A positive body image gives substance to the concept of a dynamic speaking voice.

Another important element involved in the experiencing of the speaking voice on the physical level is the forming of precise kinesthetic images, or what has been called "thinking the voice." This means developing the ability to think of a desirable voice quality in association with the physical sensation of muscle, feeling, and breathing action that produces it. This association of auditory image and physical sensation will help to carry thoughts into the physical process of speech and assure a firmer use of the voice and speech muscles.

The speaking voice is an expression of the body, of its health, its vitality, and its balance; and body awareness is the foundation of voice and speech consciousness.

As self-awareness also means perception of one's feelings, body awareness helps here, for feelings exist simultaneously on many levels. In fact, body awareness is basic to both the understanding and the expression of emotive life. Movement of the body muscles when speaking can help us to get in touch with the feelings that the words may be hiding. Feelings are involved with the voluntary muscles to the degree that an individual can willfully hold in a feeling by holding muscles tense. We frequently see this suppression of feeling manifested as high-chest breathing and limited voice production. Conversely, it is possible to produce a feeling by assuming the appropriate appearance of that feeling in the eyes, and in the muscles of the face and body, cooperative with the breath. Even though feeling and its bodily manifestation are generally produced simultaneously, we can produce a body action and thus indirectly produce a feeling. For body actions are subject to the direct control of will power and feelings are not. For instance, one can induce a feeling of confidence by holding the head high, and assuming the firm, straight posture, deep breathing, and determined facial expression associated with confidence, and this will be reflected in the speaking voice. For there is always more feeling life expressed in the speaking voice supported by proper body alignment and deep breathing. An individual can just as willfully, and with a great deal less effort, learn to release muscle tension, which also releases feeling life, and which in turn can be channeled into a vigorous, compelling speaking voice. The rewards are tremendous, for accompanying the energized voice is a marvelous state of well-being and of clarity. Increased feeling life is increased knowledge.

Lest it be misunderstood, we are not espousing the release of uncontrolled feelings that obstruct communication and have a deleterious effect on both speaker and listener. Any type of speech impeded by emotion is wrong for theater for it chokes and smothers the words. We are espousing the intelligible and audible projection of the speaking voice vitalized by controlled and appropriate feeling life.

Since physical awareness and activity are crucial to the release of feeling life and it is generally accepted that just about every feeling has a physical counterpart, it follows that change in either the physical domain or the affective domain is best accomplished by simultaneous change in both. This statement is not startling when we realize that we had this capability as babies and small children before the imposition of cultural taboos took their toll.

Breathing life may be considered the most important of all the factors of voice, for, indeed, all of the other factors depend on it. Breathing provides energy for body movement, is directly involved in our feeling life, and, in fact, is the beginning of body and feeling awareness. The more fully one breathes the more fully one lives.

The very naturalness of breathing seems to prevent people from considering it seriously and yet proper breathing is of vital importance to good health as well as to good voice. The function of the blood and of the circulatory system depend largely upon proper oxygenation in the lungs, as does the function of the digestive system and the nervous system. In fact, every organ and body part depends upon the blood for nourishment and improperly oxygenated blood has a harmful effect upon the entire body. When the body suffers a lack of oxygen nutrition, the digestive system cannot properly digest and assimilate food, the nervous system cannot properly generate, store, and transmit energy, and the respiratory system is weakened and is susceptible to disease. A dynamic speaking voice under such conditions would be impossible.

Yoga has contributed a great deal to the understanding and art of breathing and the yogic method uses many excellent exercises for cleansing the breath, vitalizing the nerves, stimulating the lung cells, and so forth. It also teaches that the complete, deeply centered breath acts as a massage agent for the gentle exercising and stimulation of the stomach, the liver, and other internal organs. In addition, Yoga teaches that correct breathing habits increase mental and spiritual growth, and that breath control is self-control.

Western culture recognizes that breathing expresses our inner state and, further, that quieting the breath is an excellent method for relaxing the mind and body. Simply focusing on the breathing process can foster relaxation. To just lie quietly and comfortably, letting the breath flow in and out with no attempt to control it, is soothing and rhythmically hypnotic.

Proper breathing is, of course, central to the production of human voice and speech for it must convey both the underlying feeling of the message and the logic and resonances of the words. For the speaker, the breath is the connection between the mind and the body, between the thought, the emotion, and the energy to project them. The simple intention of communicating an idea sends the breath down to the power center of energy and emotion which then sends it back up and out to the listener. When the breath goes down for energy, if there is feeling present the breath makes it available. This unbroken flow of energized and emotionalized breath, filling the resonators and precisely shaped by the articulators, is the essential condition of dynamic expression.

Just as it is necessary to learn how to use the body, so it is necessary to learn how to use the mind. It is our mental attitude toward what we are doing that determines in large measure just how well we do it. "There is nothing either good or bad, but thinking makes it so" is a pertinent Shakespearean quote. Emerson said, "A man is what he thinks about all day long." Lincoln said, "Most folks are about as happy as they make up their minds to be." And it could be added that most folks are about as successful as they make up their minds to be.

Certainly, thought is powerful. Any achievement, internal or external, must first happen in the mind. If every creation of the mind of man were removed from the earth we would be back living in trees, without benefit of clothes, houses, or automobiles. Such things as books and music, submarines and spaceships, computers and miracle drugs—in fact, all the artistic, scientific, and technological achievements that we enjoy—were first a thought in someone's mind.

This remarkable mind has two levels, the conscious mind that thinks and the subconscious mind that acts. Whatever one thinks with the conscious mind will be accepted and acted upon by the subconscious mind. How you think today can determine your tomorrow. Applied negatively, this principle is the cause of failure and frustration; applied positively it is the cause of success and happiness.

The conscious mind reasons things out and makes choices. The subconscious mind neither reasons things out nor makes choices but is remarkable in what it does do. When the conscious mind is asleep or occupied, the subconscious mind carries on the breathing, blood circulation, and other body functions through processes independent of the conscious mind. For the actor it is important to realize that the subconscious mind is the seat of emotion and intuition. It is the memory bank of thoughts and experiences. Freeing and using the subconscious mind is a significant principle of Stanislavski's advice to the actor. He states that it is through the conscious mind that we contact the subconscious mind, and that all truthful actions are a blending of the two. Also, as this author knows from personal experience, the subconscious mind has the capacity to communicate with another mind over a distance of miles. And relative to this study, the subconscious mind functions precisely to help bring personal desires to fruition. If it is given the right suggestions by the conscious mind it will cooperate in facilitating voice and speech improvement.

The exercises in this book must be performed with a positive mental attitude. Become objective about your self and your working progress; objectivity is impersonal, realistic, and broadening; subjectivity is personal, unrealistic and inhibiting. Know what you want to achieve and tell yourself that you are going to achieve it. There is no sense at all in going after something you don't want or that you know is wrong for you. Think about what you need and want to do and become aware of the part of self that keeps you from doing it. Then set up your objectives and go after them, positively, never negatively. Use the mind to help alter your perceptions of what voice is and then react to it. Use the positive mental intention to reach the members of the audience seated in the last row of the top balcony and the body will instinctively respond with deeper breathing, muscles in a firmer condition, and a smaller mouth opening so that pressure may build up behind the words.

And, by all means, use the practical expedient of the daily repetition of your positive thoughts. Repetition is a powerful force. It has been employed throughout history to effect some extraordinary phenomena. So that if you are blessed with a healthy body, and then apply the healthy mental expedient of telling yourself over and over again that your speaking voice is going to express what you want it to, it will. Since it is impossible to think of more than one thing at a time, you will be screening out defeating thoughts by the simple resource of focusing on positive ones.

Maintaining a constant, positive image of yourself as the speaker you want to be unifies the energies of breathing, of body, of feeling, and of awareness in the present, and this total involvement produces power and progress. "The fault, dear Brutus, is not in our stars, But in ourselves that we are underlings." It is the powerful force of self, organized and focused, that produces results. The difference between an artist and a great artist is that a great artist knows how to command attention and how to communicate, and that means "getting it all together."

We are opened to new perceptions, strengths, and possibilities when we allow ourselves to become totally involved in experiential activities that help to expand the personality and that contain within them the element of spontaneity, and therefore the possibility of change. The greatest opportunities for improvement in voice and speech are available when the emphasis is not on learning a body of facts, but on experiencing the speaking voice in every possible way, learning to communicate in a wide range of situations, roles, and relationships. Analyses should not be about what one *might* be doing, but about what one *is* doing.

In group work there should be positive reinforcement from immediate feedback. Intensely interactive dyads or small groups should consistently encourage individual members, and group members can learn from each other while reading or speaking aloud, or joining together in choral speaking materials that focus on specific factors of expression and interpretation. Barriers to effective communication can be broken down through the physical contact of such activities as back-slapping or head and back massages, and through encouragement to reveal more of the self through sharing bits of literature that contain personal philosophies or favored experiences.

There should be the constant challenge to, first, shed the inertia of old habits of anticipating and steering the speaking voice and, second, to free the speaking voice and let it go where it will, to reach out, to expand, to explore new possibilities. There should be the constant attempt to transcend one's own self-concept and to experience the impossible, allowing the self to burst through the restraining barriers of accumulated memories, conclusions, and reactions to the unrestricted field of discovery and creativity. And there should be the constant experiment of new interpretations to traditional written materials to discover fresh meaning and truthful expression. Such principles are the basis of this work, which embraces the use of techniques and the imagination to develop a new perception of the self, of the speaking voice, of the self as the speaking voice.

This book cannot teach you anything, nor can any other book or instructor. You learn by *doing* and *being*. The self is roused to an idea of itself through experiencing and through self-discovery, through total organic involvement. Success also requires order and focus, and this text tries to provide these essentials. If you open your self to the experience and the force of the activities, you can alter and expand your self-image. You can free and actualize your self by transcending your usual inertia, inhibitions and momentum. Your will to transcend familiar habits and perceptions is a powerful force. It will mold transcendent experiences and perceptions into realized potential, into the actualization of the total self. Will your self to concentrate on new upsurges of energy and experiential glimmerings so that they will become part of your behavior of being. Don't permit the matrix of improbability, your own inertia, and the momentum of your environment to deter you from functioning optimally; don't let it alienate you from your own experience and potential. Don't conform either to a static conception of your self, or to the determined opinions of others. Break out; experience; discover. To realize your full potential as an actor you must experience levels of being that transcend the modal level. Typical human experience is limited, fragmented, and separates you from your self. You must be self-assertive in your efforts to overcome any denigration of your right to feel, fantasize, and conceptualize your self as individual and whole. Complying with outside pressures can only reduce your experiences and opportunities to grow and change. The potential for transcendence is within you. Use your imagination and your will to concentrate your efforts to go beyond the expected, habitual possibility. Try for the unexpected. Persistently allow your self to discover, to be surprised, to rise above. Unify and focus all of the latent power within you to generate a new self-concept that will allow you to function optimally and dynamically. Develop your capability to perceive, to create, and to respond totally to every immediate moment. It is a significant part of an actor's talent that he experiences and communicates his entire, unified self.

· 2 ·

SELF-AWARENESS:
Body and Feeling Life

A DYNAMIC SPEAKING VOICE MEANS dynamic body life. You must become more aware of your body life and recognize that a healthy body is basic to effective self-expression. You must realize that an uptight or listless body can completely deny and defeat what your words are trying to communicate.

An actor has two basic means of communicating the life of his role: the way he speaks his lines, and the way he uses his body. And since the body houses the speaking voice, its energy and emotion, the implication is clear. The body is central in acting. It is central to the audience's understanding of the character the actor is portraying, and must, therefore, be freed of personal physical mannerisms and chronic muscle tension so that the character may be truthfully interpreted and communicated. The body is also central in that it must be kept in a healthy condition to support the arduous demands of acting. Complex studio work, long rehearsals, and the requirements of performance all make great demands on the body. Actors who play such commanding roles as King Lear or Blanche DuBois know this, and strengthen their bodies in preparation. Most serious acting students swim, play hand-ball, jog, or engage in other physical activities regularly, in addition to their physical studio work. Actors must keep their bodies healthy, strong, and flexible. They must learn to develop awareness of their body life and listen to the information it provides—telling them when the body is weak and needs strengthening, when the body is tense generally, telling them where the body tensions are specifically located, and when it is time to relax.

A dynamic speaking voice also means dynamic affective life. The actor must become aware of his feelings and recognize the central role they play in effective interpersonal relationships and communication, both on stage and off. A flat, emotionless voice can deny and defeat the intention of the actor's spoken words.

In achieving self-awareness, feelings often have to be rediscovered. Our knowledge of our feelings is never very specific and, in fact, feelings are too often considered as a thing apart. Either by training or by design feelings have been separated from the cognitive and physical domains and many actors have to struggle to regain affective awareness, and then have to struggle even harder to allow themselves to channel feeling life into their speaking performances. The affective domain must be incorporated as an integral part of the whole self and channeled into the speaking voice.

The actor, or anyone else who allows himself to feel, lives and functions with a heightened awareness. We must welcome and use our feeling life, just as we enjoy and use our body life. Happily, they are mutually supportive and dependent, one on the other. We can no more realize our feeling life without bodies, than we can appreciate our body life without feelings. In all of the exercises and experiential activities set out in this text, as well as in all of your studio and performance work, you must learn to develop and channel your feeling life. Let affective energy enrich and support the spoken text.

STRETCH-AND-YAWN

One of the best ways to become more aware of self by experiencing body and feeling life is to stretch and yawn, simultaneously and luxuriously. The stretch-and-yawn should be done slowly and sensuously, allowing ample time to fully enjoy the deep breathing occasioned by the yawns and the altered state of consciousness that results from discovering the inner feeling life. Enjoy the physical relaxation and the emotional pleasure of this expansive, tension-releasing experience. Stand tall and allow sufficient space to stretch in all directions. And as you stretch-and-yawn in slow motion, feel that the entire body is yawning as well as stretching. Inhale slow yawns and exhale audible sounds of pleasure as you easily stretch the arms and hands straight over the head; then, keeping the arms and hands straight over the head, bend from the waist and stretch first to the right and then to the left. Bending forward from the waist, stretch-and-yawn the arms and hands straight out in front, making one continuous flat line of the back and arms; and then, bending from the waist with the feet widely separated, stretch-and-yawn over first the right leg and then the left leg, allowing time to experience the deeply yawned breath all the way down to the bottom of the left lung when you are stretching over the right leg, and all the way down to the bottom of the right lung when you are stretching over the left leg. The amount of time required for this exercise will vary with the need; five minutes is usually sufficient, but it can be carried on longer.

The sheer relaxing enjoyment of freeing the muscles of unnecessary tensions and of experiencing the resultant free flow of deeply centered feeling and vocal life make this a rewarding activity. You can use it in every phase of your training — in studio work, rehearsals, or as part of a warm-up before performance. The experience of the activity has been described by students in various ways, but I especially like the expression of the student who said, "I feel like I'm letting myself out!" And this is, of course, exactly what you are doing. You feel when you are finished as if you are filling more space, and doing it dynamically. In fact, it is of benefit to enjoy the good feeling of the vitalized self for a long moment at the end of the exercise. This long, quiet moment will help to secure in the consciousness the new perception of the self as *being* rather than *doing,* of the energy and the power of the self in the immediate present. The eyes should be closed for the quiet moment, and then slowly opened and the altered consciousness of self should be maintained as visual stimuli are gradually included in the consciousness. If you are working with a group, you should continue to maintain the altered self perception as you momentarily look into the eyes of everyone in the group and share the feelings of heightened awareness in the present moment.

OPENING UP

Positive group dynamics play an important part in the productivity of any working community, whether composed of actors or non-actors, and an instructor, director, or group leader should help to facilitate comfortable relationships.

With a group meeting for the first time it is essential to establish a positive group feeling immediately by getting acquainted. To be free, and to be productive, individuals need to be able to let go of their defenses and to know that others are genuinely supportive of their efforts. It has been stated by many who work in the field of human potential that we acquire our self-concept largely from our relations with others, and that it is this self-concept that influences our verbal and non-verbal behavior towards others. Therefore, mutual support and trust is essential and should be immediately established if group members are to be productive and creative. Taking the time to share the present moment with others, as in the stretch-and-yawn experience above, is one way of breaking down barriers.

Learning and remembering people's names is another way of opening people up to themselves and each other. People should move about, taking time to greet everyone by holding their hands, smiling, and exchanging names. Each exchange should be lively, and should contain the dynamic of sharing the present moment with another person. When all in the group have greeted and been greeted in return, the group can then stand in a circle and have each member in turn name everyone else in the group. It is reassuring to have people remember your name, and this last part is both a good memory and a good listening exercise. The first part of the exercise, the greeting exchange, works well even with a group who already know each others' names. Each individual sharing of a moment with a smile and a greeting, serves as a clearing house for the mind and is a way of shedding irrelevant concerns and of bringing each person closer to the group project. Cohesiveness can be further strengthened by then having members form a tight circle, and with all the hands held together in a pile and with eyes closed, having each one allow himself to experience the group energy in the present. A couple of minutes is usually long enough for the group energy experience.

Another exercise for learning names at the introductory meeting of a new group or cast is to have everyone stand in a wide circle and then have each person in turn call out his or her first name; for instance, "I'm Joe!" The rest of the group will then respond by enthusiastically waving with both arms and hands and calling out, "Hello, Joe!" The vigorous verbal response and waving helps to open everyone up by getting the breath and feelings flowing, aided, of course, by the elevated rib cage. This experience works very well with a new production cast if done in the large theater where the production is to take place. It not only gets people acquainted and begins to open them to each other and to the play experience, but it immediately establishes a consciousness of the body condition needed to fill the theater vocally. The cast should be encouraged to maintain this body condition with the subsequent first read-through of the play. The drooping table-talk body posture permitted at most read-throughs is detrimental to the entire production. Actors very quickly fall into set patterns of speaking their lines associated with the body condition of the initial reading, and time is wasted trying to correct these bad habits at later rehearsals. At the very first verbal encounter with a play, lines should be read with the simultaneous awareness of the appropriate body and vocal life needed to project them.

A variation of the above activity, if done in a theater, is to have the cast form two lines, one on the stage and one in the very back of the auditorium where the audience normally sits. This variation can include the calling out of names as above, and in later rehearsals can include the projection of key words that each person feels are pivotal to the script, or symbolic words not from the script, but which for each person in turn express an image or conception of the play as they perceive it. This activity generally produces a deeper understanding of the play for everyone and, once again, reinforces a consciousness of the body condition necessary for theater projection. Individual lines from the play can be spoken in this physical set-up also, alternating with a line from a person on the stage, then a line from someone in the back of the theater, and so on. And as a visual aid to the concept of line projection, it is helpful for each person when speaking to push straight out with both hands toward the people in the opposite row. This gives each speaker a visual concept of what he wants his voice to be doing; he has a visual image of extending his words and reaching the listening group facing him. It is advisable for the perception of this concept to have the two lines change places after everyone has spoken once and to repeat the activity so that each member of the cast has the opportunity to speak from the stage.

Creativity and productivity can benefit from the increased self-discovery resulting from a variety of experiences and activities. Every activity will not mutually benefit every person but, on the other hand, the monotony of a few repeated activities can deaden the entire group. Experiences and activities need to be varied, surprising, and demanding to maintain interest and enthusiasm.

To experience the awareness of body and feeling life, vigorous physical exercises are a must and should be done at the beginning of every work session and as breaks in long rehearsals. Vigorous physical exercises will loosen tense muscles, induce deep breathing, get the blood flowing, and release energy and emotions — all of which are fundamental to the dynamic speaking voice needed by the actor.

The amount of benefit you derive from the exercises is, of course, dependent on how you approach them. Someone has said that there are basically two types of people in the world; there is one type that approaches life as if it were a battle; there is a second type that approaches life as if it were a game. To develop a perspective through which you can become productive and through which you can more happily resolve problems, I urge that you approach each activity as if it were a game — or better still, as if it were play. Play denotes greater spontaneity and less need for the mastery of skills and competitiveness.

One of my professors once told a delightful story of watching a race run by American Indian males. Taking part, to his amazement, were young men in the prime of health, little boys, and old men on crutches. The American Indian, it seems, is only in competition with himself, and the goal is not to get to the finish line ahead of everyone else, but just to get there. This story about the American Indians makes a good point, for it is not easy to understand the psychosocial structure of competitiveness. Nor is it easy to predict whether individual self-assertion against the competitive efforts of the group will release the productive potential, or whether it will inhibit productivity and take away the enjoyment of the work.

As with the American Indians, just getting there is the primary goal of the actor and so I suggest occasional play periods to lighten the mood of laborious gravity that pervades so much of theater work. It is, after all, self-defeating to the individual actor to let his problems engulf him. Nor is it of benefit to the rest of the group with whom he may be interacting. A grim, uptight attitude toward a goal can be the very obstacle that prohibits the achievement of that goal. Such an attitude can create tension that will tighten body muscles, which in turn will inhibit deep breathing and lock in feelings, and all productivity will come to a halt. Play is, after all, enjoyable and, as Harold Greenwald states in his fine article "Play and Self-Development" in the book *Ways of Growth,*[1] a playful attitude is infinitely more creative and productive than the tension produced by the hard-driven, hard-driving "make-it-at-all-costs" attitude. A playful attitude is a way of coping with individual problems by enabling us to look for their lighter side; it makes it possible for us to accept the absurdities of the situations in which we find ourselves. A playful attitude gives us a lighthearted, humorous perspective by which we can do our work and enjoy it. It releases tensions and gets the creative juices of energy and of emotion flowing. Play, be it the attitude or the activity, opens people up

---

[1]*Ways of Growth,* edited by Herbert Otto and John Mann (New York: Grossman, 1968).

and brings them into contact with one another; it reinforces the group spirit which is essential to successful production; it centers attention in the here-and-now; and it increases the awareness of body and feeling life, as well as of energy and rhythm, all fundamental components of a dynamic speaking voice.

In all of the following exercises, as with most of the activities suggested in this book, it is necessary to move freely and not to encumber the body with tight-fitting articles of clothing, so be certain to remove excess jackets and loosen tight belts. Wear a leotard or other comfortable clothing and flexible ballet slippers. Stay loose.

JOGGING

One of the best of the physical exercises that can be done in studio work is jogging. This can be done around in a circle or just in place, but it should be done vigorously, pulling up the knees and elevating the arms. It should be done with the accompaniment of either a voice count, or other spoken materials such as the articulation jingles which will limber the speech muscles at the same time, or loosely running speeches from a script. With all of the spoken materials a wide range of intonation should be used. There should be the feeling of a free voice, moving easily inside, and as if the words were bouncing from the head to the lower belly. The length of time for jogging will vary, but three or four minutes is usually enough to start with, and this can be increased in subsequent work sessions. At the conclusion of the activity it is important to repeat whatever spoken materials were used while standing quietly, reproducing the same wide range of intonation, the free voice moving easily.

Whenever you engage in vigorous physical activity simultaneously with the use of the speaking voice the voice will be free and flow easily. The voice movement will not be inhibited by muscle tension, since the muscles will also be free and moving as the result of the activity, and the words will bounce out easily. This sort of activity should give you the feeling that the entire body is speaking, rather than the feeling that it is somewhere in the throat that the speaking voice is housed.

BOUNCING BALLS

Another activity that works similarly to jogging in that it allows you to experience body and feeling life, as well as freeing vocal sound, is to stand and imagine that you are a rubber ball. Be specific as to what color ball you are, and also imagine that you have a noise-maker bouncing around inside you. Use your imagination as you release the sounds of the noise-maker inside you while bouncing up and down with both feet together twenty or thirty times. Maintain a light-hearted, playful attitude with this activity and let the voice go where it will. Bounce easily and enjoy the buoyant feeling of rising and floating in the air. Let the sounds rise and float too. Short speeches can also be done while bouncing. And, as with jogging, the importance of the exercise is that the perception of body and feeling life is channeled into the spoken words, and that the whole process is flowing as freely when you repeat the spoken words standing quietly at the end of the activity.

If the floor is carpeted or mats are available, this exercise can be done on the floor. You begin by lying on your back. Pull your knees up to your chest and embrace them with your arms, once again imagining that you are a brightly colored rubber ball. Then you roll from side to side, and all around, releasing the sounds of the noise-maker inside you. Use your imagination and if you are a red ball make red sounds, if you are a blue ball make blue sounds, and so forth. Roll around easily, and if you are working in a group and happen to roll into another ball, simply bounce off it and roll in another direction. To maintain the perception that you are a rubber ball rolling around the floor and bouncing off of the other balls, it

seems to work best to use only the noise-maker sounds. These maintain the play spirit of the activity in the encounters with other ball-persons and keep things moving. However all of the body and feeling life and free-moving vocal sound should be channeled into lines or short speeches at the conclusion of the activity. The goal of all of this activity is, after all, to support and enrich the spoken word and this must never be lost sight of. The exercises can and should be fun; if they are not fun they accomplish very little in the way of self-discovery. But the ultimate end of the free-flowing energy and emotion is to speak your lines truthfully, freely, and dynamically.

RUNNING

Running can be fun, too, and can be helpful in enabling you to experience body and feeling life, as well as freeing the voice from muscle constriction. A couple of fairly recent books on the subject of running also praise the increased awareness of spiritual life as one of the benefits to be derived.

If running with a group, it is best to form as wide a circle as possible, leaving room around the outer edge for faster runners. You start at a moderate pace, build speed gradually, and accompany the running with vocal sounds. The sounds can include sustained, open vowel sounds—although the pitches on these should be varied within a wide range; or you can sing a song, or rhythmically chant something like "Go! Go! Go! Go!" Running and speaking or singing in rhythm helps you to feel the energy and rhythm of the words in the body. Whatever the vocal sounds may be, start them lightly and as the increasingly faster running pace produces greater awareness of body energy, slowly blend body energy and vocal sound into increased vocal volume. But don't think of this as getting louder. Never use the word *loud* to yourself. Instead, think expansively of the voice as getting wider and deeper and intensifying the sounds. And, here again, when you stop running speak some lines with your bigger voice. It is always the carry-over that is the point of the activity, when you let your self enjoy the physical, mental, and spiritual exhilaration as an integral part of spoken words. The time limit for the running activity is variable, but five minutes is generally long enough to produce the desired results.

A variation of the running exercise is to pretend that you are an airplane, running with your arms straight out and making gliding noises as you dip and soar in the wind. This especially helps deep breathing, since the raised arms keep the rib cage up and out at the sides, and it also includes a more extravagant pitch range. Speeches done immediately following this activity often have exciting interpretations.

Another interesting variation is to run as if you were a bird flying in the air, making all sorts of bird noises and chirps. Here again, the continuous flapping of wings and gliding help to free the breath and get it deeply centered, and the various bird chirps include more use of the articulation muscles, so the following lines and speeches are generally more precisely shaped and more intelligible. For it must always be kept in mind that, fun though these activities may and should be, the ultimate aim is to make you a more effective speaker.

FOLLOW THE LEADER

The "leader" for this activity should be chosen for his imaginative mind, his spirit of fun, and his ability to lead in spontaneous and varied movements that fit the group, the environment, and the music (if it is used). Accompanying the body movements there should be sounds and/or words, as varied and with as much range as possible. The sounds and/or words should be sustained and the resonances felt in the body, as you move about the room or theater.

Another way to perform this exercise is to stand in a circle, and to have each in turn perform within his own space. Each in turn will engage in movement simultaneously with a spoken word, and the rest of the group will then imitate the word-movement. Words should be chosen for their interpretive value, such as *flow, shake, sway, whirl* — or *wind, cloud, sky, trees* — or *beautiful, electric, round, tall*. Here again, the point of the exercise is to experience the energy of the sounds in the words. You must feel that it is the entire body speaking, as you let the sound resonances communicate themselves to you.

To focus on pure sound, without associated meanings, it is good, as a variation, to perform this activity using nonsense words. This usually brings your performance entirely into the physical and affective domains, and enables you to really experience the quality and power of the sounds. Let the sounds flow through your body, generating energy and feeling. Running sounds together in this fashion, accompanied by slow, sensuous movement will increase your feel and appreciation of them, and increase your ability to use them to interpret meaning.

This second variation is of great benefit in working alone when you are trying to generate emotional meaning and body support for sounds and words. This process communicates important body and feeling information to the mind and increases your ability to express words and phrases as a total communication of the self. You can truly become your voice in this exercise and be able to express exactly what you mean; for the voice will be a harmonious blend of mental, physical, and emotional power. Just let the vocal sounds go. Don't try; let them happen to you. Let the quality and the quantity of sounds surprise you. Voice is, after all, matter in motion, and can be a powerful influence on you, on your words, and on your audience.

DANCING

Another way to transcend the limitations of ordinary consciousness and generate dynamic body life is by dancing. Rhythms and cycles direct the energy of our biological being, indeed of the world of nature that surrounds us, and most everyone is exhilarated by moving in time to music. Rhythmic dancing is a delightful means of self-expression and of integrating body movement and feeling life. Find songs that you know and let your body respond freely to the rhythms as you sing and express your feelings with your spontaneous movements. Feel your self enjoying the rhythmic expression. If you choose to dance to songs to which you don't know the words just sing *la la la,* but sing. Use your voice and body in as many varied rhythms as you can. Let your self out. Dance your way to a keener sense of self-awareness. All rhythmic exercises, and particularly dancing, will sharpen your perceptions and imagination, and help you to realize and communicate your self. And you'll have fun doing it, which generates energy.

With today's free-style dancing as a model you can dance alone, or in pairs, or as a group. For the inhibited "I can't dance" individual the patterned dances work fine. Square dancing, or any type of folk dance, will get everyone involved and produce a friendly, cooperative atmosphere. Or there is "Ballin' the Jack" for which there is music, and in which the lyrics dictate the body movements.

SIMPLE GYMNASTICS

Still another way to increase your awareness of body and feeling life and of rhythm, to raise your energy level, and to free your voice is by doing simple gymnastics. Do them rhythmically to a voice count and in a spirit of enjoyment, not with the mechanical physical culture approach of simply going through the motions. Remember as you do the exercises that it is the perception of the body doing the speaking that you want to maintain, and that means sustaining the vowels and continuant consonants long enough to experience their resonances in the body. Below are three of the best exercises to evoke the choreography of free vocal sound, deeply supportive breathing, and the altered consciousness of body and emotive energy.

1. Stand straight with feet together and arms at the sides. Jump the feet wide apart and raise the outstretched arms to shoulder level as you intone the word "One!" Jump the feet together and drop the arms to starting position as you intone the word "Two!" Continue this to the count of twenty.

2. Stand with feet widely separated and arms straight out to the sides at shoulder level. Bend and touch the fingers of your right hand to your left foot as you intone the word "One!" Return to the starting position as you intone the word "Two!" Bend and touch the fingers of your left hand to your right foot as you intone the word "Three!" Return to the starting position as you intone the word "Four!" Continue this to the count of twenty.

3. Stand with feet widely separated and arms straight out to the sides at shoulder level. Jump your feet together and raise your arms straight over your head as you intone the word "One!" Jump and return your feet and arms to starting position as you intone the word "Two!" Continue this for the count of twenty.

Making the physical commitment to the above activities will open you to self-discovery. You will realize new avenues of self-expression and you will enjoy doing them. Because speaking dynamically is a pleasure, people sometimes mislead themselves into thinking it is a luxury; that it is a fun thing to be used occasionally but is not essential. That, for the actor, is stupid and shortsighted. The speaking voice that you need for the stage must become a permanent part of your equipment, not something you put on for a performance like make-up. In the first place, it doesn't work that way. The speaking voice that you need for the stage must be integrated into daily use or it will not be available to resonate the total humanity of your character. The speaking voice that you need for the stage must be free and readily available so that you can properly focus on *what* you are saying, not *how*. So let your self honestly and freely discover every possible vocal nuance and alternative for expressing meaning. And do it enthusiastically. Enthusiasm resonates much more widely than doggedness.

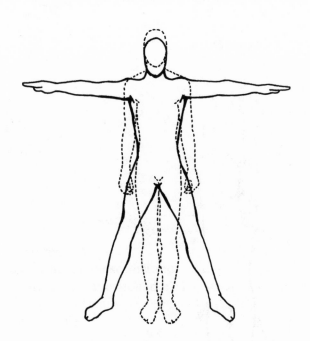

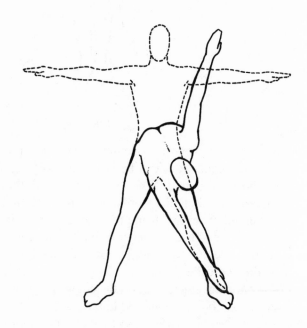

23

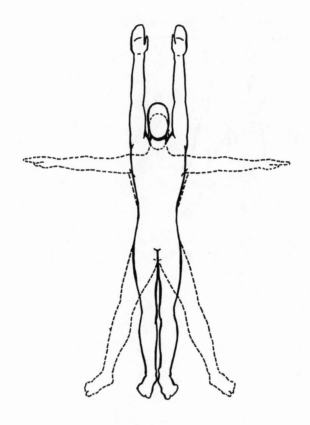

WORKING IN PAIRS

Two people working together is the usual procedure in studio scene study, but scene-work can be very uninteresting if the actors are too literal, too word-bound. Too often actors think they are acting when they are merely speaking the words, when they are, in fact, using the words to hide behind instead of using them as a channel for honest emotion. This type of acting is usually accompanied by a generalized excitement rather than the specific emotion(s) of the character portrayed; in fact, it shouldn't be called acting at all. For the audience's attention is not focused on the character but on the actor. The words must be colored with honest, specific emotions and to facilitate this, as well as to intensify acting relationships, it helps when the two actors in a scene engage in a physical activity through which they can communicate feelings and relate while speaking lines, and which expands the focus from just a literal exchange to a total one. One of the best of these activities is the widely used

Mirror Exercise which, in addition to reinforcing the above-named factors, will concentrate the actors and scene in the immediate moment of performance. Since the Mirror Exercise is widely known and used, I won't outline the pattern here.

Another activity that works well when the characters are young, such as Romeo and Juliet, or playful, such as Rosalind and Orlando, is Patty-Cake. The words of the jingle can be used to start, and in case you've forgotten, here they are.

> Patty-cake, patty-cake, baker's man,
> Bake me a cake as fast as you can;
> Pat it and shape it and put it in a pan;
> Patty-cake, patty-cake, baker's man.

Or you can begin with a number-count immediately to establish the rhythm. Patty-caking is basically a six-count rhythm, partners facing each other. On the count of "one" you clap your own hands together; on the count of "two" you simultaneously clap your right hand to your partner's left and your left hand to your partner's right, fingers pointing upward; on the count of "three" you clap your own hands together; on the count of "four" you clap your right hand to your partner's right; on the count of "five" you clap your own hands together; and on the count of "six" you clap your left hand to your partner's left. Then you begin all over again, and repeat the sequence enough times to master it. Sustain the vowels and continuant consonants on the word count; let them resonate through your body and flow out and blend with your partner's word count. The activity should then be repeated a couple of times without the audible word count, and finally it should be continued as you speak the lines of the scene.

Repeating a scene and patty-caking immediately following usually elicits some interesting results. Splitting the focus while speaking and performing the physical activity will have expanded the communication to something more than mere words; the relationship will have resonance and immediacy, and the words will be imbued with vitality and feeling as well as with literal meaning.

Another effective means of integrating physical and emotional interaction with the spoken exchange of a scene is Arm-Wrestling. This particularly strengthens relationships of conflict or power-play, such as Benedick and Beatrice, or Angelo and Isabella. In this interaction both actors lie on the floor on their stomachs, facing each other. Then you both raise your right forearms so that they are touching, with elbows on the floor; you interlock thumbs and clasp hands. At the signal to begin, you

try to force your partner's right arm down toward your left while running the lines of the scene. If you down your partner's arm quickly or he downs yours, just keep on starting over again. And if the scene is a long one, you should stop halfway through and change to wrestling with the left arms. If the scene is a short one, it should be repeated with this change to left arms. But, whether you are wrestling with right or left arms, do it slowly enough to be aware of the words in the body. Allow the time to experience the words simultaneously with the body condition that is producing them. Be aware that all of you is speaking. Then immediately run the scene in a standing position and try to maintain this perception.

This interaction also produces some exciting line interpretations. I frequently ask the rest of the group to close their eyes and listen while one pair is working, and, without exception, they are amazed at the increase of vocal energy and range, as well as at the more complete emotional meaning of the spoken words. It is helpful to tape these exchanges so that the participating actors may get immediate feedback, which will encourage them to continue to strive for total communication.

The voice and speech students in my classes frequently applaud each other, and I encourage it. If you feel like applauding, you should. It is enjoyable as an avenue of self-expression, and it will stimulate your heart and lung action and help to keep the juices and the enthusiasm flowing. Maintaining the energy level and the enthusiasm are necessary to productivity, be it in speech class or anywhere else. And heartily shouting *Bravo!* or other verbal plaudits is all right too. Applause is mother's milk to the actor and can help to develop the all-important element of self-confidence and to strengthen the ego, which is, after all, part of the actor's talent.

Another pleasurable experience that integrates and resonates the various elements of the self, that, indeed, opens you up to your self and to others, is laughing. This experience can trigger significant new perceptions of the self, by stilling the restless mind and releasing vital physical sensations. And to the speaking voice, laughing is elixir; it relaxes the voice muscles in the lower belly, and is one of the most effective means of getting the voice deeply rooted and centered.

If you are one of those who has difficulty initiating an honest, easy-flowing laugh, and who can't seem to get the source deeper than a high-chest rasp or chuckle, then I suggest the following. First, elevate the rib cage by laying your hands on the back part of your hips with the thumbs pointed forward. Then open your mouth by dropping the jaw in a *ha* position. Now sigh, easily and deeply; let yourself enjoy it all the way down to the lower belly. Sigh twice in this manner, and the third time you begin to sigh, but halfway through you turn it into an easy laugh. Don't try too hard; just let it happen. Just relax and keep on laughing and you will find that your laughter feeds on itself and will ventilate your body sensations to an altered state of consciousness. You will be infected by the sound and feel of mirthful expression and you will infect others as well. Don't think; just feel. Laugh at your self laughing. If you need a ridiculous mental image to keep you going, use one; but keep laughing for four or five minutes at least. Your body will encourage you if you let it; it will so enjoy the pleasurable, relaxed sensation that it will keep sending you messages to continue. And as you experience the body enjoying itself, be aware that it is the entire body that is producing the vocal sound that is resonating inside you and is easing its way out. Both physically and psychologically, this is an exhilarating experience, besides doing wonderful things for the speaking voice. It should be done frequently. "Laugh it off" is one of the wisest phrases ever uttered; laughter relaxes and frees you. And when you speak your lines immediately after a session of honest, prolonged laughter, you will find that they are enriched and supported by the energy of deeply centered breathing and vitality, by the feeling life of the body.

If you are to capture and hold an audience your speaking voice must be an expression of the unified power of your body and feeling life. To command attention you must become increasingly aware of these factors and learn to coordinate their use with supportive breathing and the spoken words. Body and feeling life are, of course, the basis for your characterization and for the words spoken. Maintain persistently your heightened awareness of your self. Channeling these vital forces will not only lighten the burden of self-expression, but make it easier and more enjoyable to express your self.

In any given moment, right now or following one of the experiential activities, close your eyes and be aware of how you feel. Imagine that you are smiling all over, with every muscle of your body, and let yourself bathe luxuriously in the warm body feeling that this image generates. Feel your body energy. Experience your self feeling. Begin to move slowly and sensuously and to express that feeling with body language. Let your voice softly respond to the movement of the feeling and the body. Let your voice express how you feel. Move rhythmically and enjoy the rich experience of vocal sound and feeling life that is resonating inside you. Infect your self with your radiant feelings and let the voice go where it will, gradually intensifying and expanding the feeling voice until you achieve a real high. Open your self to the vibrations of vocal sound and body feeling and let them flow. When you feel really high, and as if every body cell is experiencing and producing the free-flowing voice, begin to gradually distill your vocalized feeling into an essence. Wrap your arms around your self and hug it close, as you rock back and forth, feeling that vibrant essence in every part of your body, from your head to your feet. Slowly rock your self to a standstill, but continue to let the integrated body, feeling, and vocal life express your essence. Maintain the awareness of the feeling vocal self as you slowly open your eyes and channel the integrated whole into some lines.

The experiences suggested in this chapter and in subsequent ones will trigger significant states of awareness, intuition, spontaneity, and self-discovery. Allowing yourself to interact with your body and feeling life will center your strength and focus your intentions. The stimulus and the response are both, and at once, your own. The conscious and subconscious minds are integrated simultaneously with the physical and affective domains. And this concentration of your internal forces is the key to your actualization of self and the ultimate achievement of your goals. Your speaking voice will be free to express all that you want and need it to; you will have become your speaking voice.

• 3 •

SELF-AWARENESS:
Relaxation and Energy

INCREASED SELF-AWARENESS BRINGS INCREASED KNOWLEDGE that the human body is a complex organism; it also brings the self-assurance that many of its complex functions are subject to self-control.

One such complex function is that of controlling tension in the muscles of the body, which can mean the increase of efficiency and productivity, not only in the speaking voice but in every phase of acting life. Control of muscle tension means that body energy is conserved; excessive, uncontrolled muscle tension means that body energy is wasted. Control of body tension is a significant consideration for all training in voice and speech for the actor, for what is the purpose of such training if it isn't to increase the energy and effectiveness of the speaking voice and of the body in which the speaking voice is housed. Energy that is bound up in tense muscles is energy that is unavailable to power the speaking voice because it is inhibiting the breath and feeling life from flowing freely. Training in muscle-tension control, therefore, must include the ability to generally relax the muscles in the entire body, and to specifically relax the muscles in the voice and speech areas.

Basic causes of excessive muscle tensions are neither easily determined nor easily removed, and are acknowledged by psychotherapists as being the results of many factors, among them heredity, instincts, and habits. This text doesn't presume to delve into these causes, but it does accept the responsibility to try to lessen some of the effects.

29

For the actor, chronic tension states are often produced by either a hard-driving determination to succeed in a highly competitive profession, or by excessive and severe self-evaluations, or by a combination of both. It is extremely important for the actor to learn that the determination and self-evaluations necessary for success can also be the very factors that produce the tensions that will limit that success. Therefore, determination and self-evaluation must be tempered with reason. You must develop the self-control to change bad tension habits, the self-awareness to recognize extreme tension states when they exist, and the honest self-appraisal that will deny the self-justification of tension states. It is only the neurotic who rationalizes the reasons for his tensions, who believes that they are necessary to him, and who comes to depend on them. Muscle contraction requires the energy of effort and to waste energy in tense states of muscle constriction is senseless. We also know that excessive tension can cause a variety of bodily diseases. Energy must be made available for positive effort. An acting career is strenuous at best and takes all the energy you can muster. The speaking voice of the actor is subject to a great many tensions. Many character roles and actions are tension-producing, as is the underlying motivation of the actor to do it all perfectly. But if your tension is excessive during a performance, it will interfere with that performance, limiting the effectiveness of your ability to realize the total humanity of your character.

In other words, the causes of your tensions are within your self; happily, the means of controlling your tensions are also within. Psychotherapists tell us that there are many types of inner muscle-control, but the important one for the actor to learn is to directly experience his muscle sensations: when his muscles are enduring the strain of excessive tension, when they are enjoying the comfort of relaxation, when they are in a dynamic state of readiness with the proper degree of tonicity, and to be able to tell the differences.

The muscle tissues of the body are the focus of the awareness training. Muscle tissues are tensed and shortened; they are relaxed and lengthened. By these means we are able to move and function, and it is the awareness of these means that we must have for the most efficient use of our muscles. Get inside your self and learn as much as possible through concentration. Concentration means exclusion; it means learning to focus despite whatever else may be going on around you. Experience your body muscles. Be aware that it is you that is living inside the body, and is causing the tensions. Be aware of the tensions and the meaning of them. As you are lying still, be aware that everything inside you is constantly moving and changing. Change is the only certainty in this world and, through stillness, you become aware of your inner movements, of the rhythm and energy of physiological pulses, of constantly changing tension in the muscle fibers.

It has been said that the life of the mind, which includes imagination and memory, as well as all forms of feeling life, depends on specific muscle actions. Transcendental Meditation and other forms of meditation have proven that being still and quieting the mind also relaxes the muscles, as well as the respiratory and cardiovascular systems and other bodily functions. It seems reasonable then to expect that one can develop awareness of these psycho-physiologic actions and be able to develop the muscle-sense to use the organism wisely and not let it get into over-tense states. Training for the conservation of muscular energy means both mental and neuromuscular awareness of where the tension spots are located and being able to release them. The goal of the training is immediate control in action, whereby the individual can recognize the proper degree of tension necessary to perform specific actions, can recognize and free excessive amounts of tension that inhibit actions, and thus be able to regulate the organism according to what works best.

You must develop an awareness of what tension is when you experience it, without justification or condemnation. To be aware that you are in a tense state is the first step to becoming free of tension. If you are unaware of your state of tension, you try harder, which can only worsen the tension. Don't even try to experience body sensations; just let them happen. There should be no effort involved. Trying not to feel tense is self-defeating, because that just imposes more tension. You want to simply observe the sensations of tension within, and this requires the concentration of an alert mind, since tension-states are constantly changing. And don't talk, if you would really turn in on your self. Don't depend on words or other symbols. An alert mind is not the result of mental assertions but of quiet self-observations and awareness. Imposing preconceived notions on your body state, your own or someone else's, will only lessen your ability to *be,* to achieve total self-realization.

The necessity of lessening excessive muscle tension is an important one, too important to neglect, and this text has provided some specific structured experiences to help you. But reading the exercises won't do the trick. The need and the means to improve tension control are within you. I can only tell you what I have personally experienced and observed others experiencing, and what I know will work, giving the opportunity. The application of the prescribed experiences and the self-discovery must be yours, along with the gradual elimination of constricting habitual responses. To realize and communicate the total humanity of any character means that you have to free the total self: the mental, emotional, and bodily energy. And, as we have previously stated, these factors are interdependent and interpenetrating. If the mind is quiet the muscles will relax; if the muscles are relaxed, the mind will be quieted, and along with the emotions, will enable you to freely express the life of your character, without your own effort getting in the way. It must be the character's speaking voice we hear, not yours; and likewise, it must be the character's effort we see, not yours. The habitual muscle-tensing preparations for self-expression tend generally to inhibit the complete freedom of expression. You must not try to make it happen, but keep the muscles loose and let it happen. This concept of letting the expression happen by its own power is, as I understand it, a fundamental principle of the excellent Alexander technique; it is certainly the basis of self-realization, and of fine acting.

TENSION AWARENESS

To begin your experience of tension awareness, lie or sit in a relaxed position. Now close your eyes and be aware of the silence around you. Feel it. Hear it. Don't expect anything; just receive and experience the silence. Let it clear your head of excess mental baggage. Let it sharpen your perceptions. For a long moment allow your self to experience your self in the silence. Experience your self in the present moment. Be aware of your easy, rhythmic breathing. Focus on your self.

Tightly clench both fists, and then rigidly hold that tense position. For a long moment be aware of the sensation of excessive muscle tension in your clenched fists as well as in the forearms. Be aware that the tension also involves the muscles in the upper arms. Hold the tense position until you are acutely aware of the locked-in energy and of the resulting discomfort.

Now, very slowly release the tension from the arms, hands, and fingers by gradually unclenching the fists. Be aware of every second of the slow release of tension and of the freeing of energy, and for a long moment experience the sensation of the muscles when they are free of the excessive tension. Enjoy the comfortable, relaxed feelings of the muscles.

To better understand the relationship of mental activity and muscle tension, continue to enjoy the sensation of relaxation by thinking of yourself lying on a warm, sandy beach, or sailing, skiing, or otherwise engaging in some activity that you particularly enjoy. Mentally project your self into the scene. Smile at the pleasure of your thoughts. Feel the entire body smiling and be keenly aware of the pleasurable sensation of dynamic tonicity in the muscles of the body.

Tell yourself that you can't be where you want to be, doing what you enjoy, because there is some other tedious, unpleasant task that you must do instead. Let this be the most disliked task you can think of, and see yourself doing it. And now be aware of the different feeling in the muscles of the body. Experience the unpleasant sensation of increased muscle tension, the lack of ease and comfort in the body feeling. As a result of your mental conflict your body will reflect sensations of strain and tightness, and your breathing will be inhibited. Allow yourself to experience this unpleasant state of tension for a long enough time to imprint it in your conscious awareness, and to store it in your memory bank so that you will be able to recognize both cause and effect in the future.

Once again think of yourself as engaging in the activity that you particularly enjoy. Take time to totally involve yourself and smile at the pleasure of your thoughts. Be aware of the body muscles slowly relaxing and of the deeper breathing and flow of feeling life that result. And, once again, allow yourself to experience the sensation for a long enough time to be able to recall both cause and effect in future situations, to be consciously aware of the relationship of mental activity, feeling life, and muscle tension.

This psycho-physiological principle is fundamental to all experiences of relaxation. The state of body tension and feeling life is largely dependent on the state of the mind. Mental conflict is reflected in the body conflict of excessive muscle tension and wasted energy; and the greater the conflict the greater the tension and waste. As was stated in the first chapter, it is necessary to learn how to use the mind. Right mental activity is a powerful force. It is the organizing factor that makes the difference. In the following relaxation experiences, let your mind work for you.

The experiences in relaxation are a blend of Yoga, of the sensory awareness techniques of Bernard Gunther, of emotional release through deep breathing, of mind over matter, and of various exercises picked up in studio work along the way. Any experiences that have brought new perceptions and change to my students have been incorporated in this text.

Bear in mind, too, that I do not use the term *relaxation* as meaning "flaccidity." Flaccid muscles are flabby, weak, lacking in power and force. By relaxed muscles, I mean those muscles that are in a dynamic state of readiness, with the proper degree of tonicity or tension: that is, muscles that are neither excessively tense nor flabby, but have the right amount of tension to perform with power and flexibility.

TENSION AWARENESS AND RELEASE

Lying or sitting comfortably with eyes closed and with straight back, neck, and head, slowly curl your toes under and tense the muscles in your feet and toes. Hold the tension in the muscles of the feet and toes, as you slowly add tension in the muscles of the calves of the legs, the thighs of the legs, the buttocks and lower belly, the trunk of the body, the fingers, hands, forearms, upper arms, shoulder girdle, neck and face. Hold the position in your entire head and body long enough to experience the tension and the resulting inhibition of breathing, feeling life, and energy.

Now very slowly release the tension from the facial muscles, then the muscles of the neck, the shoulder girdle, arms, hands, and fingers, the trunk of the body, the buttocks and lower belly, the thighs, the calves of the legs, and finally release the tension from the muscles of the feet and toes.

In all of the body parts, the important factor is to apply the tension slowly enough to be able to experience the effect, and that you then release the tension even more slowly in order to experience every instant of the release and of the ever increasing freedom and the flow of breathing, feeling life, and energy. And remember that the experience must be to tense up and relax down, the important part being the latter. As you relax down, visualize the tension as flowing from the head, down through the body, legs, and feet, and finally out and away. Then lie or sit quietly for a long moment and experience your relaxed self, and enjoy your easy, deep breathing and free-flowing energy and feeling life.

As a variation of the above exercise, lie or sit comfortably with eyes closed and with straight back, neck, and head. Now for a few moments put your focus on your breathing, and let the hypnotic regularity of inhalation-exhalation calm you and increase your awareness of your body and feeling life. Then slowly explore your body for tension spots. Start with the feet and work upward, allowing yourself time to experience the muscles in the feet, the calves of the legs, the thighs, the buttocks and lower belly, the trunk of the body, the hands, arms, and shoulder girdle, and the neck and face. And as you slowly examine each area, if you feel there is tension there, slowly increase that tension, hold the tense position for a long moment, and then more slowly release the tension. Systematically search out each tension spot and remove the block to energy flow.

And when you have removed all the tension blocks be aware of your self in the free state, a channel of dynamic, free-flowing energy. Allow your self to enjoy this perception for a long moment.

Still another variation of the above exercise is to do it with movement. As you walk in an easy, relaxed manner, slowly tense the muscles of the face. Hold the tense position long enough to experience the discomfort and constriction that results, and then slowly release the tension from the facial muscles, being aware of every instant of the slow release of tension and the freeing of energy, and for a long moment allow your self to experience the sensation of the muscles when they are comfortably relaxed.

Repeat the experience with the muscles of the neck, then the muscles of the arms and hands, the muscles of the trunk of the body, the muscles of the lower belly and buttocks, and the muscles of the legs, the muscles of the feet and toes. And with each separate group of muscles use the sequence of first slowly increasing the tension, holding the tense position long enough to realize the effect, slowly experiencing every instant of the tension release, and then the long moment of experiencing the muscles when they are comfortably relaxed.

A total focus and keen awareness is fundamental to the success of the above experiences and to the development of your ability to recognize and control states of tension and energy flow. Don't engage in any of the experiences mindlessly. Project the whole of your mental focus and the awareness of your feeling life and body sensation into the experiences, especially into the final step in the sequence. Always allow time for your entire self to recognize and record for all time the consciousness of body musculature free of tension, in a dynamic state of readiness to express whatever you will. Self-awareness was discussed more fully in chapters one and two. It doesn't end there. Self-awareness is fundamental to the success of every step of your training. It is vital to the development of every phase of voice and speech improvement.

PSYCHO-PHYSICAL EXPERIENCES IN RELAXATION

We know that there is a relationship between mental activity and muscle tension. You have experienced the relationship in the above experience of imagining your self as first engaging in an activity that you particularly enjoy, and then as having to perform an unpleasant task instead. Now let the experience of mental activity work for you.

Lie flat on your back on the floor, raising your head slightly with the use of a book, a pillow, or some article of clothing folded into pillow size, and with your arms lying on the floor beside you. To make certain that your back is as flat as possible, first pull up your knees toward the ceiling until your feet are flat on the floor. Stretch and flatten the back in this position, particularly the lower back. When your back is completely and comfortably relaxed in this position, let your feet slide forward until your legs are also lying on the floor. Your legs and feet should fall easily outward to the sides.

Now take a long moment to be aware of your relationship to the floor. Is the floor holding you or are you holding onto your self with your own tension? Follow with 1 or 2.

1. Lie quietly with eyes closed. Let go. Allow your self to relax. Feel the heavy weight of your feet and legs and imagine that they are sinking into the floor. Take as much time as you need to let them slowly sink, and until you have a sensation of completely weightless legs and feet. Allow your self to enjoy the sensation. Then feel the heavy weight of the buttocks, and slowly let them sink into the floor. Allow your self to enjoy the sensation of weightless buttocks, legs, and feet. Now be aware of the heavy weight of the trunk of your body. Let that sink into the floor, and enjoy the sensation of weightless trunk, buttocks, legs and feet. Continue next with the arms, hands, and fingers, and last of all, with the head. Feel the heavy weight of each part separately, let it slowly sink into the floor, and then lie quietly and experience the sensation of weightlessness. And when you have relaxed your entire body take a long moment to luxuriate in the weightless feeling of your self blending with the floor.

2. Lie quietly with eyes closed. Let go. Allow your self to relax. Let your body spread slowly outward, along the surface of the floor. Imagine that every part of you is becoming wider and wider as you slowly spread outward to the sides. Now imagine your spine lengthening and your head easing itself farther outward, as you spread from top to bottom. Be aware of your self as covering more and more floor space as you continue to spread in all directions. And when you have relaxed your entire body take a long moment to enjoy the sensation of weightlessness and freedom.

DEEPENING RELAXATION

The following experiences may be used as a follow-up for 1 or 2 above, or as a first step in your psycho-physical release of tension and energy flow. As in the above experiences, the results are dependent on the relationship of mental activity and muscle tension, and on the total awareness of your mind, your body sensation and feeling life.

1. Lie flat on your back with your eyes closed. For specific body position follow the directions in the introduction to the psycho-physical experiences above. Now imagine that you are lying on a warm, sandy beach. Feel the sun on your body and the warm sand under you. See (in your mind's eye) the blue sky, fluffy white clouds, and flying sea gulls. Hear the sea gulls calling and hear the rhythmic breaking of the waves on the sand. Taste the salty sea spray on your lips. Experience your self as part of the life-giving warmth and energy of nature. Allow your self plenty of time to realize the deepening relaxation that this experience brings. Enjoy the feeling of dynamic body and feeling life, the awareness of vital energy flowing inside you.

2. Lie flat on your back with your eyes closed. For specific body position follow the directions in the introduction to the psycho-physical experiences above. Now imagine that you are floating on your back in a pool. Let go your own hold on your body and enjoy the feeling of weightlessness as you allow the water to support you. Spread your arms and legs and experience the buoyant energy and movement of the water as it cradles you and gently rocks you on its surface. Feel the warm water and sun against your body. See (in your mind's eye) the blue sky and white clouds overhead, and hear the rhythmic lapping of the water against the sides of the pool. Experience your own body energy and rhythms as blending with the water and the sun, as part of all nature. Allow your self to luxuriate in the deepening relaxation of your body. Enjoy a long moment of well-being, of weightlessness and freedom.

3. This experience may be engaged in either in a comfortable sitting position or lying flat on your back. If you lie down follow the specific body-position directions in the introduction to the psycho-physical experiences above. Now close your eyes and fully experience the quiet strength of your inner self, of your inner energy and rhythms. Intensify your awareness of your inner core and deepen your relaxation as you slowly count down from ten to one. Silently say "ten" to yourself and take time to realize a long moment of deepening relaxation. Silently say "nine" and realize another long moment of even deeper relaxation. Continue the slow countdown until you reach "one," allowing your self time to experience the deepening relaxation with each number. And at the finish, take a long moment to enjoy the relaxed feeling deep inside you, and the resulting flow of warmth and energy that vitalizes your entire body.

When you engage in any of the three experiences above, or in 1 or 2 of the psycho-physical experiences, it is important that you be constantly aware, second by second, of each slight increase or decrease in tension. It is only through such keen sensitivity that you can accurately monitor your tension states and learn to control them.

SLAP-MASSAGE

The dynamically alive feeling of readiness which is the result of the proper degree of tonicity can best be experienced by using slapping and massage exercises. Slapping and massage experiences are used in a great many actor-training and other such physical fitness programs and induce a marvelous sensation of vital self-awareness in the immediate moment, of keen sensitivity to muscle tone, to feeling and body life. There is something almost miraculous that happens from the "laying on of hands," from the careful stroking and manipulation of the body muscles. Energy and warmth are generated and produce an extraordinary feeling of physical well-being. It is believed by some specialists in this field that differing body parts have differing energy potentials, for instance, the hands and the eyes. It is certainly possible to increase the warmth and energy in the hands by rubbing the palms vigorously together and this should always be the preliminary step for the person administering the slap-massage in the following exercises.

The group will separate into pairs, with one person seated in a straight chair with eyes closed and arms hanging loosely at the sides. The other person will stand behind the chair and vigorously slap the seated partner, first the front, back and sides of the shoulder girdle, and then the shoulders and all the way down the arms and hands. When this is completed, the standing partner begins once again with the shoulder girdle and slowly and firmly massages this area, and then the arms and hands. For voice students, it is beneficial if both partners easily hum with lips closed and simultaneously engage in a slow chewing motion during the period of the exercise. For both participants the hum-chew can help to free the voice and begin the process of experiencing the audible self.

The focus should next shift to the head, with both partners continuing to hum-chew, and with the standing partner first finger-tapping the seated partner's head, including the forehead and cheeks, and then massaging the same areas.

Both partners next change to the audible expression of soft, sustained, open vowel sounds. The seated partner lets his head drop forward onto his chest, and the standing partner massages the seated partner's spine, beginning at the base of the skull and working his way all the way down to

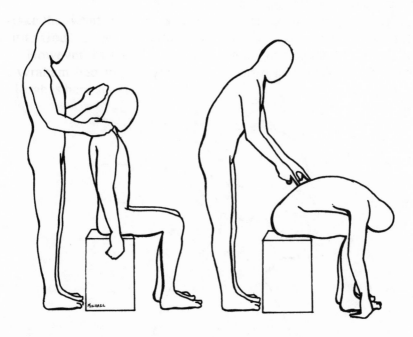

the tail bone. During the spine massage, the seated partner will let the
weight of the head and shoulders slowly pull him down until he is lying
on his own thighs. After the seated partner has fallen forward and the
standing partner has massaged, with the fingers of both hands close in to
the spine on each side, all the way to the tail bone, the seated partner's
back should then be vigorously slapped all over and then massaged.

Both partners then stop vocalizing, and the seated partner must put his
entire focus on the bottom-most vertebra, then the second, the third, and
so forth, and on the image of stacking up his vertebrae, as he slowly
raises himself back to a vertical position, and while his standing partner is
slowly walking up his spine with a firm pressure of alternating first and
middle fingers close in on each side of the vertebrae. This final step must
be slow and concentrated for both partners, all the way up and including
the seven cervical vertebrae in the back of the neck. The standing partner
must never press right *on* the vertebrae; the walk-up should be firm,
measured movement on each side of the vertebrae where there are some
pressure points for releasing energy. The seated partner must focus on the

image of the vertebrae being stacked one on top of the other and pulling him up, and not on the muscles.

When the spine-walk is completed and the seated partner is sitting upright the standing partner will then lay his hands on the sides of his partner's neck, fingers pointing downward, and slowly slide his hands and fingers upward behind his partner's ears two or three times, suggesting to

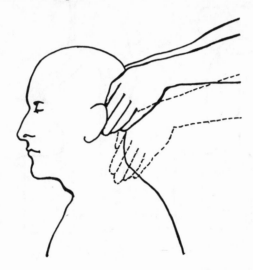

his seated partner that his head is floating upward out of his shoulder girdle, and that his spine is lengthening and straightening. The seated partner should keep his eyes closed and record this vitalized perception of himself for a long moment before slowly opening his eyes. He should focus on this same perception for another long moment, first seated and then standing, with eyes open, and then the two partners should change places, and the exercise is repeated.

This is an excellent warm-up, both in studio work and rehearsals, and, if there are no available straight chairs, it can be done with both partners standing. In this instance, the partner receiving the slap-massage simply falls forward from the waist following the head massage and should slightly bend his knees out to the side to maintain his balance, and since he does not have the support of a chair, the back slap-massage can be of shorter duration.

If there is a rug on the floor, or if there are practice mats available, massages can also be done with one partner lying face down with arms at his sides, with the manipulating partner working over him. This has the advantage of also being able to slap and massage the buttocks and legs. It is not, however, as beneficial to the head and neck, and to the front of the shoulder girdle and arms. The partner being worked on can receive a much more thorough slap-massage to the above-mentioned body parts if he is seated in a chair. There is the added advantage that when he falls forward from the waist (either sitting or standing), his face and neck muscles easily relax due to the pull of gravity. Also, when he is hanging down, the vocalized hum-chews or open vowel sounds flow right into the head, along with the blood and its supply of oxygen, and a wonderfully full, resonant tone develops. This tone is further amplified and supported by the deeper breathing which results from the lower ribs opening out in this position, and because it is almost impossible to engage in high-chest breathing while hanging forward.

This combination of slapping, finger-tapping, and massage administered by a considerate partner, along with the relaxing, forward hang, is of great benefit in getting rid of excess tension, in generating energy, and in getting in touch with basic body and feeling life.

In the discussion and practice of tension awareness and release we must necessarily concentrate on the muscles, which tends to make us think of ourselves mainly as physical beings. We need, in fact, to realize that the human body, which appears to be a solid mass of bones, muscles and other tissues, is actually a mass of myriads of tiny cells which are constantly moving. Each cell is composed of tiny, moving molecules; each molecule is composed of tinier, moving atoms; each atom is composed of even tinier elements, which are infinitesimal sparks of rapidly rotating energy. Every muscle, bone, tissue, and blood cell is, therefore, a storehouse of vital power.

Tension release must also be perceived in terms of its effect, which is energization and energy flow. And energy must be perceived, not only in terms of the food and oxygen we take into our bodies from the outside, but also in terms of our own internal life force.

All of our body movements and postures, be they walking, standing, sitting, raising our arms, or whatever, are produced by the conscious willing of energy to the appropriate muscles. Raise your head and look at the ceiling. Now lift your arms toward the ceiling. It is the conscious directing of energy to specific muscles that has enabled you to make both of these movements, and if you hold the position long enough you will experience the result of muscle energization when you drop the head and arms into their original position. Especially in the arms you will feel a vibrant, prickly sensation and oftentimes a buoyancy which creates a feeling that the arms are floating.

The following exercises are designed to increase the awareness of energy, and to help in its intensification, direction, and control.

ENERGY AWARENESS AND INTENSIFICATION

Lie flat on your back, raising your head slightly with the use of a book, a pillow, or some article of clothing folded into pillow size, and with your arms lying on the floor beside you. Make certain that your lower back is as flat as possible and that your legs and feet are falling easily outward to the sides. Precede all of the following experiences with 1 or 2 from the Psycho-Physical Experiences in Relaxation or with 1, 2, or 3 from the experiences in Deepening Relaxation.

When you are completely relaxed, with eyes closed, take a long moment to fully experience the deep inner energy of your breathing center. Now take another long moment to fully experience the energy in the atmosphere around you. Feel it on your face and hands, on your arms and legs, on any exposed part of your body. Be aware that everything in the universe is energy and rhythm. Experience your self as part of it. As you inhale, feel that you are breathing in energy from the atmosphere around you. As you exhale, feel that you are breathing out your own inner supply of energy. Very slowly and easily, breathe in external energy and breathe out internal energy for at least five minutes, or for as long as it takes for you to experience your internal energy blending with the external energy. Allow your self a long moment to enjoy this feeling of wholeness, of your self as blending with the energy and rhythm of the atmosphere around you, of day and night, of the tides, of the seasons, of the orbiting planets, of all of nature, of the universe.

A second experience in energy awareness and intensification involves the element of sound vibrations. Once again, lie flat on your back and follow the directions in the introductory paragraph above.

When you are completely relaxed, with eyes closed, take a long moment to fully experience the deep inner energy of your breathing center. Now be aware of any sounds you hear outside the room you are in. Don't try to identify or name the sounds. Just allow your self to receive their vibrations and experience them. Next be aware of any sounds you hear inside the room. Receive their vibrations and experience them. Now be aware of any sounds you hear within your self. Tune in and listen to your self exist. Experience any sound vibrations within your head, your chest, or your belly for a long moment. Slowly and gradually let your inner sound vibrations blend with the sound vibrations you have received from the outside. Let all the sound vibrations blend into one dominant sound, and experience its strength and power. Now imagine that you are slowly absorbing the energy from the sound into every body cell. Experience the energy flowing to and through every part of your body. Allow your self a long moment to enjoy the resulting sensation of dynamic vitality with your eyes closed, then slowly open your eyes and try to maintain the perception of your self as a bundle of vibrating energy.

A variation of the experience in energy awareness and intensification involving sound vibrations requires the use of music. Following the preliminaries of a relaxation exercise you lie quietly and listen to a tape or recording of a fully orchestrated selection (with lots of string and woodwind instruments). You must not use a selection in which words are being sung. Unfamiliar music is best, something with no previous associations. As you listen to the selection don't try to follow a melody line or think about the tonal patterns. Just let your self experience the sound vibrations as you receive them. Feel your self breathing in the sound vibrations through every pore in your skin, and imagine that this energy is coursing throughout your entire body, vitalizing every bone, muscle, tissue, and blood cell. Blend with the energy of the music, and when the music ends be aware of your energized self, first with your eyes closed and then with them open.

Another way to intensify your energy supply involves the process of centering. This should be preceded by experience 3 under Deepening Relaxation. When you have completed the slow countdown, and taken a long moment to enjoy the relaxed feeling deep inside you, imagine that you are slowly pulling in all of your scattered energies and forces and focusing them inward on your self. Don't send. Don't receive. Just ground your self, until you have an awareness of nothing but a totally unified you. Now look deep inside your self. You have within you an essence that is uniquely you, that makes you different from everyone else in the world, and that is the spark of your potential power. Find your spark. See in your mind a spot of bright color. See nothing else. Watch it slowly grow larger and brighter, and feel it getting warmer and warmer. Relax and concentrate on your radiant center as it slowly expands, permeating first the trunk of your body, and then outward to your arms and legs, electrifying your fingers and toes, and to the top of your head. Experience radiant energy in every cell in your entire body. Feel that you have *become* a mass of radiant energy. And, once again, enjoy that experience for a long moment with your eyes closed, and maintain the feeling for a long moment with your eyes open.

In all of the experiences related to energy awareness and intensification, it is helpful to use the analogy of the battery. See your self, like a battery, as a connected group of cells storing an electrical charge and capable of furnishing current. And also like the battery, see your self as needing occasional recharging.

If these exercises are done with a group, once everyone is recharged it is a benefit for the group to share the experience of furnishing a current. These experiences are designed, after all, for the purpose of playing, whose end requires the flow of energy between players, and between players and audience.

To experience group energy flow, sit or stand quietly in a fairly tight circle, close your eyes and hold hands with the person on either side of you. For a long moment fully experience your deeply centered breathing and your own radiant energy. For another long moment receive and experience the energy generated by the people on either side of you. Then slowly expand your consciousness of energy flow, until you receive and experience the energy generated by the entire group. Breathe in the group energy. Breathe out your own energy. Feel energy flowing in and out through every pore as you blend with the group. Experience your self as one with the group, as one with all humanity. Now open your eyes and maintain this perception of oneness with the group as you look deep into the eyes of the other group members and share with them your supercharged feelings of free-flowing energy and humanity.

Another dynamic experience of group energy flow is group chanting. This can be used as an exercise in itself, or as a follow-up to the experience above.

The group will stand in a tight circle, and each member will extend his arms outward and encircle the shoulders of the person on each side of him. Through the interlocking of arms with the two people on the other sides of your neighbors, you are actually making physical contact with four other members of the group.

The entire group will stand quietly with eyes closed for a long moment and experience the energy flow through the arms and bodies of the people they are physically contacting, and then slowly expand their consciousness of energy flow from the entire group.

At a cue from the instructor or group leader, the group will begin to bounce easily at the knees, and softly and rhythmically chant in unison: "Go! Go! Go! Go!" Gradually the volume and intensity of the chant should increase until it reaches a peak, and then just as gradually the volume and intensity should decrease into stillness and cessation of movement.

The group should continue to stand with arms interlocked for a long moment and share the experience of group energy and exhilaration. At another cue from the instructor or group leader, the group will then open its collective eyes and maintain this perception of group energy and oneness as long looks are shared between group members.

Any chant can be used in this experience, such as a poetic image for a play or project the group might be working on. Chanting is also useful for intensifying individual energy if you happen to be working alone. The simple expedient of chanting one's own name has been used successfully many times in this respect, always making sure that you use the format of starting softly and rhythmically, of gradually increasing the volume and intensity to a peak, and then just as gradually decreasing the sound to absolute stillness, and then holding onto the feeling for a long moment.

"Tension Awareness and Release" and "Energy Awareness and Intensification" are, of course, simply two sides of the same coin. To comprehend tension we must comprehend energy, for tension is energy potential. Tension is energy that is confined.

There are many exercises for the release of tension and energy flow, such as holding a folded newspaper with both hands and vigorously striking a table while shouting loudly about something, such as "My Pet Peeve!" There are as many variations of this particular exercise as there are practitioners to advocate them. Some suggest loud shouting to the accompaniment of pounding a bed or pillow with one's fists. Others suggest getting on one's knees and shouting while pounding the floor. With any of these instances, the potential energy that is confined in excessively tense muscles is released for more productive use.

On the other hand, there are Yogic exercises that suggest energizing tired or flaccid muscles through the process of consciously tensing muscles in various parts of the body, and then relaxing them. In this instance, energy is consciously directed to limp or fatigued muscles and the energy potential is increased. The first exercise under Tension Awareness and Release (above) can also be used toward this end.

In any instance, it is basically a matter of creating in the muscles the proper degree of tension that is necessary for the muscles to function optimally. And for all of us the method of maintaining this optimal condition will vary with circumstances. There will be times when we need to release tension from taut muscles so that energy will flow, and there will be times when we need to increase tension in weak muscles to supply them with energy.

The underlying factor necessary to the achievement and maintenance of optimal muscle tonicity is self-awareness. Total mental and neuromuscular focus is required to develop the muscle-sense to use the organism wisely by conserving and controlling energy.

Energy is matter in motion. It is the undulating glide of fish in a glassy stream, and the rising, dipping, and circling of birds on their spreading wings. It is the burning radiance of the sun, and the surging pulses of the seas. Energy is the flow of the human voice, rhythmically rising and falling in waves, and the human organism that houses it. Everything in nature is energy, matter in motion, and, even while viewing the separate parts, should be comprehended as a whole. The speaking voice and the human organism that houses it are one entity. This holistic principle is one of the bases on which this text is founded, and your voice will change dramatically once you grasp it. In continuing the study of voice and speech improvement, it will be necessary to consider separate factors of the speaking voice, but the ultimate goal of the study will be your perception of these factors as an integrated, single unit.

· 4 ·

SELF-REALIZATION:
The Breathing Process

A DYNAMIC SPEAKING VOICE MEANS dynamic breathing life. It means becoming increasingly aware of breathing energy and rhythm, of breathing patterns and depth. Breathing is the energy that strengthens and unifies all the other energies. Because of its working relationship with the blood stream in supplying oxygen to the body, breathing means life itself. Because of its working relationship with the voluntary nervous system which we consciously direct, and the autonomic nervous system which we don't, breathing connects the conscious with the unconscious self and represents a source of inner strength and control. Because of its working relationship with body posture, breathing relates to improved health, poise, and appearance. Because of its working relationship with the muscles and the emotions, breathing represents a channel for dynamic self-expression.

The awareness of integrated body life, feeling life, and breathing life can put you in contact with—and in control of—your self. And when you experience this contact, when you become aware of your self as controlling what you speak, you will be more alive to the realities of the present. Dynamic people live in the present and are keenly aware of themselves acting within the present. People have dynamic speaking voices because they allow themselves to be dynamic people.

The breathing process involves the torso of the body, from the shoulder girdle to the pelvic girdle. The diaphragm, a large dome-shaped muscle

47

that is attached to the edges of the lower ribs, divides the torso into the upper thoracic cavity (chest) and the lower abdominal cavity.

The upper thoracic cavity houses mainly the heart and lungs, and these organs are encircled by the rib cage, consisting of twelve pairs of ribs. All of the twelve pairs of ribs are attached to the spine in the back, but the manner in which the ribs are attached in the front permits considerable movement in the lower thorax. The upper seven pairs of ribs are attached to the sternum (breast bone), the lower three pairs of ribs are fused outward together by cartilage, and the bottom two pairs of ribs are completely unattached. The ribs are further attached by the intercostals, an intricate arrangement of internal and external muscles. Interdependent actions of tension and relaxation of the intercostal muscles move the rib cage upward and outward during inhalation, and permit the rib cage to move downward and inward during exhalation.

Following each exhalation, the diaphragm relaxes upward into a domed position under the bottom ribs. When the next inhalation begins, the diaphragm contracts, flattens, and pushes down on the stomach and other organs in the abdominal cavity which causes the abdominal muscles to protrude. This diaphragmatic action happens simultaneously with the action of the intercostal muscles as described above. (See Figure 4.1.) The combined actions of the diaphragmatic muscle and the intercostal muscles increase the size of the chest cavity and decrease the air pressure in the lungs, creating a partial vacuum. To equalize the air pressure in the lungs, air immediately flows in through the oral and nasal cavities, the trachea (windpipe), the bronchial tubes and the smaller bronchioles, and fills the alveoli (air sacs) of which the lungs are made.

In exhalation, the intercostal muscles relax and the ribs move downward and inward, the diaphragm relaxes and moves upward, aided by the inward movement and push of the abdominal muscles and organs. The chest cavity is thus reduced in size and the air is forced out. The lungs, being of a somewhat elastic composition, are completely passive in this process. Everything depends on the muscles.

It is through the free and natural use of the intercostal muscles and diaphragm, and the other muscles of the chest, abdomen, and back that one attains maximum lung expansion with all of the life-giving properties and vocal power that this affords. It is the firm, controlled support of these muscles in exhalation that provides the sustained voice capability to project long, intricate phrases. Maximum vocal power and sustention require

FIGURE 4.1.

MOVEMENT OF THE DIAPHRAGM IN BREATHING

A. Diaphragm rises and relaxes at end of exhalation. B. Diaphragm contracts and lowers in inhalation.

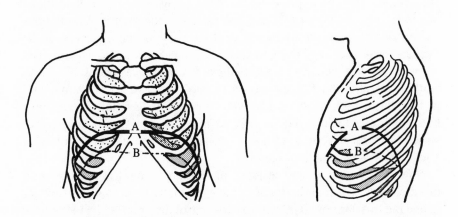

full, free use of all the muscles from the shoulder girdle to the pelvic girdle during the process of respiration. Anything less means that the actor is inhibited from expressing the total humanity of his character.

By far the most common respiration problems are involved with those individuals using only high, clavicular or midchest breathing in which the action of both the diaphragm and the lower rib cage is restricted. This type of breathing permits only limited air intake and results in minimal powers of expression and projection. The added effort of trying to supply the body's oxygen needs with this inhibited type of breathing also produces hypertension in the pharynx (throat), the larynx (voice box), the soft palate and tongue, and this results in limited vocal range and unpleasant voice qualities. Most of the types of voice problems that we label variously as thin, breathy, harsh, or strident can be corrected by learning to breathe freely and fully. This natural manner of breathing also helps to eliminate hypertension in the muscle of the jaw and the tongue, as well as those in and around the larynx.

Another respiration problem occurs with those individuals using only abdominal breathing in which the rib cage seems to move hardly at all.

This type of breathing also permits only limited air intake, produces its own tensions, and results in restricted vocal power. Fortunately this problem is much less common and when it does occur it is often as the result of improper training. Questioning usually reveals the fact that abdominal breathing has been encouraged as the proper support for the voice.

To determine whether or not you are breathing freely and fully, I suggest that you first jog in place or otherwise engage in some form of vigorous physical activity for two or three minutes, and then lie flat on your back. Loosen any tight articles of clothing such as belts, jackets, neckties, and brassieres, and if your shoes have high heels, remove them. The vigorous physical activity energizes the breathing process, loosening tight clothing permits the full expansion of the muscles of respiration, and getting rid of high heels enables you to put your feet flat on the floor, knees pointing toward the ceiling, so that you can flatten your lower back. Also, raise your head about an inch with the use of a pillow, a book, or a folded article of clothing.

Now close your eyes and be aware of your breathing. Empty your mind of all else and concentrate totally on the rhythmic process of air flowing in and out of your nostrils. Don't try to control the process. Just let it happen. Be an observer.

Lay one hand on your upper chest and lay the other hand over the midriff. As you continue to relax under the spell of your rhythmic breathing, be aware of which hand moves first and which hand moves most. If you're really relaxed and are a normal breather, you will experience the hand over the midriff area moving first and higher. Remain in this position long enough for the sensation of movement and tension connected with natural, free breathing to fully penetrate your consciousness. You are receiving this kinesthetic sensation through the nerve ends in your muscles, tendons, and joints and you must concentrate on the sensation if you want to establish control of the process. You must form a kinesthetic image of the process of effective breathing associated with the condition and sensation of the muscles that produce it. The image must be realized simultaneously in the mind and body.

To better understand why there is more breathing movement in the midriff area, look inside your chest cavity with your mind's eye. See that, while all twelve pairs of your ribs are attached to your spine in the back, they are not all attached to your sternum (breast bone) in the front. Put your fingers at the top of the sternum and run them slowly down it. Be aware that the V-shaped separation of the ribs at the bottom of the ster-

num is due to the fact that the ninth rib is fused outward from the eighth rib, the tenth rib is fused outward from the ninth rib, and that the eleventh and twelfth ribs are completely unattached (floating ribs). See that the lungs are wider at the bottom than they are at the top. Then be aware that the body was designed for deep breathing. The arrangement of the ribs and the shape of the lungs both permit greater movement in the midriff area.

With fingers spread, lay both hands flat on the midriff. For a long moment experience the deep center and the fullness of your breathing through the rhythmic rise and fall of the muscles beneath your hands. Be aware of the breath flowing in and out through your nostrils as the result of this muscular movement. Now lay your hands on the floor at your side and continue for a long moment to concentrate on your kinesthetic image of the breathing process associated with its physical sensation.

To increase your awareness of the action of the rib cage in respiration, turn your fingers in toward the palms of your hands as if you were going to make a fist and then place the outside of the fingers against the lower ribs on each side. As you continue to focus solely on your breathing, experience the sensation of the lower ribs swinging upward and outward during inhalation and then swinging downward and inward during exhalation. Once again, remain in this position long enough for the movement and tension that you feel through the nerve endings in your muscles, tendons, and joints to fully penetrate your consciousness.

Now move the fingers up and place them against the ribs under the armpits. Be aware that there is much less movement in the upper part of the rib cage. The body was designed for full, deeply centered breathing, and this fact must be firmly imprinted on the mind and fixed in the kinesthetic memory. To bring about this necessary awareness, it may be necessary for you to repeat this imprint-conditioning experience for many days.

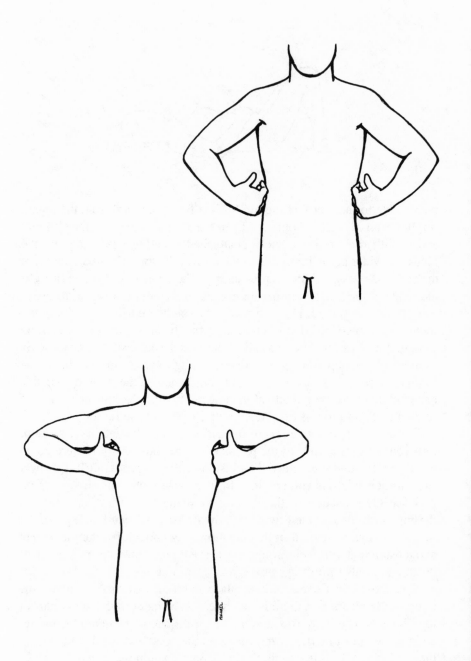

It is very easy to slip back into bad breathing habits, and these habits must be monitored constantly at first. I suggest to my students that they repeat this entire experience every day for at least a month, then cut down to perhaps two or three times a week, and for maintenance purposes after that to give themselves a regular weekly check-up. And with this particular experience, as well as with those experiences that follow, an important factor is the carryover into the daily activities concerned with moving and speaking in an upright position.

Following the period of breathing awareness done on your back on the floor, there should be an immediate continuing period of breathing awareness done in a sitting or standing position, or both. To firmly fix the sensation of full, natural breathing in the mind and the kinesthetic memory, you must continue to concentrate on the experience as you move about and speak; this focus should continue for at least ten minutes, or for as long as you can, and for as many times as you can throughout the day and evening. Imprint-conditioning, so vital to the acquisition of improved breathing habits, needs frequent short periods of conscious awareness.

Of all of the muscles involved in the process of total respiration, it is generally the intercostal muscles of the lower ribs, the muscles of the abdomen and lower back that need strengthening. These muscles must be encouraged to fully expand for maximum vocal power and for effective control in the projection of long phrases.

LOWER RIB AND BACK MUSCLE CONDITIONING

To strengthen the action of the muscles between the lower ribs and in the lower back, as well as to increase sensitivity to this important factor of the breathing process, the following practice is recommended.

Stand up straight or sit up as tall as you can in a straight chair. Let your head fall forward and let its weight slowly pull your shoulders and upper body down until the combined weight forces you to fall forward easily and with a complete exhalation. (If you are standing you will feel that you are being held up by a string at the base of the spine. If you are sitting, the trunk of your body will be lying on your thighs.) Breathe out all of your air and close your mouth. Then clamp the fingers of one hand on your nostrils so that you cannot breathe in, slowly pull yourself upright, let go of your nose, and experience the expansion in the deepest part of you as the air surges in. You should feel the ribs swing up and out, as well as the muscles of your lower back and abdomen.

To narrow the focus of the action, however, you will repeat the exercise of falling forward, exhaling all of your air, and clamping your fingers on your nose, but do not pull yourself upright. Continue to hang forward from the waist if you are standing, or lie on your thighs if you are sitting and, with closed mouth and nose, hold that position until you feel the need to breathe in. Then let go of your nose and experience the air surging in. Since abdominal breathing is somewhat inhibited due to being bent over, the expansion of the rib cage and the lower back should be much stronger and more pronounced.

Repeat the second step of staying bent over until you have let go of your nostrils and breathed in, and then repeat the first step of slowly pulling yourself upright, letting go of your nostrils and inhaling. Be aware of the expansion of the rib cage and lower back muscles in both cases and monitor the relative movements of each posture. It is to be expected that doing the exercises two or three times in the forward position will encourage the rib and lower back muscles to expand more fully, and that this will carry over when the exercise is repeated in an upright position.

Strengthening the action of the muscles between the lower ribs and in the lower back can also be done effectively by working in pairs.

A will sit tall in a straight chair, with eyes closed, and then lean forward from the waist, maintaining the straight back and resting forearms on the thighs. *B* will stand behind *A* with hands firmly on the lower ribs in *A*'s back, fingers curling around the ribs on each side. (This exercise may

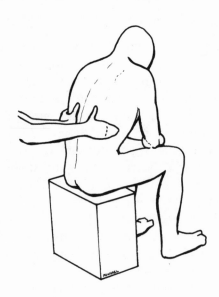

also be done with both members seated on the floor in yoga fashion, one behind the other.)

A will breathe in deeply, and then exhale every bit of air. The complete exhalation should feel as if the stomach muscles are being flattened against the backbone, and that position should be held. A should be aware while holding that position that the body is accumulating carbon dioxide and increasing its need for oxygen, and that he has to impose tension on the respiration muscles to prevent the body from inhaling air. A must also be aware, however, that he is the one imposing the tension, that he is in complete control, so there is no need to panic. When the felt need for an inhalation becomes strong enough, A will easily release the imposed tension on the muscles and enjoy the experience of the air surging in and the ribs and lower back expanding enthusiastically. A key concept in this exercise is that the imposed tension is released easily. This factor is readily accomplished if the position is not held so long that panic sets in and the needed inhalation is hastily gulped. It must be thought of as an easy letting-go of muscle tension. Only this method of release will let air flow in freely. Trying to quickly pull in air imposes further tension on the lower back and rib muscles and the air will fill only the upper chest, completely defeating the purpose of the exercise.

It is important to the success of this experience that both members quietly concentrate on A's lower back and rib expansion, exchanging only necessary feedback. For example, B may need information regarding the placement and degree of firmness of his hands on A's back, being aware that the hands are placed there to aid A's focus and not to inhibit breathing. And A should receive feedback as to the degree his rib cage swings out at the sides and back.

After A has breathed in and out two or three times and information has been exchanged, A and B will change places and repeat the exercise. To eliminate any possible effects of hyperventilation, the exercise should never be done by any one person more than three times in succession. Usually twice is sufficient at one sitting, and if more work is needed to condition the rib and back muscles the practice can be repeated later in the work session, or used on successive days.

After A and B have both experienced the exercise, each person in the group should sit straight with eyes closed, lean forward with forearms resting on the thighs, and concentrate on trying to reproduce the entire experience including the hold at the end of the exhalation, for a maximum of two times. Each person should then try to reproduce the experience of the expanded action of the lower rib and back muscles, breathing naturally, and without the hold at the end of the exhalation, but still leaning forward with forearms resting on the thighs.

As a final step, maintenance of the expanded muscle action should be extended to an upright position, either sitting or standing, or both. Let the vital sensation of full, free breathing integrate with the increased awareness of body and feeling life that inevitably accompanies this experience when it is properly practiced. When the eyes are opened it should extend to a sharing of this increased vitality with others in the group. This increased sensitivity and self-realization should extend into your daily activities. Behavior has to be relearned and brought under conscious control. The comprehension of the anatomical and physiological reasons for full, natural breathing and the kinesthetic sensations connected with the process must become a constant, disciplined consideration in your daily use of your self.

BREATHING CAPACITY AND CONTROL

Muscle strength, flexibility, and coordination are important factors in the control of breathing. These factors are just as important to the actor as they are to the athlete, and for an individual to be effective in either field, frequent periods of attention must be devoted to the development of these factors. This is particularly true for the actor or any other type of public speaker, and for a curious reason. The athlete, in almost any sport you can name, realizes the need for muscle building because he uses his muscles in a way different from his everyday activities. To achieve perfection, therefore, the athlete is generally willing, if not eager, to work diligently at conditioning his muscles. For the actor or other public speaker, however, breathing is something he does all the time. He doesn't even have to think about it. The fact that he speaks all day long using the muscles of respiration, too often produces a casual "why bother" attitude and it frequently requires constant reminding that speaking in performance demands far greater muscle strength than that needed for speaking in everyday situations.

To begin the development of muscle control in respiration you should lie flat on your back. This horizontal position is the way the body breathes naturally and the way the body breathes best. When you are lying down you are better able to relax and this horizontal position also eliminates the counter-productive problem of gravity pull that takes place when you sit or stand.

Once again, loosen any tight articles of clothing, remove high heels so that you can put your feet flat on the floor and point your knees toward the ceiling, and raise your head about an inch or so.

Now close your eyes and be aware of your breathing. Empty your mind and focus on the rhythmic process of air flowing in and out of your nostrils simultaneously with the movement of your respiration muscles. For a long moment be an observer and just let it happen. This particular experience is immensely satisfying and relaxing, puts you in touch with your body and feeling life, and produces a unifying self-awareness, which is a necessary first step to self-realization.

To express your self effectively, however, there must be a conscious control of these unified factors. In effective expression, body and feeling life, along with mental and spiritual life, are channeled into the exhaled breath. Breath control is self control. So now take control of your breath and of your self.

Breathing comfortably and easily, inhale for the silent count of five, then exhale for the silent count of six. Inhale for the count of six, exhale for the count of seven. Inhale for the count of seven, exhale for the count of eight, and so on, increasing the count of the exhalation by one each time, until you feel that you have reached a comfortable capacity.

Since the more you breathe out the more you are able to breathe in, this exercise is excellent for breath capacity, as well as breath control. The key to the success of this exercise is that it be done slowly and easily, and that you do not try to extend your capacity to the point where you are uncomfortable. In trying to extend beyond your maximum capacity, you put a strain on the respiration muscles and impose unnecessary tension that lessens your ability to control exhalation. Try it just once and you will understand this particular phenomenon. Inhale until you feel comfortably full, and then continue to inhale until you experience uncomfortable strain in the muscles. And when you exhale you will find that the muscles, in their need to be rid of the excess tension, will very quickly relax back to the position where they are comfortable, accompanied by a burst of exhaled breath. This burst is wasted breath, and this experience of straining your capacity is one that you should remember when you speak lines. Before you can even begin to control the breath in supporting your words, you will have lost quite a portion of it in one great puff.

This is a needless expenditure of energy, both in exhaled breath and muscle tension.

When you have demonstrated to your own satisfaction the elements of comfortable capacity and control in a horizontal position, you then repeat the exercise in a vertical position, first sitting and then standing. In fact, as your comfortable capacity and your control of it increases, you will be able to easily perform the exercise sitting or standing.

Another practice that aids the development of breath capacity and control is that of the breath count while walking. The counting in the exercise, as with the one above is, of course, done silently in the mind, since it is practically impossible to speak aloud while inhaling. This exercise can be done as you walk down the street alone, or with a group, circling about in a large room.

In group practice, the instructor or group leader will give a signal to begin, such as "One, two, three, go!" and the group will rhythmically, and in unison, walk forward to the following count: inhale "two, three, four," hold "two, three, four," exhale "two, three, four," relax "two, three, four." Walk confidently and easily as if you knew where you were going.

Used individually or in group practice, the exercise should be repeated six or eight times with a total count of four; then repeated with a total count of six, then of eight, and so on. The highest total count depends on how fast you are walking and counting.

But even if the total count seems to be getting too high for certain individuals, simply making the physical adjustment to accommodate it provides further development in control. For instance, when inhaling for the count of ten you simply take in the breath more slowly than you would for a lower total count of four or six; and, of course, the same principle applies when you let the breath out. That is breath control—the conscious direction of the movement of the respiration muscles to regulate incoming and outgoing breath. Just consider how well this will serve you in speaking long passages in performance. This logically brings us to another important factor.

The process of breathing to sustain life differs from that of breathing to sustain speech. In the first instance, the two phases of inhalation and exhalation are relatively equal in length; this is not true in the second instance. In speaking, the inhalation phase is shortened and the exhalation phase is lengthened. In fact, in long speeches we must learn to get a full, deep breath to start and to never let all the breath out. The initial wide expansion of the lower rib and back muscles should not be allowed to diminish by much before you take in quick, little compensatory breaths, timing them to coordinate with logical pauses in the speech. You can develop this skill by counting aloud in longer and longer sequences.

Begin your practice on your back with head slightly elevated, feet flat on the floor, eyes closed, and not bound by any tight clothing. Put your concentration totally on the breathing process until its hypnotic rhythm relaxes you and you are breathing easily and freely.

Now let your self inhale fully and comfortably and count to ten; take a quick breath and count to eleven; take a quick breath and count to ten; take a quick breath and count to twelve; take a quick breath and count to ten; take a quick breath and count to thirteen; and so on, ten then fourteen, ten then fifteen, and as far as you can go with ease.

The two factors to be developed are (1) the comfortable control of longer and longer phrases, all the way to the last, sustained number in the phrase, and (2) the quick little intake of breath before each phrase. By sustaining longer and longer phrases you are developing control of the breathing muscles; by sustaining the final number in each sequence you are developing the habit of projecting final words in your lines instead of letting them drop so that they can't be heard, which is a far too common occurrence with actors. By not letting all the breath out and taking little compensatory breaths instead, you are maintaining not only breath support but body strength.

The element of body strength can be demonstrated very easily. Select a heavy piece of furniture in your room and prepare to lift it. You will find that the body takes in a full, deep breath automatically and that the vocal folds in the larynx close to prevent that breath from escaping. This combination of full breath and energized muscles due to expansion tension has given the body a firmness and strength it does not normally have.

Now let your self experience the reverse effect. Start counting, but this time don't stop to take a quick breath when the ribs begin to sag. Keep counting until you completely run out of breath and be aware of two significant results. First of all, your body will be so weak when you finish counting that you couldn't possibly lift a piece of furniture; you will find that you have undue strain in your arm muscles if you lift so much as a book. Second, the absence of breath and body support will have forced you to try and project your speech from the throat, causing excessive tension in the muscles in that area as well as in the upper chest, jaw, tongue, and palate, and producing a strident, unpleasant voice quality.

For all the above reasons, it should be clear at this point that the best voice production is achieved with full natural breathing and with comfortable capacity and muscle control. Also, you must practice the exercise of counting in long phrases interspaced with quick breaths in the sitting and/or standing position. We begin exercises for breathing and voice production in a horizontal position for the reason that the process works best in this position. Once the process is fixed in the mind and the kinesthetic memory, however, it is the carry-over of the imprint-conditioning into actual performance postures that is important.

BREATHING AND POSTURE

It should also be clear at this point that full, natural breathing is impossible without the proper body posture. Prove it to your self. Sit down and imagine that you are very tired. Use your imagination to dramatize your self in any fatigue-producing situation—the end of a busy workday, after a long, tiring rehearsal, or what you will. Let the fatigue impose itself on your body. Let the head sink into the shoulder girdle, and then let the entire weight of the head, shoulders, and trunk of the body sag over the pelvic girdle. Close your eyes and tell your self that it is a great effort to sit at all, that what you really want to do is lie down and sleep. Hold this position for a long moment and while still holding it try to take a full breath. Try again. Try harder and be aware that your body wants to straighten up. Begin one more inhalation and slowly lift and straighten your body, allowing the air to flow in and fill you deeply. Be aware of your elongated spine and of the separation between the lower ribs and the pelvis as you now breathe fully. Imagine that your head is floating upward; let it float you to a standing position.

For a long moment enjoy the freedom of full, uninhibited breathing, and imprint the sensation in the kinesthetic memory and the conscious mind. Tell your self that you are not making your self stand upright but that you are letting it happen. The idea that you are making it happen imposes unnecessary tension on the body muscles and can inhibit the very thing you are trying to accomplish. Experience the breath flowing in and out without any necessary effort from you and focus on your spine with your head floating on top of it. Think tall. Think that it is the skeletal structure that is supporting you; think of the muscles as hanging loosely from the skeletal structure; think of the head as suspended; then think of your entire self as lighter than air, floating in space.

BECOMING A PUPPET

An excellent experience to produce body lightness and improved posture is to imagine that you are a puppet. See yourself not as bones and muscles, but as thin, narrow pieces of wood, loosely held together by pieces of string. Now imagine that there is a puppeteer standing on a platform above you and that he is holding you up straight by a string attached to your head, by strings attached to your shoulders and wrists, and another string attached to the base of your spine.

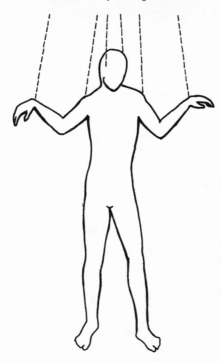

Imagine first that there is a puppeteer above you who pulls up the strings attached to your wrists and bounces your arms around in the air, then drops them. Now imagine that the puppeteer pulls up the strings attached to your head and shoulders and bounces you up and down off the floor.

Now imagine that the puppeteer loosens the string attached to the top of your head and your head falls forward, that he loosens the strings attached to your shoulders and the upper part of your body falls forward, and that you are suspended only by the string attached to the base of the spine.

Now imagine that he pulls up the trunk of your body by the shoulder strings, and pulls up your head by the head string, and that he once again pulls up the strings attached to your head and shoulders and bounces you up and down off the floor.

This concept of your self as merely loosely connected slats of wood, being moved about by someone else's effort, is a very useful one when you are tired and your muscles feel sluggish and heavy. It helps to achieve the feeling of lightness and buoyancy so necessary to good posture.

Many of the exercises of chapter 2 are also helpful in achieving a feeling of body lightness, exercises such as jogging, running, and bouncing balls. Particularly helpful is the stretch-and-yawn. Reread the instructions and perform this exercise fully and then continue with the following variation, which is loosely based on a Yoga exercise.

LADDER STRETCH

Standing comfortably with your feet separated about the width of your shoulders, think of your head floating upward on top of your tall, straight spine. Now lift your arms straight out to the sides at shoulder height and breathe easily in and out two or three times. The elevated arms help the rib cage to expand and your breathing should be deep and full.

Now lift your arms straight up overhead and imagine that you are pulling your self up by the rungs of a ladder. Keep stretching and breathing easily as you grasp a rung with the right hand, then a higher one with the left hand, a higher one with the right hand, and so on. Coordinate one full inhalation with the stretch of each rung. Do not look up as you do this, but maintain an eyes-front position with a straight back that enables you to experience the spine stretching. After climbing six or eight rungs, stand quietly with both arms straight up and experience two or three full, deep breaths. After the exercise, and in this body position, the muscles in the lower back and abdomen should be relaxed and, together with the muscles connecting the lower ribs, will expand easily to allow deep respiration.

Be aware of the elevated rib cage and comfortably maintain it in this position as you let the hands fall from the wrists, let the forearms fall from the elbow and then let the upper arms fall from the shoulders. As you stand with arms hanging down at the sides, maintain the image of your straight spine and your head floating upward, followed by the rib cage, and the total easy respiration that results.

You can quickly contrast good postural breathing with bad by letting the rib cage sag and the trunk of the body press down on the pelvis. One inhibited breath will inform you that this is wrong for the respiration process, and one glance in a mirror will also inform you that it is wrong for a dynamic appearance. So let your final impression be a positive one and straighten your spine and let your head and rib cage float upward to the position where you can once again experience total, easy respiration.

The arms-straight-over-head stretch is not only an aid to correct posture and total respiration but does a marvelous job of energizing the entire body, particularly when one is lying flat on one's back.

Lying completely flat, stretch your arms and hands as far as possible and your legs, feet, and toes as far as possible while inhaling slowly and deeply. Stop stretching and relax as you slowly exhale.

Once again slowly inhale while stretching your arms all the way to the finger tips, but this time stretch the back of your legs and your heels, pulling the toes back toward you. Stop stretching and relax as you slowly exhale. For a long moment enjoy the resulting feeling of well-being and vitality, and try to maintain the feeling when you stand.

This exercise is also effective when done with a partner, who stands in back of your head, grips your hands and pulls to help you stretch your arms as you inhale, and stops pulling as you exhale so that you can relax. And if there is a third person gripping your ankles and pulling to help stretch your legs at the same time, so much the better. But be it one or two partners, the pulls must be coordinated with inhalations, and they must be done firmly but gently.

Posture and respiration can also be improved, and the rib cage be given a good stretch, by laying the two hands, with fingers interlaced, on top of your head and slowly breathing in and out once or twice.

Then let your head fall forward and your hands slide to the back of your head and hang there with elbows pointing toward the floor, as you breathe into your back. Imagine that you are both widening and lengthening your back as you fill it with air at least twice.

Now let your elbows open like wings and fall to the back, simultaneously with the head cradled in the clasped hands, as you breathe into and expand your chest in the front. Imagine that you are both widening and lengthening the chest as you fill it with air at least twice.

Finish the exercise as you started it, with the head and body straight up, the hands on top of the head, and breathing in and out once or twice, after which you maintain the head and body position, drop the arms, and continue to breathe easily and fully as you move into your daily activities.

The slap-massage exercise in chapter 3 is also conducive to improved posture and respiration, particularly the spine-walk. Focus on the spine, however, can also be reinforced without the help of a partner in the following manner. Keep your eyes straight ahead, as you stretch your arms straight up over your head. Keeping the arms straight up, drop first the hands, then the forearms, then the upper arms.

Now drop the head onto the chest, and let the weight of the head, and then the arms and shoulders, pull you slowly down until you fall forward easily from the waist. Let the knees bend slightly and imagine that you are held up by a string at the base of the spine.

Next, put your focus on the bottom-most vertebra and imagine that you are stacking the second vertebra on top of it, the third on top of the second, the fourth on top of the third, and so on up as you slowly pull yourself back into an upright position. For the entire pull-up, keep your focus on your spine as your center and support, and don't forget the seven cervical vertebrae in the back of the neck that pull the head upright. For a

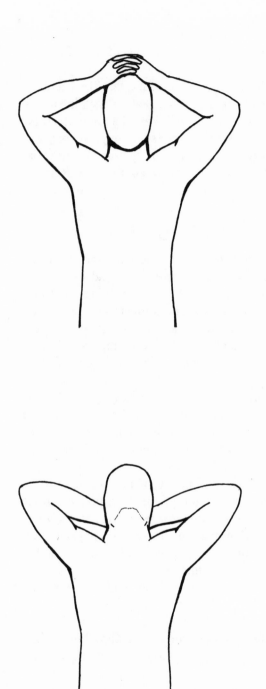

long moment stand tall with your head floating upward, and focus on your spine.

Now close your eyes, and as you inhale, imagine that the energy is flowing into your spine. Hold your breath at the peak of each inhalation and imagine that your spine is being energized from the tailbone all the way up the back of the neck. Conclude the exercise when you experience your spine as a column of energy. Then open your eyes and try to maintain that image as you move about and perform your daily tasks. Remember always that your strength is in your back, that the spine contains the energy of the life force.

PSYCHO-PHYSICAL CONDITIONING

In beginning your study of voice production, it is necessary to isolate specific factors and to practice exercises to strengthen and expand the muscles of respiration and to improve posture, thus enabling you to induce and use complete, natural breathing. The ultimate goal, however, is to integrate these improved factors with those of energy and an adequate amount of body tension into new self-awareness. Improper, limited breathing is, after all, only a symptom of a cause that is rooted solidly in the mind and the body. Improper breathing is changed through psychophysiological conditioning. As you progress in your study, you will think less and less in terms of taking a breath, and more and more in terms of replenishing total energy. The thought of "taking a breath" has a curiously inhibiting effect on the body. The word "take" implies effort and translates into muscular tension.

The perception of the breath, and ultimately of the voice, must be thought of in terms of total self-energy and rhythm. Daily practice of the foregoing exercises will eventually fix this new perception in the mind and in the kinesthetic memory. Command of this psycho-physiological mechanism will give you the control you need and transform your ability to use your self. The simple act of breathing, for instance, when done with an accompanying, positive mental image can transform you into a dynamo.

Either sitting or standing upright, with eyes closed, breathe easily in and out, and be aware just of the increased body and feeling life that full breathing produces. Concentrate totally on experiencing the energy, rhythm, and feeling life in every part of the body.

Use your concentration now to intensify your energy supply and to enhance your self-concept. As you slowly inhale, imagine that you are pulling in energy through every pore in your skin. See energy coursing throughout your entire body, and hold the peak of your inhalation long enough to feel that every body cell is vitalized, then inhale your energized breath. Breathe in external energy, vitalize the body, breathe out internal energy. Repeat this as many times as needed, until you feel supercharged.

You can imagine an inflow of power, purpose, poise, peace, command, or whatever you will. Energy as an image works well for the reason that after you have breathed in external energy through every pore in the skin, and then breathed out your own internal energy for a long enough period, you will suddenly become aware that it's all one. Your realization of your self and of the atmosphere around you as all part of the unifying force of natural energy will come as a spiritual illumination. You will find that you have stopped counting, and that your power feels no boundaries. Creative impulses will be stimulated, as will the energy and desire to explore them.

Hold onto this new perception of your self for as long as you possibly can to imprint it on your psycho-physical mechanism, and then very slowly open your eyes and imprint it on your visual world. The impact of the visual world won't dampen your illumination if you keep reminding your self that objects that catch your eye have no power whatsoever. The forces that have power are things we can't see — love, truth, honor, hate, greed, and jealousy. Remind your self that the force of love can accomplish miracles, even though you can't see it. We see birds fly, leaves flutter, and waves roll, but we can't see the energy that is powering them. Be mindful that you too are powered by energy, as is your speaking voice, and you must constantly repeat this to your self until it becomes a fixation. Your speaking voice is whatever you are at any given moment, at whatever level of energy.

You will have to assign your self daily periods to imprint this new perception, for no one can function at this level of intensity for all his waking hours. Also, there will be other considerations and forces, many of them negative, that will intrude on your conscious thought. But a daily, quiet practice of this experience can make a difference, in you and in your speaking voice, which are, after all, one entity. And some reading of Yogic theory related to the unseen forces as your real strength will help to reinforce your practice.

If you have only a short period in which to recharge your battery, say before a rehearsal or performance, or if you have trouble grasping the above scientific facts, you can get a charge using a different image.

This experience will be effective either lying on your back, or sitting or standing tall. In either posture, close your eyes, breathe through your nostrils, and imagine that you are a balloon of a lovely, gay color. Make the color specific.

As you slowly inhale, experience your self becoming larger and larger, and more and more buoyant until you are floating and weaving gently back and forth.

As you slowly exhale, experience your self becoming smaller and smaller, drifting downward, and becoming finally flat and limp. This phase of the experience works best if you are sitting or lying on your back, as you can more completely achieve the feeling of being totally empty of air, and the important factor of relaxation can be integrated into the breathing cycle. And be aware that the more completely you relax after each exhalation, the deeper and fuller will be the next inhalation. This factor is also worthy of imprint.

Repeat this experience five or six times, or until you feel free of excess tension and are aware of feeling life flowing freely through the body.

Now inhale slowly again, and imagine that each inhalation expands the balloon larger and larger, and that you don't diminish your size as you exhale. With each inhalation see your self getting larger and rounder, and maintain that image and weave gently back and forth as you exhale. When you feel completely light and buoyant, and have achieved a lovely high as the result of releasing and expanding the self, open your eyes slowly and imprint this self-image on your visual environment.

Any psycho-physical experience should be followed, wherever possible, by the following experience, which reinforces the factors of energizing muscles, relaxation, concentration, creativity, the ability to risk and experiment, self-control, posture, total respiration, and the enhancing of the self-concept.

Stand tall with your eyes open and looking straight ahead. Now stretch your arms straight overhead, flatten your hands, palms up, and imagine that you are pushing against the ceiling with the palms of your hands. Do not look up. See your self peripherally as filling all of that space, feet very solidly on the floor, and hands firmly pressed against the ceiling. Maintain this posture until the perception of your self as filling the space from floor to ceiling is clear and fixed. Then maintain this perception as you let your arms fall easily at your sides. Imprint the perception of your self as floor-to-ceiling persona for a long, long moment.

Now stretch your arms out to the sides, at shoulder height, and with the fingers pointing straight up, imagine that the palms of your hands are pressing against the wall. Feel the texture of the wall against your hands, as you make one slow, complete turn. Keep your eyes straight ahead, and see your self peripherally as filling all of that space, wall to wall, as you slowly turn. When you complete the turn, maintain this perception as you let your arms fall easily at your sides. Imprint the perception of your self as wall-to-wall, floor-to-ceiling persona for a long, long moment as you stand quietly. Continue to maintain and imprint the perception as you move slowly about the room.

If you have executed this psycho-physical experience properly, you will have a glorious high. You will feel that you have let your self out, extended your sphere of influence and domination, and that you are in complete control of your sphere and of your self.

Maximum development and control of breathing for voice production means maximum functioning and control of all of the elements that make up the psycho-physiological mechanism. It means ever-increasing self-awareness of body and feeling life, of body energy and tension, of muscle flexibility and control, of body posture and rhythms, and of the self-concept. The breath that powers the speaking voice is a composite of all of these elements.

· 5 ·

SELF-REALIZATION:
Voice Production

THE VOICE IS DIRECTED ENERGY, an instrument of changing and infinite design. Voice releases energy in a continuous flow from the power center of the respiration muscles — energy moving upward and vibrating against the vocal folds, resonated and amplified in the cavities and bones of the chest, throat, and head, and issuing at last from the mouth where it is shaped by the lips, tongue, soft palate, and jaw. Voice production constitutes the sum of muscle energy, nervous energy, emotional energy, and the energy of the breath. Total respiration is only one of many coordinated processes that produce vocal sound.

That total respiration is the basis for effective voice production, however, must be kept constantly in mind, and the practice of total respiration must be continued as we study and integrate other factors of voice production.

Exhaled breath furnishes the power for the vocal tone which is vibrated in the larynx (voice box); this process is called *phonation*. The basic tone vibrated in the larynx is amplified and intensified in the resonating chambers in the head, throat, and chest; this process is called *resonation*. And while the study of voice production must necessarily be more concerned with function than with structure, it is important to understand the structure of a mechanism if we would use it efficiently.

The larynx is suspended from the *hyoid bone*, which is, in turn, suspended from the roots of the tongue. The larynx is supported from

71

underneath by the trachea (windpipe) on which it sits and to which it is attached. The larynx is, in effect, the top part of the trachea; together they form one continuous tube through which air passes in and out of the body. The skeletal framework of the larynx is made up of cartilages which gradually harden and lose their flexibility as we grow older, and this hardening process affects the quality, pitch, and flexibility of the voice in older people. The parts of the larynx discussed below are only those parts that are needed to understand the process of phonation.

The *cricoid cartilage* forms both the base of the larynx and the top ring of the trachea. It looks very much like a signet ring, with the wide part in the back and the narrow part in the front.

The *thyroid cartilage* that we call the Adam's apple, is a wedge-like structure and is joined to the cricoid cartilage on the sides by two horns. This attachment is in the form of a hinge-like device which enables the thyroid cartilage to tilt back and forth on the cricoid cartilage.

The *vocal folds*, which vibrate to make the basic vocal tone, are attached to the center of the thyroid cartilage in the front, and to the inside wall of the thyroid cartilage on the sides.

The *glottis* is the opening between the vocal folds.

The *arytenoid cartilages* are two pyramid-shaped structures to which the vocal folds are attached in the back. They rest on the wide part of the cricoid cartilage in the back and are loosely attached to it, permitting a

FIGURE 5.1.

PRINCIPAL PARTS OF THE LARYNX.

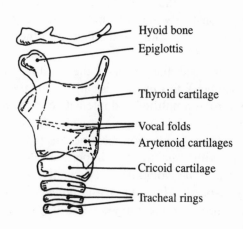

Hyoid bone
Epiglottis

Thyroid cartilage

Vocal folds
Arytenoid cartilages

Cricoid cartilage

Tracheal rings

movement which combines both sliding and rotation to open the vocal folds in breathing and to close them in phonation.

The *intrinsic muscles* have attachments inside the larynx and are primarily responsible for the production of vocal sound. They form an intricate system of abductor and adductor muscles which separate and bring together the arytenoids and vocal folds, and of tensor and relaxer muscles which elongate and shorten the vocal folds to produce the many rapid changes necessary in speech production. Their control of the vocal folds is further coordinated with the function of the arytenoid cartilages, the thyroid cartilage, and the muscles that connect the thyroid, cricoid, and arytenoid cartilages. The sole function of the instrinsic muscles is their effect on the shape and size of the glottis and on the vibratory behavior of the muscles that make up the vocal folds.

The *extrinsic muscles* have at least one attachment to structures outside the larynx and are primarily responsible for supporting the larynx and holding it in position, and for moving it up and down. The movements of these muscles are more directly related to biological functions; for instance the elevator muscles move the larynx up when we swallow, and the depressor muscles move the larynx down when we yawn. However, they do aid the process of phonation by changing the position of the larynx in relation to the pharynx, thereby altering the size of the pharyngeal resonating cavity.

The primary biological function of the larynx, like that of the breathing mechanism, is to sustain life. The process of respiration supplies life-giving oxygen to the body, and the vocal folds in the larynx close to contain air in the lungs during such physical exertions as childbirth, the elimination of body waste, and for heavy lifting. The vocal folds also close when we swallow to prevent food from entering the respiratory tract. Voice, therefore, is a secondary use, or what is known as an "overlaid function," of the larynx. As part of their evolutionary development, humans have made use of the larynx to produce vocal sound.

As stated previously, however, the important consideration for the student of voice production is the way in which the larynx is used. It is practically impossible to visualize the structure and comprehend the physiology of the larynx from a word description and a few diagrams; the functioning of the mechanism is extremely complicated and involved. What matters is that the vocal folds are the vibrating structure that produces vocal sound; that this process involves the complex, integrated action of many, tiny muscles; and that this action requires a minimal amount of energy. In other words, we are concerned once again with adequate muscle tension, but on a much smaller scale.

When you are relaxed and breathing easily, the larynx is generally not overly tensed. It is unfortunately true, however, that anxiety-producing situations translate into muscle tension in the area of the jaw, the shoulder girdle, and the pharynx, and that the proximity of this combined tension increases the tension in the larynx and has a deleterious effect on the voice. If continued for long periods, hypertension in the larynx can produce small lumps, or nodules, on the vocal folds, which negatively effect voice quality, and may have to be removed by a laryngologist. Excessive muscle tension in the larynx, coupled with bad breathing habits, is the cause of such vocal qualities as harshness, hoarseness, stridency, and glottal attacks.

On the other hand, insufficient muscle tension in the larynx, coupled with bad breathing habits, can also cause nodules, and results in producing such vocal qualities as breathiness and huskiness.

It becomes obvious then that good vocal tone is produced by the proper degree of muscle tension in the larynx, combined with full, firm breath support; and, in fact, it is impossible to maintain adequate laryngeal tension without proper breathing. It must be kept in mind that the production of the basic vocal tone in the larynx requires very little effort in that specific organ. The effort required for vibrating the vocal folds must be thought of as coming from the breath support in the trunk of the body. The vocal tone is powered by the muscles of the lower thorax and back, and the muscles of the abdomen, and the larynx is simply a passageway where the exhaled breath is changed into the medium of vocal sound by the vibrating vocal folds. Maintaining this concept will keep the larynx and the throat from becoming overly tense, particularly when volume is increased for purposes of projection.

The ability to increase volume without an accompanying rise in pitch and unpleasant voice quality indicates a properly used vocal mechanism; it is, also, too rarely found. Generally when an actor is asked to speak louder, his increase in breath pressure is accompanied by a higher pitch. This is especially true if he is using high-chest breathing, when the muscles in the throat become too tense and interfere with the action of the vocal folds. An increase in volume should be produced by an increase in breath intensity and a slight readjustment of the vocal folds against the increased breath so that there is no change in pitch or vocal quality. This coordinated process of increased breath pressure and the compensation of vocal-fold alignment must be constantly monitored for a long time for it to become habitual. Naturally, the actor will want to use a wide pitch range of inflation and melody and of stressing key words in expressing the total humanity of his character. But he does not want all of his words pitched so high that they become thin, unpleasant, and unintelligible.

The actor's goal is a voice that is full, resonant, and so expressive that it can easily involve the minds and emotions of an audience. This means a combination of kinesthetic awareness and ear training. It means fixing firmly in the kinesthetic memory the body condition of power and support in the breathing muscles and a throat and larynx free of excess tension; it means, at the same time, experiencing the quality of voice that this body condition produces.

To determine how you are using your larynx, it is important that you become better acquainted with it. Lay the fingers of one hand on the thyroid cartilage in the front of the neck. Now swallow and feel it move up. Yawn and feel it move down. Leave the fingers in place and breathe easily for a moment; then allow your self a full breath, vocalize an *m*, and feel the activity in the larynx as the vocal folds come together and vibrate. Now encircle the entire front of the neck with the palm of the hand and fingers. Your thumb will be pointing toward one ear and your first finger toward the other. Allow your self another full breath and phonate again on a sustained *m*. Be aware of the vibration of the larynx from the phonating

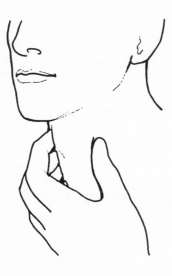

m, but you should feel no accompanying tension in the muscles of the neck, inside or out. Leave the fingers in place easily for another moment, then once again get a deep breath and phonate an *m*. The muscle tension in the neck should not increase when you vocalize. The degree of muscle tonicity required to hold the neck and head erect does not need to be increased for you to produce vocal tone. On the contrary, increased tension in the muscles of the neck and throat will interfere with the free action of the vocal folds in the larynx. This condition must be monitored daily, and certainly before a speaking performance. If you feel increased tension in the muscles not directly involved with the phonation process, now or at any time, then the following exercises should help you.

YAWNING FOR THROAT TENSION

Yawning is one of the best ways to free your throat of excess tension. In fact, the stretch-and-yawn exercise in chapter 2 should be extended at this point to include an awareness of the throat and neck muscles. Yawn and stretch slowly enough to enjoy the relaxed muscle sensation and resulting flow of body feeling life, as well as benefiting from the deep, full breathing so important in good phonation. And when you bend forward from the waist and stretch-and-yawn over your legs, be certain that your head has fallen forward and the muscles of the neck are relaxed.

Yawning can, of course, be done without the vigorous body stretch. Either standing or sitting, let the head float upward out of the shoulder girdle, tilt it forward ever so slightly, and then yawn. Remember that the neck and throat muscles will realize only limited benefits from yawning with the head sunk into the shoulder girdle and tilted backward.

And when you yawn be aware of that lovely open throat feeling. Memorize it. Imprint it in your mind and in your muscle awareness. That is the feeling you should try to maintain when you are speaking. For instance, when you have indulged your self in several relaxing, luxurious yawns, try the following.

Do your last full yawn with special attention to the slow, opening stretch of the muscles in the throat, bearing in mind that it is a slight, easy stretch that you want, and that it is not to force the larynx down. You do not want to depress the larynx and cause the production of a throaty, muffled voice. Easy does it. Now close your lips and yawn again, as you do when you're trying to conceal a yawn from others. Do this in slow stages in order to experience the gradual stretch of the throat muscles. And, finally, with lips still closed, initiate the first slight stretch of a yawn, but don't complete it. Make certain that the stretch is so slight that the larynx is not depressed. This last slight stretch is the open-throat feeling that permits free passage of the vocal sound, and that allows maximum pharyngeal resonance.

MONITORING THROAT TENSION

When you finish the above sequence, maintain the internal sensation of the open throat and encircle the front of the neck again with the palm of the hand and the fingers. Close your eyes and be aware of the degree of tonicity in the throat and neck muscles as you easily inhale; be certain that you are sitting tall so that you may experience a full inhalation without tension in the respiration muscles.

Now on your exhalation count to ten in a conversational tone. Let the breathing muscles relax at the completion of the exhalation. Allow your self to inhale easily again, and exhale on the spoken count of fifteen. Repeat this sequence, counting to twenty, and so on for as high a count as you can comfortably sustain with breath. This monitored sequence can then be repeated as you speak some lines, but continue to monitor for breath support, the open-throat feeling, and that you are not depressing the larynx. And since this experience is one of the best to improve voice production, it should be done frequently.

Any of the previous exercises that are done lying on your back with your head slightly elevated, or leaning forward with the head hanging down are helpful in relaxing the muscles in the neck and throat, and your awareness of muscle tension will gradually include this as your work progresses.

INCREASING VOLUME

To improve your ability to increase volume without raising your basic pitch, it is suggested that you try the following exercise, which is simply an extension of the above experience.

When you feel that you can maintain a comfortable control of breath support and a proper degree of tension in the neck and throat muscles without depressing the larynx as you count and speak lines, try the following.

Count to ten or speak a line at a conversational level, then repeat it a bit louder on the same pitch, being certain that you maintain comfortable breath support and monitor tension in the area beneath your hand. Speak the count or the line as many times as you can maintaining the same pitch, and make each utterance somewhat louder than the one before. Don't try for too much volume at first, and if you begin to experience tension in either the breathing muscles or the laryngeal area, stop, and speak the count or the line several more times at gradually decreasing volume.

This exercise should be done with very slight increases and decreases of volume to begin, and when this is mastered try for greater increases and decreases; for instance, speak first as if to someone close to you, and then as if in a large theater full of people, and alternate these two levels until you accustom the muscles of respiration to these abrupt changes with ease.

CHEWING AN M

Another exercise that works very well at freeing the larynx and throat muscles of excess tension is to chew a sustained *m*. Start with a full, comfortable breath, close your lips, and slowly and easily chew the *m*. Use a soft, light voice so that you experience it in the head resonators, and slightly move the pitch up and down. Make this pitch range narrow to start, and then gradually widen it to higher and lower pitches. Attaining a wider pitch range and experiencing the head resonators will be facilitated by pushing your closed lips forward each time you drop your jaw in chewing; this action will work the tone forward into the oral and nasal cavities, as well as the sinuses and the sounding board of the facial skeletal structure.

This is quite remarkably effective in what it can accomplish. Not only does it improve phonation and resonation, but the process of articulation is profitably advanced if you actively engage the lips and tongue in the chewing process. And if you are powering this combined activity with deep, comfortable breathing, you are producing a full, free, resonant vocal sound of the quality you are seeking.

This exercise also has the happy faculty of helping you to achieve the proper degree of tension in the muscles of the throat and laryngeal area, whether your problem is too much tension or whether it is not enough tension. For instance, the slow, easy performance of the exercise using a soft vocal sound as outlined above, will help you to get rid of excess tension. The same exercise, performed with more vigor and a somewhat louder vocal sound will help you to energize flaccid muscles and produce adequate tonicity and firmness so that your speaking voice will be vibrant and clear, and not sluggish and muffled. This latter condition is generally the case when you first get up, and if you have to perform shortly after you arise your flaccid muscles can be helped by a vigorously chewed *m*.

RESONATION

This basic vocal tone, powered by the breathing muscles and phonated in the larynx, receives its fullness and quality through the process of resonation. This basic vocal tone at the vocal fold level is rather weak and thin, but it is amplified and resonated principally in the pharyngeal, oral, and nasal cavities. Whether or not there is such a thing as true chest resonance is in doubt. Certainly the soft, spongy lungs can do nothing but dampen sound. However, the trachea and bronchial tubes which branch off from it are of a size and shape to provide resonance, although these same factors of size and shape are fixed and the range of frequencies to which these resonators can respond is limited to the pitches most closely approaching the natural frequencies of the cavities. This means that the trachea and bronchi will only reinforce some pitch levels, and others not at all.

However, there is no doubt that the skeletal walls of the chest and back function as an excellent sounding board, as well as the skeletal structures of the head. You can readily determine the presence of sound vibrations in the chest if you lay your hands flat on the sternum and ribs while sustaining an *m* or an open vowel sound, and you can feel sound vibrations in someone else if you lean an ear against their sternum in the front and against their spine, between the shoulder blades, in the back. This is more noticeable on low pitches, and is believed to be the result of vocal fold vibrations which reach the vertebrae in the back, and are thus conducted through the ribs to the sternum in the front, reinforcing the basic laryngeal tone. We do know that no specific techniques or exercises will improve chest resonance, with the possible exception of the body posture and muscle function of total respiration.

The *pharyngeal resonator* extends from the area behind the larynx upward to the area behind the nasal cavity, and is generally thought of in terms of the laryngopharynx (the area behind the larynx), the oropharynx (the area behind the oral cavity, and the nasopharynx (the area behind the nasal cavity).

There are three important factors to be considered in relation to pharyngeal resonance. The first of these is its anatomical position. Being directly behind the larynx, it provides immediate reinforcement for the basic laryngeal tone, amplifying this fundamental tone as well as lower overtones, and also acts somewhat like a megaphone or band shell in the outward direction of vocal sound. The second consideration of the pharynx is its adjustability as to size, which can be modified by the contraction or expansion of its muscle tissue, by the action of the tongue and velum (soft palate), and by the position of the epiglottis, a leaf-shaped cartilage which is attached to the front inner wall of the thyroid cartilage and which normally assumes an upright position against the base of the tongue during phonation and respiration. These modifications provide amplification of the different frequencies of specific vowel sounds, and affect the quality of the voice. The third consideration is related to the texture of the muscular walls of the pharynx, which also affects vocal quality. The proper degree of muscle tonus and the open throat are the desired factors which produce full, pleasing, resonant sounds. Excessive tension in the pharyngeal muscles produces a harsh, unpleasant voice, and conversely, too little tension, or flaccid muscles, will produce a dampened, inefficient resonance.

The *oral resonator* is probably the most important resonator because of its remarkable ability to vary in size and shape. This variability is due to the mobility of the tongue, the soft palate, the oropharynx, the lower jaw, and the lips. All of these combine in the precise shaping of sounds and words, and in the function of the oral cavity as a significant resonator.

It is the precise positioning of the above-mentioned parts of the oral cavity that clearly defines the sounds of speech, the flexibility of these parts that permits the linking and flow of sounds and words in intelligible speech, and the adjustability of these parts in determining the size and shape of the oral cavity produces maximum oral resonance. If there is sufficient breath pressure, and a relaxed open throat, and if the chewing muscles in the sides of the face are properly relaxed to allow the jaw to drop and increase the size of the oral cavity, there should be a full, vibrant resonance in the mouth.

Altering the size of the cavity by dropping the jaw also adds to the brilliance of the vocal sound by placing it farther forward in the mouth. My research has uncovered very little that seems to explain the added brilliance and clarity of frontal placement, but no one disputes the practice of frontality as a desirable technique in voice and speech production. As an image and a device, it works. Try it for your self. Say the *ah* sound in the word *hot*, and as you do, think of placing it in the back of the mouth, right against the wall of the throat. Say it several times, and close your eyes, so that you can feel the sound as well as listen to it more keenly. Now say it several more times, and think of placing it in the front of the mouth, between the teeth and lips, and notice the difference in the quality of the sound. Where the first production, placed consciously in the throat, was muffled and dull, the second production, placed in the front, had more clarity and brilliance.

Obviously this mental image results in some physiological adjustments that vary the oral resonance, the significant consideration being not what they are, but what they do. I have yet to work with an individual whose speaking voice was not improved by focusing on the front of the mouth, and whose oral resonance was not improved by the primarily frontal articulation process.

The *nasal resonators*, or nasal cavities, are not adjustable as to size, and are primarily notable for resonating the three nasal consonants, *m*, *n*, and [ŋ] as in the word *bring*. It is also acknowledged that vowel sounds have some degree of nasal resonance, but that this varies with the proximity of nasal consonants to the vowels; for instance, the vowel sound in the word *bed* will have less nasal resonance than the same vowel in the word *men*. It is also acknowledged that a tense jaw and consequent small oral cavity produces an increase in nasal resonance by forcing some of the sound cut through the nasal passages. This increase in nasal resonance is negatively defined as nasality, and can produce an undesirable voice quality, particularly when it is combined with the strident quality of excessive throat tension.

The term nasality actually has a wider meaning, denoting both too much nasal resonance on vowels, and too little nasal resonance, or denasalization, which produces a dull quality, lacking brilliance.

Nasal resonance is largely determined by the combined function of the velum (soft palate), the pharyngeal wall, and the pillars that form the sides of the aperture between the mouth and the throat. When the velum is elevated, the pharyngeal wall and pillars approximate it and the opening between the mouth and nasal cavities is closed, and vocal sound cannot move into the nasal resonators. When the velum is open, the vocal sound can receive additional resonance from the nasal resonators, which will be beneficial to the tone if there is not too much nasal resonance which causes an imbalance of resonance. This is usually the result of the tight jaw and consequent small oral cavity we mentioned above.

RESONANCE BALANCE

The proper balance of adequate nasal, oral, and pharyngeal resonance is generally attained by the proper training in opening the mouth and throat, in striving for the frontal placement of the vocal sound, in properly articulating sounds and words, and in supporting the whole with total respiration.

For instance, the exercise of chewing an *m*, which was used to demonstrate the achievement of the proper degree of tension in the muscles of the throat and laryngeal area, can also be used in part to demonstrate resonance balance, and to begin to put the entire process of voice production together.

Start with an upright posture, head floating upward out of the shoulder girdle and rib cage floating upward from the pelvic girdle to allow for deep, easy breathing. Close your lips, and at the peak of a comfortable inhalation, exhale on a chewed *m*, which you open into an *ah*. Written out, it would probably look something like this: *m-m-m-m-m-a-a-a-a-ah*.

Repeat this a few times, and imagine that the *ah* sound is placed well forward in the mouth. Be certain that the jaw drops easily while chewing the *m*, and on the *ah* sound, to achieve maximum oral resonance; and, also, that you maintain a relaxed, open-throat feeling to achieve maximum pharyngeal resonance; and vary the pitch as you repeat the exercise. And that should produce a balance of resonance on the *ah* sound, within the oral, pharyngeal, and nasal resonators.

To familiarize your self with the sensation of resonance balance, and to fix it in your total mind and body consciousness, repeat the exercise with your eyes closed, and gradually shorten the chewed *m* until you are saying *ma-a-ah*, *ma-a-ah*, *ma-a-ah*, and thus concentrating entirely on the resonance balance you experience on the open vowel sound as you sustain it.

Acquiring the proper feel and awareness of resonance balance is not always easy, but once again negative practice can help. As with breathing, posture, or any other factor of voice production, consciously doing something wrong can provide clues as to what you shouldn't be doing.

Using the open vowel sound of *ah*, first tighten your jaw and tense the muscles in the throat, breathe in and then breathe out, phonating the sound. Be aware that you not only have limited oral and pharyngeal resonance and a strident unpleasant quality to the sound, but that much of the sound is forced out through the nasal passages, resulting in an imbalance of resonance, with the major portion of the resonance being in the nasal resonators.

Now loosen and drop the jaw, but maintain the throat tension, and phonate the *ah* again, and be aware that the major resonance is in the oral and nasal cavities: once again, an imbalance.

Now open the throat by initiating a yawn, but don't complete it; maintain the loose jaw, hold your nose and make the sound again, being aware that you have a fully resonated sound in the oral and pharyngeal resonators, but that it is lacking the brilliance of the nasal resonator: another imbalance.

And finally, let go of your nose, maintain the open throat and loose jaw, and resonate the sound again, and be aware of the balance of resonance in the three major resonators when they are functioning with maximum efficiency, and of how the sound is reinforced by vibrations in the body structure of the head and chest when it is free of muscle constriction. The voice must be thus freed of any restrictions if it is to express the nuances of language and the humanity of a character.

The exercise of chewing an *m* and then opening it out should be practiced with all of the vowel sounds. Always be certain that you assume the upright posture as outlined in the beginning of this exercise, and that your voice production is supported by deep, full breath support. Chew the *m* slowly and experience the enlarged oral cavity that results every time you drop your jaw in chewing and the opening stretch of the throat muscles that accompanies it. Be aware too that this combined activity places the sound well forward in the mouth, and that the sound is further reinforced by head and chest vibrations. More on this in the next chapter on vowel study.

It is one of the fundamental concepts of this text that voice production will not change dramatically until it is perceived in a different way. So many people perceive voice production as something that takes place in the throat; they clutch their throats with their hands and wail, "Oh, my voice! It's terrible! Can't you do something about it?" And, of course, such perceptions are very limited ones. Voice production must be thought of as a process that involves your body from the groin to the top of the head. The breath power is mainly centered in the area of the diaphragm and lower ribs, but involves muscle support in the lower belly and back, and includes the upper thighs. The throat is an open passageway where vocal tone is initiated in the larynx, and the tone is further resonated in the principle resonators and the bony structure all the way to the top of the head. The entire area from the groin to the top of the head can be thought of as a spherical object such as an egg, or perhaps a balloon in which the mouth is the opening. Training in voice production requires the use of the imagination as well as the practice of techniques. Both are equally important.

Exercises in developing capacity and control of total respiration, in opening the mouth and throat for balanced resonance, in frontal placement of the vocal sound, and all the rest, are analogous to the scales and finger exercises of the pianist and the bar exercises of the ballet dancer. These exercises need to be done daily and with utmost concentration on the development of individual factors. This daily practice is mandatory for the pianist and the ballet dancer and it should be for the actor. Muscles must be trained and toned to the peak of efficiency so that the performing artist doesn't have to think about them, but is free to concentrate on interpreting the piano concerto, the *pas de deux*, or the verbal expression of a character. Practice must always be distinguished from performance.

When the actor steps onto the stage, the muscle exercises that result in the peak condition of the body, coupled with the conditioning of the psycho-physical mechanism that results in the perception of self as a mass of vibrating energy, filling the theater, wall-to-wall and floor-to-ceiling, will allow the actor complete freedom to concentrate on the interpretation of the role. In an actual performance the total focus must be on *what* you are saying, not on *how* you are saying it. The how is reserved for practice periods only, and if done properly and with regularity, provides the ability and freedom for the what.

EAR-STOPPELS

Once again, be it said that the *how* requires both physical training and new perceptions. The way you perceive your voice determines how well and how freely you use it. To this end I suggest the use of several devices, the first one suggested here being Ear-Stoppels. These are available at most drugstores, and are generally purchased for use when swimming or to shut out noise. They usually come with directions, but if not, knead them with your fingers until you have a cone shape with a point at one end. You insert the pointed end into your ear and flatten the rest of the cone on top of it. They shut out most noise, but you will be able to hear voices if they are loud enough.

Ear-Stoppels are not to be used to listen to your self. They are used in order that you may experience the voice in a new way, that you feel the resonated sounds in new places, and that you don't anticipate your voice. Anticipation of what your voice will sound like and how it will feel when you speak is one of the barriers to changing it. Most people are unaware of this phenomenon, but it exists on a subconscious level. It is responsible for the fact that people continue to speak with the same vocal range and patterns, usually very limited, and with the same voice placement, usually in the throat, and that this repetition digs the grooves of the patterns and placement deeper and deeper until, like a broken needle, their needles get stuck. They anticipate a certain sound and a certain feel, and that's what they get. And that's what they will continue to get until they change their expectations and their vocal experience. Ear-Stoppels will help to do this.

Not only are the expectations and inner experience of the voice changed, but the unanticipated sensations will encourage you to experiment. You will find that the new, intensified feeling of the voice will encourage you to experiment, to manipulate, to extend; you will enjoy exploring new resonance centers and increased pitch range. There will be no habitual anticipation to stop your voice from moving freely—up, down, and forward. This experience is analogous to the conditioned responses of the breathing muscles, which can be improved readily by altering the body conditions under which the responses take place, such as lying on your back, falling forward from the waist, and other variations of posture and movement.

When we change our body-set and our mind-set we can change our habitual, anticipated responses, and when this is accomplished, and not until, we can free our breathing patterns and our speaking voices to explore new forms of expression. This is the sine qua non of voice improvement.

To change the expectations and experience of vocal sound, and to alter the conditions under which these take place, try the following exercises.

USING EAR-STOPPELS

Insert your Ear-Stoppels, repeat the exercise of chewing an *m*, and opening it out on *ah*: as in *m-m-m-m-a-a-a-a-ah*. Be sure that your tongue is lying flat in the bottom of the mouth with the tongue tip touching the bottom teeth on the *ah*. Repeat this several times, until you have a good frontal placement on the *ah*. Allow a full, comfortable inhalation before you start each repetition, and constantly monitor for throat tension. You can easily combine these two factors by inhaling through the nose, and while you are inhaling with the lips closed, simultaneously ease open the back of the throat as in the first stages of a yawn. Make this one gesture; and if you do it consciously during practice periods for a long enough time, you will make it a conditioned response that will carry over into performance, even when you are inhaling through your mouth.

After you have repeated the exercise sustaining both the chewed *m* and the *ah*, gradually shorten the chewed *m* until you are saying *ma-a-ah*, and sustaining only the vowel sound. Now, on a series of *ma-a-ahs*, explore your pitch range. Start low and go high; then start high and go low. But don't force the pitches. Simply use a free, light tone and let the voice go where it will easily. Let your imagination aid the free movement of the voice, and think that you have a new, musical toy with which you are experimenting. Or imagine that you are massaging the inside of your head and especially your face and chest, with sound vibrations. Play with the sounds and enjoy the experience, which is always intensified by closing your eyes.

Repeat the entire exercise using *m-m-m-m-m-o-o-o-o-o*, then a series of *m-o-o-os*; *m-m-m-m-m-e-e-e-e-e*, then a series of *m-e-e-es*. And, finally, play with the word *moonbeam*. Enjoy the combined resonances of the vowels and nasal sounds; experience them moving around in your head and vibrating in your chest. Wet your lips with the tip of your tongue, and say it again, tasting it on your tongue and feeling it on your lips. With eyes closed, form an auditory image of the movement and resonances of the sounds and the word. And when your image is firmly fixed, remove the Ear-Stoppels, but keep repeating the word *moonbeam*, as you continue to imprint your new image.

You will be amazed at the way your voice feels when you remove the Ear-Stoppels. You will experience new openness, new freedom, and new placement. And if you don't, you'll be the first not to. Everyone is invariably astonished at the different sound and feel of the voice, their own and others. These insignificant looking ear plugs can dramatically change your voice production and your perception of it. And their practical application to words in a script is obvious.

With your Ear-Stoppels in and eyes closed, play with the vowel sounds and continuant *l* and nasal sounds in Lorenzo's line, "How sweet the moon-light sleeps upon this bank!" You've already experienced the vowels in *sweet, moon*, and *sleeps;* now experience some of the others in the line. Feel them, and taste them, and run them up and down your pitch range. Then remove the Ear-Stoppels and say it several times with your changed production and perception. The difference will be particularly apparent if you tape the line before you do the exercise, and then immediately on removing the Ear-Stoppels.

This particular device should be used with great frequency, and is very helpful in moving a tired, or weak voice out of the throat and getting it forward and into the resonators. The device also develops an affinity for sounds and words, for their energy and function. But, first and foremost, the device can completely change your concept of voice — of what it is and what you can do with it. I suggest using them in your daily practice, with one caution — that you may become uncomfortable if you use them too long at one time. This has happened with a few of my students, who don't seem to be able to give a specific reason for their discomfort, but who use the device quite happily for short periods.

An extension of the above exercise is to combine it with increased body awareness. This is a group activity and can be done with two or three people working together.

If two people work together, A will be doing the exercises above, while B is slapping A's back and/or vigorously massaging A's spine from top to bottom with the heel of his hand. A should constantly vary the pitch and focus on feeling the sound in the spot where B is massaging; A should also vigorously slap with both hands, up and down the sternum in the front. While B is slapping and massaging A's spine, B should also be humming and chewing an *m* with Ear-Stoppels in, as the activity of using his arms will also help him to experience the vibrations in his body.

A should conclude the exercise by removing the Ear-Stoppels and repeating the words or lines, while both A and B continue to slap. Then A and B should change places, and repeat the entire exercise.

If three people work together, A will be doing the exercises above, while B slaps and massages his back, and C slaps A's sternum, rib cage, and belly in the front; both B and C should be chewing an *m* with Ear-Stoppels in. This leaves A's hands free to finger-tap the head, which is done by bending the fingers and tapping both hands at the same time — beginning with the top of the head, then the back and sides, and then the forehead and the rest of the face. Neither A's finger-tapping nor B's and C's slapping should be done so hard that it hurts; nor should it be done so lightly that it has no effect. Firm but bouncy is the answer, so that A produces a vitalized, tingling sensation in the trunk of the body and the head. Lines spoken following slapping and finger-tapping and the use of Ear-Stoppels have a whole new sound and feel to them. B and C will, of course, each take their turn at being slapped and massaged by two other people.

This exercise is a marvelous energizer, brings a new sensitivity to vocal sounds and vibrations, provides spoken words with an organic connection of body and feeling life, and induces an exciting new self-awareness. The experience will transform your perception of the condition, nature, and function of voice.

This exercise is very effective for warm-ups before a rehearsal or performance, with or without Ear-Stoppels, and as a final activity can include a group slapping experience. This is done with the entire group forming a circle, with each member slapping the back in front of him, and with everyone chewing an *m* or vocalizing on sustained open vowels, using varying pitch range. The circle must be tight enough to allow each member a comfortable slapping position. Eyes should be closed to maintain inner focus, heads should be slightly forward to avoid strain in the throat, and breathing should be full and comfortable. Full breathing is facilitated in this instance because of the physical activity.

The exercise should conclude at a cue from the group leader to stop slapping and to let the vocal sounds gradually decrease to stillness. The group should then remain quietly in position and, for a long moment, be aware of the energy generated by the group activity and vocal sound. This experience both animates the individual and inspires group strength and unity.

THE FALL-FORWARD

The fall-forward also combines very well with the use of Ear-Stoppels to free and resonate the voice. The exercise can, of course, be done without the Ear-Stoppels, particularly when your new perception of voice production is firmly imprinted.

Stand tall and stretch your arms straight up over your head. Now drop the hands, then the forearms, then the upper arms, then the head, and then fall easily forward from the waist, with arms and head hanging loosely down. Now chew an *m* and/or experiment with pitch variations and sustained sounds on some lines, as in the exercises above. While hanging down, bounce easily up and down, and from side to side, and imagine that you are shaking the voice onto the lips, and into all the resonators in the head. After bouncing in all directions for a few moments, maintain an up-and-down bounce while slowly pulling the body to an upright position. Continue the production of sounds or words during the pull-up and be certain that your head hangs heavy throughout and is only pulled up after the back is straight. Then repeat your lines in a standing position with the Ear-Stoppels in, and then with them out. It is always the carryover into the upright speaking posture that matters, and which must always be kept in mind.

If you are working on a long speech, it is helpful to the carryover to fall forward and bounce a line or two, then in one big bounce bring your self to an upright position, let the head float upward, and repeat the lines while standing straight. Then fall forward and bounce on another line or two, bounce up straight and speak these lines in turn, and so on. Don't pause between the lines bounced on the forward fall and the lines spoken upright and don't allow the rib-cage to sag. Inhale as you bounce to an

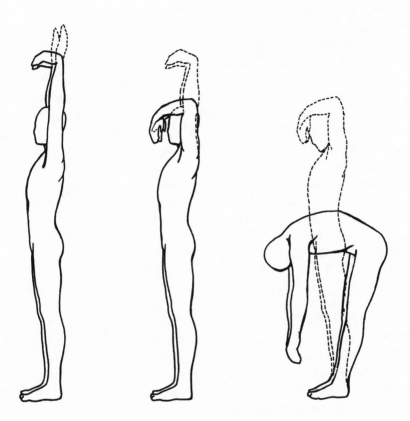

upright position and take advantage of the deep breath induced by the posture and activity of the fall forward; speak the line immediately upon assuming the upright position, welding your words together with your full breath as you project them. It is ever and always the carryover that is important.

You may experience a wonderfully free, resonant voice, a wide pitch range, and good frontal placement of the voice while performing the exercise(s), and that is just great and is what the exercises are all about. But the goal of all of the exercises is to be able to experience and maintain these same factors when you actually perform. This means concentrating on altered perceptions and new responses. Experiencing full breathing, open throat, and a resonant voice placed well forward while vigorously active is only the means. Experiencing these same optimal conditions when performing is the end. And if you perform the exercises with total commitment, concentration, and enthusiasm the end will certainly justify the means.

Another device suggested by this text to aid you in freeing the voice from muscle constriction and in experiencing it in a new way should be fairly obvious at this point; it is movement. The voice is, after all, a product of body muscles which supply the breath, phonate the basic tone, and shape the words, and it is body cavities that resonate the basic tone. Voice is also a product of body tension and emotions, and there is an inverse correlation between excessive muscle tension and expressed emotions. The voice is an expression of the whole self, is an integral part of that self, and not an isolated phenomenon. If we are to improve our voices we must consider the well-being of the entire organism. Body movement serves the primary function of waking up the whole being.

Body movement aids circulation, increases the energy level of the body, eases tensions, releases emotions, and loosens the voice to move with flexibility and freedom. Body exercises improve posture, tone, and strengthen the whole speaking instrument, and integrate mind, body, and emotions in speaking. Improved voice production is the result of this holistic approach. The speaking voice must be shaken free from its habitual, limited body production and this happens most effectively when the body is moving and is animated. Trying to improve the vocal process when one assumes a habitual standing position provides only minimal results. The body will too readily take on the familiar body-set of being motionless, with all its inhibitions, tensions, and postural quirks. And this is true for a very long time, or at least until you have radically changed your perceptions of voice, and fixed these perceptions permanently in your kinesthetic memory. Even then, you will need to engage in periodic exercises to vitalize the body and voice and bring the whole self to a peak condition.

This approach has been the basis for previous exercises and for those that now follow. Keep in mind, however, that it is the carry-over from the exercises into the actual speaking performance that is the goal of the effort.

The variations of the fall-forward are some of the best exercises for the well-being of the body and the voice. They energize the body, encourage deep breathing, and reverse the pull of gravity so that blood flows into the head and the voice flows into the head resonators. Bear in mind that when you are standing up the head is above the heart and gravity pulls the blood and the voice down, away from the head. If you hang down long enough, you will experience not only a frontally placed, resonant voice, but also relaxed muscles in the face and lips as a result of the reverse gravity pull. And, of course, the heavy head hanging loosely down will relax the muscles of the neck and of the pharynx. However, the increased blood flow to the head and the increased oxygen from deeper breathing can cause discomfort if you hang forward too long, so this exercise should be used only in moderation. In addition, there will be times when you are dressed in a costume that does not permit this sort of movement. Therefore, we offer some exercises that may be done in an upright position.

SWIVEL

Stand in an upright position, with head and rib cage floating upward to encourage full breathing and an open throat. Stretch your arms straight up over your head to lift the rib cage. Now drop the hands, then the forearms, and leaving the rib cage up, drop the upper arms. Let the arms and hands hang loose and limp at your sides.

With or without the Ear-Stoppels (you must be able to judge when you need these to reinforce resonance and tone placement), chew an *m* or sustain open vowel sounds on varying pitches as you swivel the trunk of the body, first to the left and then to the right, flinging the arms freely with the motion. After a few minutes of this, speak some lines while swiveling the body and flinging the arms.

Do this exercise vigorously but easily, and concentrate (it helps to close your eyes) on the experience of your voice moving freely inside you. Continue for long enough to imprint the experience and then gradually stop swiveling but continue speaking, and try to maintain the same feeling of the free voice when the body is quiet. Several repetitions of the exercise can bring about this maintenance of production. As was suggested in the previous exercise, it is effective in working on a long speech to swivel one or two lines, repeat them when the body is quiet, then swivel one or two more lines, repeat them when the body is quiet, and so on. It can not be overstated that it is the carryover to the performance that is important.

UMBRELLA

An interesting variation of the swivel exercise, in that it provides a mental image, is to imagine that your spine is the center shaft of an

umbrella with the handle pointing down. Imagine that your ribs form
the spokes of the umbrella and that they are closed, lying flat against
the shaft.

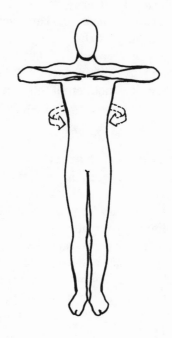

Elevate your bent elbows out to the side, at almost shoulder height, and
rapidly and easily shake the spokes of your umbrella open. Shake them up
and out, as you chew an *m*, sustain open vowels, speak or sing. Alternate
shaking a line free and then repeating it without shaking. Or try shaking
just on the words which should be stressed. In all cases allow your self to
fully experience the moving energies and vibrations of the sounds in the
body. Experiment with pitch range, with volume, and with the sustention
of sounds that you might not normally stress. Discover new things about
your vocal instrument and your text. And don't forget the carryover.

ARM, LEG, AND HEAD SWINGS

Another effective variation is to swivel the trunk of the body with the
arms straight out to the sides, shoulder high. As you produce sounds or
words, swivel the trunk of the body to the left so that the right arm swings
to the front, and the left arm swings to the back. Then swivel the body to

the right so that the left arm swings to the front and the right arm swings to the back. Repeat this six or eight times, then add the following movements.

As you swivel the body to the left and the right arm swings to the front, swing your left leg up and to the right. As you swivel the body to the right

and the left arm swings to the front, swing your right leg up and to the left. Repeat these movements six or eight times.

Now add the head movement, which should turn in the same direction as the leg. When your left leg swings toward the right, so will your head; when your right leg swings toward the left, so will your head.

Repeat the combined movements six or eight times, and let the production of sounds or words continue uninterrupted when you stop the movement. This exercise is excellent in freeing you from the bondage of a too literal expression of words. The necessary concentration on involved movements enables you to experience the energy of the words and allows them to flow more freely. The words will be coming through a physical movement, and not just dropping word by word from your mouth.

ARM SWINGS

Still another variation of arm movements, without the swivel this time, is to stand straight and lift your arms straight out to the sides, shoulder high. Now produce sounds or words, using a wide pitch range, as you swing your arms in circles. First swing the arms toward the front, then straight up and over your head, down the back as low as you can, and up

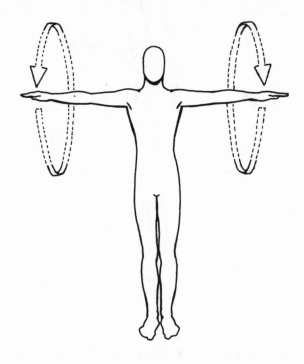

toward the front again. Make the circles wide and vigorous, with a similar pitch range, as you repeat this ten or twelve times.

Then circle in the opposite direction; swing your arms down and toward the back, up and over toward the front, down and toward the back again. Repeat this ten or twelve times, and finish with ten or twelve swings in the reversed, initial pattern; and when you finally drop your arms at your sides, continue speaking with the energy and wide range that you used during the arm swings, always concentrating on the experience of the free voice while exercising so that you can the more easily imprint it in mind and body.

The above exercises will not only free the voice, but will expand the rib cage, accelerate circulation and respiration, ease tensions, release emotions, and will result in a feeling that the whole body is speaking. You will connect to the voice and words organically, experiencing their power and substance in the body.

It is of equal importance, of course, to exercise the muscles of the neck and face, to relieve them of excess tension, to increase their flexibility, and to experience them in a new way. Excessive and often chronic, tension in the neck, shoulder girdle, and jaw is a problem for nearly everyone.

The neck muscles, in combination with the vertebrae of the neck, balance and support a head weighing approximately ten pounds. Food and air pass through the passageways of the neck to sustain the life of the body. Nerve messages from the brain and blood are also channeled through the neck. For bodily health as well as for good voice production, therefore, it is necessary to maintain an adequate degree of muscle tonus in this area. There is a positive correlation between adequate neck tension and dynamic voice production. Exercises for the neck muscles are generally an important part of toning up the vocal mechanism before performing.

NECK EASE

Head-rolls, to relax the neck muscles, are usually required in most training programs, but they should be done slowly and easily, and it is best to ease into them with a few simple head-drops as suggested below.

Sit or stand tall, with your head floating upward out of your shoulder girdle. Close your eyes to shut out any visual distractions that might prevent you from concentrating on the experience as you perform it.

Allow a full, comfortable inhalation and open your throat as you inhale. At the peak of the inhalation, let your head fall forward toward your chest. Don't put it there, which requires muscle tension; just release the tension in the muscles and let the head fall.

On your exhalation, very slowly chew an *m*, working the lips well forward each time your jaw drops in chewing, and each time experience the easy stretch of the throat muscles and the flexing of the muscles in the neck, as you slowly pull your head back to an upright position by stacking up the vertebrae in the back of the neck.

Let your head float upward once again, as well as the rib cage, open the lips, and let your jaw hang down loosely. Imagine that your entire body is floating upward, with the exception of the eyelids and the jaw. Allow a full, comfortable inhalation as you let your heavy head fall straight back, and on your exhalation sustain an *ah*. Initiate the sound easily and be sure there is no preliminary glottal click in the larynx. This happens if the exhalation is begun with too much force; the breath must be released slowly and evenly. Repeat the *ah* twice more with head hanging back, and experience the lovely open-throat feeling in this position.

Leave the jaw hanging down and maintain the open-throat experience. As you float your head back to an upright position, inhale and repeat *ah* several times more.

Leave your jaw hanging loose and breathe through your mouth, as you let your left ear fall toward your left shoulder. Bounce your head slightly in this position and feel an easy stretch in the muscles on the right side of the neck. Now float your head straight up again, then let your right ear

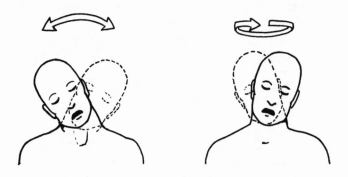

fall toward your right shoulder. Bounce your head slightly in this position and feel an easy stretch in the muscles on the left side of the neck. These stretches should feel just as pleasurable as those you feel in your back when you stretch your arms over your head; they are intended to ease tension and that is what you should feel.

Let your head float upward once again and experience your head bouncing around in the air. Imagine that your neck is a solid mass of rubber and do some very slight head rolls on top of it, with the jaw hanging loosely and breathing through the mouth.

Now extend the head rolls, by keeping the neck in an upright position and dropping the head forward, jaw hanging down. Swivel your jaw toward your left shoulder, then straight up as your head falls to the back. With the head hanging back, swivel your jaw toward your right shoulder, then down toward your chest as the head falls forward again in the front, and let the neck muscles relax forward as well.

With the neck and head relaxed forward, inhale and audibly sigh a couple of times, then float the head upward and repeat the entire exercise in the opposite direction: swivel the jaw first to the right.

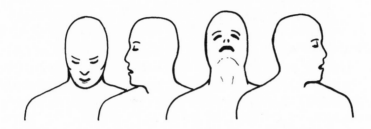

The above exercise is one of the best means of relaxing neck muscles, but the entire experience needs time and careful attention, and must be done slowly. The exercise will very quickly reveal any tension spots in the neck muscles, and if you feel any of these, ease up. Maintain comfortable, full breathing throughout, and don't force. The tension spots can be relaxed by slow, careful stretching of the muscles only and not by throwing the head around randomly and rapidly as so many people are wont to do. In fact, medical research reveals that wildly tossing the head around at a rapid rate can damage the muscles, nerves, and other tissues. So take some time, exercise careful attention, and concentrate totally on the experience and on slow, deep breathing, and you will be rewarded by relaxed muscles in the neck and throat.

This exercise also aids the processes of phonation and resonation. If you use the combination of the chewed *m* and open this into the *ah*, *o*, or *oo*, as in previous exercises, the slow, relaxed movement of the muscles completely frees the vocal sound to move into resonating areas that combine with the changing postures to produce new vibratory sensations. The slow, careful stretching of neck muscles should be mastered first, however, and completely imprinted in your conscious and kinesthetic memories before employing sustained vocal sounds throughout. Sustained sounds and even lines can be used, but to do them too soon will work to neither the advantage of the neck relaxation nor the voice production. It is the same principle as that of first mastering the capacity and control of total respiration before attempting vocalized sounds and words. Good voice production is only possible when the structure and function of the instrument is understood and properly used. This is true of phonation and resonation as well as respiration. It is even more true of the delicate, complex area of the neck because it is involved in so many intricate physiological systems, and thus to keep the neck free of excess tension needs to be a constant consideration.

For most of us, neck tension is a chronic problem, induced, as it is, by daily niggling anxieties and fears. And unless we use our minds and imaginations constructively to rid ourselves of our anxieties, we will find it almost impossible to rid ourselves of our neck tensions. Severe cases of tense, tired neck and throat muscles are usually only helped by working with a careful, understanding partner. In this instance, the head and neck manipulations are done entirely by the partner's hands.

HEAD CRADLE

You will lie on your back, being certain that the spine is straight and the lower back is flattened by pointing your knees toward the ceiling with your feet flat on the floor. Lie either on a mat, in which case your partner crouches in back of your head, or on a table, in which case your partner may sit in a chair. In either case, your shoulders should be even with the

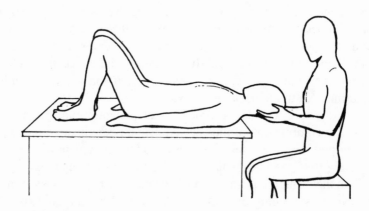

mat or the table so that your head and neck are unsupported except by your partner's hands.

Let your partner have the complete weight of your ten-pound head in his hands. Completely relax the neck muscles and breathe deeply and fully. At the same time your partner will very slowly move your head up and down, and turn it from side to side, beginning with very slight movements and gradually increasing them to bigger, more extended ones, still done slowly. Frequently, your partner should cradle your head in one of his hands and slide the other one down your spine as far as he can reach, then pull his hand gently but firmly up the spine toward your head, as if lengthening and straightening the spine.

After five or ten minutes of this manipulation, you should introduce vocalized sound. First, inhale deeply and sigh audibly, then sustain some open vowel sounds and short phrases, and do them all on soft, light tones, with deeply rooted breath support, letting the pitch go as high and as low as it will easily.

Twenty minutes of slow, considerate manipulation by a well-intentioned partner can work miracles. The concerned efforts of another person, plus the always magical "laying on of hands," usually always warms and relaxes and frees you, at least for the period of the experience, from your anxieties and thus your muscle tensions. You feel your self browsing in warmth and relaxation as if in a meadow.

Too much cannot be said about the advantages of working with a partner, provided that partner is dedicated to the task. Fortunately, this generally happens, if only for the selfish reason that he expects the same commitment from you. But when a manipulator's thoughts and energies are genuinely directed toward the well-being of the subject, remarkable improvements take place for that subject.

If you don't have a friendly partner, however, you can benefit from the energy and manipulations of your own hands. You can slap yourself vigorously with both hands, beginning with the upper chest, slapping down over the lower chest and belly, then bending forward and slapping the front and sides of the thighs, then up the back of the thighs, then the buttocks and lower back, and around to the lower belly again, and back up the front. This results in increased body and feeling awareness, and, when done in combination with sustained open vowels, or sung or spoken phrases, can vitalize and free vocal sounds. You can also perform *Shiatzu* on your own body, and give your self massages. These manipulations are especially easy to perform on the neck and face area. There are excellent books available for the specific points that should receive the *Shiatzu* finger pressure, so we won't discuss them here, but self-administered massages are quite simple, and almost impossible to do wrong. You can lay your hands almost anywhere on your body and gently knead the muscles or firmly slide the hands up and down with good effect. This is certainly true of the shoulder girdle, neck, and face areas, all of which affect the processes of phonation and resonation if they are excessively tense.

SHOULDER MASSAGE

Start with the shoulder girdle in the back, and lay your hands and fingers between the shoulder blades and close in to the spine. Now firmly and slowly pull up toward your shoulders. You will probably end up on top of the shoulder girdle about two inches from the neck. Put your hands back on the starting point and slide them up again, always slowly and firmly, and aim for the top of the shoulder girdle a little closer to the neck. Keep starting at the the same spot, and finishing closer to the spine, until your pulls come right up the back of the neck. Breathe fully and imagine that you are directing warm breath into the area under your hands.

Now place the tips of all four of the fingers on both hands on either side of the spine, as far down the back as you can reach, and massage the area with tiny circular motions six or eight times; move the finger tips up a half an inch or so and do the same, and so on up until you reach the base of the skull, at which point you will get best results by massaging only with the first two fingers of the hands. Keep directing warm breath into the area being massaged and enjoy the experience. You will feel energized and relaxed.

Now put the first three fingers of the hands on the muscles in the side of the neck, close up under the ear, and again with tiny circular motions, work your way slowly down to the shoulder girdle, breathing slowly and fully. Raise your chin slightly and massage under the lower jaw, and very gently massage down the front of the neck, slightly jiggling the larynx as you work down. And finish up by laying the thumb and fingers of one hand on your larynx and gently jiggling it from side to side as you inhale fully and exhale on easily phonated *ah* sounds. The muscles of the neck, throat, and shoulder girdle in the back should feel marvelously relaxed after this.

Now finger-tap all over the back, top, and sides of the head, and all over the face. Then with your finger tips massage, again with tiny circular motions, the forehead, the temples and all around the eyes, nose and cheeks, and the lips and jaw, letting your jaw hang down loosely. And if you are breathing fully and phonating with soft, light tones, you can easily feel the vibrations of the resonated sound, particularly in the facial resonators.

The energy of your hands, combined with the stimulated energy of the facial muscles and resonated sounds will give your face a tingling sensation and wake it up to new expressiveness. So many faces are expressionless, immobile, and like masks which reveal so little of the personality of an individual. Along with all of the body muscles, the facial muscles need to be relaxed and vitalized.

FACIAL MUSCLES

You can also vitalize facial muscles and loosen them up by slowly moving them around. Imagine that you are massaging the front of the skull with your facial muscles. Open the mouth wide, then purse the lips, raise and lower the forehead, move the jaw up and down and from side to side, moving the muscles around in every way possible. Or imagine that you are making faces at someone, even to sticking out your tongue and loosening that up as well. And finish up by blowing out your lips, on a sustained *b*, the lip-flutter. You will produce the sound you made as a child when playing at driving an automobile. This exercise for facial muscles, lips, and tongue is an excellent preparation for effective expression and the use of the articulators. The entire sequence of exercises, beginning with the shoulder girdle, increases circulation, self-awareness, induces relaxation, and, with full breath support, reinforces all the factors of voice production. That is what is so satisfying and rewarding about this discipline: all the pieces fit together.

EMOTION AND THE VOICE

All of the elements of voice production that we work on individually reinforce the whole. The sum is truly greater than its parts. If one element is neglected, the whole process of voice production suffers. And it remains now to consider one more important element of the voice process — emotion. The spoken words would be colorless and without meaning if they were not enriched by feeling life.

The depth of emotion is directly connected to the depth of breathing. If the emotions are present, the breath will make it available to you. You can easily prove this point to your self by lying on your back, with your head comfortably raised, and being certain that your spine is straight and your lower back flat by pointing your knees toward the ceiling with your feet flat on the floor. Now put one thumb at the top of the breast bone and slowly slide it down until you reach the bottom where the ribs separate outward into a V-shape. Keeping the thumb in that spot, lay the rest of the hand and fingers below it, over the area that houses the solar plexus, known as the pit of the stomach. The solar plexus is a ganglia of nerves in the abdominal cavity behind the stomach which sends out nerve impulses that are basic to the expression of audible emotions. Drop your jaw open to the *ah* position, think of something amusing and start to laugh. We've discussed the way to induce laughter in the chapter on Body and Feeling Life, so if you have trouble getting started, go back and review the process. It is basically a matter of breathing deeply, sighing a couple of times, and then halfway through a sigh, turn it into a laugh instead. Bounce the *ha-ha-ha*s off the diaphragm, and be aware of the activity beneath your hand. The real, genuine emotion of laughing is deep-seated, just like the factor of full breathing. After you've had a good laugh, which can do nothing but good for you, lie quietly for a long moment and focus on the sensation of the experience, and on the fact that the seat of the emotions is in the area beneath your hand.

Now let your facial muscles droop into the *aw* position, think of a sad image and begin to sob. To give the action some tension, imagine that you have been sobbing for a long time and are trying to get control of yourself. This is the same principle as playing a drunk on stage, in which you *are* drunk but try not to show it, which gives it a spine. Once you are sobbing freely, be aware of the activity in the area beneath your hand. The genuine emotion of sobbing, like that of laughing, is deep-seated. When you stop sobbing, lie quietly for a long moment and be aware of the relationship of deep breathing and emotion.

It is extremely important to remember this relationship when performing. Not only must you remember that deep breathing makes the emotions available in the expression of the total humanity of a character; you must also remember that passionate emotions affect your breathing. You can prove this to your self as well by lying on your back and breathing easily for a few moments, then concentrating on some person or situation that makes you very angry. Use your sense memory and recapture every detail of the situation. Put your self totally in the scene, and when you are completely involved in your anger, put your focus on your breathing. If you are genuinely experiencing intense anger, your breathing will be agitated. It may probably still be fairly deep breathing, but will be quite rapid. Then let go of the scene that caused your anger and relax as you think of something pleasant, such as sunning your self at the seashore. Notice the different breathing patterns connected with this image.

It is interesting to repeat the experiment with other induced emotions, such as fear, joy, relief, envy, and the like, and to observe how the breathing is affected, and then to remember this when you perform any of these emotions and have to express them verbally.

You must not let long, impassioned speeches freeze you so that you can't breathe. When you get overly impassioned and loud, keep hooked to the breath and channel the emotion and body tensions into the words. The words and the breathing will help get rid of emotional body tension if you use them properly. To overcome extreme emotional body tension, don't just try to speak it out, as this will jam all the tension up in the throat. Think what you're going to say, breathe into it, and let it speak itself. The effort of trying to make yourself overcome the tension block worsens the tension block and inhibits further the free flow of breath and emotions. Remember to think, breathe into the thought, and then let it speak itself! Since you cannot relieve the tension during performance by some physical activity, such as a good shake-out, this is your only recourse. Breathe into your thought, then let it flow. This is so important, being a constant acting problem, that it bears repetition.

To further the essentials of free-flowing breath and emotions, take your first opportunity offstage to have a good shakeout and fall-forward, breathe deeply, and sigh. Or stretch and yawn. Or stretch your arms straight over your head, inhale fully, then let your arms and upper body fall quickly and limply down as you sigh audibly on a long sustained sound, starting as high as you can and sliding down the scale as low as you can go. You must feel as if you were wringing your self out, and flinging the sigh in all directions. Yawning and sighing are two of the best ways to relax the body, yet keep it alert. You will feel the breathing open up and the energy and feeling life start to flow. Then use a different image, such as breathing through your forehead and experiencing a cushion of breath right behind the words in your mouth, and extending in a column all the way down to the groin.

Sometimes the only way to loosen up the power center of the body that houses the emotions and supplies the breath support is to gyrate the hips, like a belly dancer. Or if this is too difficult for you, try the slow, rhythmic hip movements of the Hawaiian hula, accompanied by the graceful movements of the arms and hands. Move and rotate your hips in the widest circles you can, pushing them way out in the front, to each side, and to the back, and let the arms undulate in graceful waves to keep the upper body loose. Hawaiian music helps, and if you don't have any available, hum a little tune. Or, if your throat needs a rest, have someone else hum as you sway and freely rotate your hips. This will greatly reduce tension in the deep breathing and emotional areas, as well as the sexual area, and after only a short time you will experience the energy of the body and feeling life flowing throughout your entire body. The voice and the body that houses it will be vitalized and relaxed.

Almost any of the physical activities we've previously discussed, such as bouncing up and down like a rubber ball or a puppet, or jogging while you sustain open sounds or speak words, will engage the breath and emotions and weld the production of sound into total self-expression. As you jog or bounce, just imagine that the sounds are bouncing from the top of the head to the groin and back again, in as wide a pitch range as possible, and until you feel that it is the entire body that is communicating.

Swaying rhythmically back and forth, as in the hula, is an excellent way for two people to rehearse lines in a scene. Just put your hands on each others' shoulders and drop your heads forward so you're not looking at each other, and dialogue. The rhythmic movement encourages you to experience the life of the words in your bodies, and they flow out easily. And you imagine that the words are enveloping your partner as you speak. You sustain the sounds of key words and wrap them around your partner's body, penetrating his skin. The scene repeated with customary movement after this experience will take on a whole new meaning. But you must first touch physically, as in the dancing movement, and then in the repeated scene, feel that you are touching with your speaking voice.

SUMMARY

Your speaking voice, and the words you use to express your self, have dramatic qualities of great power and range, and you must be as extravagant in your imaginative use of them as you possibly can. Be aware of how your full breathing life frees energy and emotions and gets them flowing through your body. Live your voice from the inside out. Experience your vocal self as free to explore, to transcend. Don't anticipate where your vocal self will take you. Be surprised! Experience your vocal self as something you've never heard before. Recognize no limitations for your vocal self. Just stop trying and let go, and trust your vocal self to spontaneously unfold. Experience nothing but enthusiasm and fascination for the process, and open up to new possibilities as you become your voice, from the top of your head to the tops of your fingers and toes. Your voice is free-flowing, expressive, lyrical movement; let it rise and soar, and transcend earthly sounds. You're a baritone who wants to sing tenor? Try it. You're a soprano who wants to sing baritone? Try it. Transcend your perceived limits of your self, and hold on fast to your new images. Become your voice.

Perceive your voice in terms of the mental, body, and emotional energy that produces it. Think precise kinesthetic images of voice as involving all of you. Hear your voice in terms of these kinesthetic images and as incorporating full, rich, dynamic sound. Think whole phrases in terms of this auditory kinesthetic image. Become your voice. Let your conscious, kinesthetic image erase from your brain the negative vibrational patterns that have formed over the years, those patterns of a passive voice. It's an active voice you want and are. Let the metaphysical happen through your imaging, so that the image becomes manifest.

Voice is an expression and extension of personality, as distinctly individual as a fingerprint. We cannot separate the voice from the other parts of a person. As infants we become bonded to our mother by the sound of her voice. Behavioral psychologists have performed tests during which other women imitate the pitch and rhythms of the real mother's voice. No baby, however, was ever fooled. When one's entire universe is represented by a voice, deception is impossible. Impressions of friends and acquaintances always involve their voices as much as their appearance. Some voices make you want to turn away from them. Others are so comforting that you long to rest inside them and let them cradle you. Voices can both hurt and endear. Voices are a means of projecting the self into the world. Through stress, phrasing, intonation, and rhythmic patterns, we project and orchestrate our inner selves. Voices transmit messages, sometimes consciously, sometimes unconsciously.

A highly trained voice expresses, seemingly effortlessly, every subtle nuance that its possessor commands. Seeming effortlessness is, of course, an illusion, the art which conceals art. But voice is far more than technical proficiency, important as that is. It is the spirit pouring forth full heart in profuse strains of unpremeditated art. This is the combustion, the spontaneity, the divine spark that surpasses technique — that individually unique and personal expression of human experience that underlies all artistic representation. We recognize a Monet painting by its impressionistic technique, subject matter, rainbow of muted color, and flood of light—just as Cézanne is distinguishable by his bold color contrasts, black outlines, and strong architectural form. Vocal art, analogously, paints, expresses, and interprets.

The voice is a key to the door of the universe. It stretches the wings of our imagination across gulfs and galaxies, then pulls us back to the deepest core of ourselves, to elemental, unclothed truth. Cultivated and freed, the human voice possesses the power to open wide the arch of limitless experience and unending discovery. Become your voice.

·6·

SELF-REALIZATION:
The Articulation Process

THE WORDS WE SPEAK ARE the result of *respiration*, in which the body inhales and exhales air; of *phonation*, in which the vocal folds in the larynx move together and are vibrated by the exhaled breath into producing a basic vocal tone; of *resonation*, in which the basic vocal tone is intensified and amplified in the cavities of the mouth, nose, and throat primarily; and of *articulation*, in which the lips, teeth, tongue, jaw, and soft palate shape the resonated tone into specific sound combinations that form words.

It is with this integrated speaking process that we now concern ourselves. For we do not cease to be aware of voice as we begin to focus on the spoken word. We don't because that is not what happens when we speak. All of the above named processes are interpenetrating and interdependent. Producing a spoken message is one coordinated process whereby ongoing vocal sound is resonated and shaped into meaningful words as it flows out through the mouth and nasal cavities. The body muscle energy of voice production is experienced simultaneously with the energy of the speech muscles as they blend into one dynamic auditory image. To experience—to feel—to be aware—continue to be key words. They also continue to become more inclusive.

In releasing and experiencing vocal energy we have worked freely with the large muscles of the body. In releasing and experiencing speech energy we will work more precisely with the smaller muscles of the articulators. Shaping vocal sound into intelligible speech requires a narrower, more meticulous focus. We need to consider the production of distinct sounds and of the linking of sounds and words in intelligible utterance. Muscles must be trained, perceptions must be altered, and limitations must be transcended.

The fundamental purpose of speech is, of course, to communicate, with sounds, words, and phrases that are audible and clear to the listener. The basic components of speech are the individual speech sounds characterized by distinct energies, placements, and functions, and which are imposed on the resonated tone by the articulators, molding the free-flowing voice into meaningful verbal messages.

The clarity of the verbal messages is dependent on the precise placement and production of the articulators; it is also dependent on the flexibility of the articulators in moving from one distinct sound to another and welding them into intelligible words and phrases. Speech is movement. Words on a printed page, including those you are now reading, are a blueprint for energetic speech gesture and action. The constantly changing positions and resonances that make up words and phrases must also be made rapidly in connected speech. Too often, however, the quick changes muddle the precision of the sounds; the sounds are not clearly articulated and speech is unclear.

You can very quickly determine your own ability to articulate sounds distinctly and rapidly by listening to your self. It helps to listen to others as well, particularly to those who have good speech. In listening to yourself it is helpful to use the Ear-Stoppels, which allow you to feel sounds as well as hear them. Speak slowly at first and feel what you are doing. Let your self experience the movement, the placement, and the energy of the individual sounds. Read aloud one or two of the paragraphs on this page and concentrate on living through the movements and vibrations of speech. Let your self undergo the articulatory sensations of sound pressures and contacts in the oral cavity. Let your self react to the feelings triggered by resonated sounds. This experience can tell you a great deal about your speech.

If you wonder why you speak the way you do, know that the determining factors are these. Assuming that the health and structure of your articulators are not abnormal, you speak the way you do because of the speech community of family, teachers, and peers that you heard and imitated as you grew up. Some of these models were good, some bad, and some were those who spoke a foreign language that included sounds not part of standard American speech.

Your speech is also affected by your ability to use your muscles. Muscular movement and coordination in individuals varies from extreme agility to extreme clumsiness. And this is just as true of the speech muscles as it is of the body muscles. Fortunately, motor skills can generally be improved by concentrated effort.

Deficient hearing can also affect your speech. Every sound has a distinct energy and quality, and if one cannot hear these discreet distinctions, it becomes almost impossible to produce them.

Personality traits are also reflected in your speech. If you are a hyperactive person who thinks and moves rapidly you probably also speak rapidly and run words together so that many sounds are slurred or omitted altogether. If you are an apathetic or overly casual person, chances are your lips and tongue are lazy and you produce words that are muddled and often indistinguishable. If you are an aggressive person you probably push out sounds and words with such force that all your listeners hear is a series of clicks and explosions. And so it goes. And while changing personalities is difficult, changing speech isn't.

Speech is a learned process, and can be relearned. In many cases, it *must* be relearned if one is to be able to function effectively in the world. Good speech is your most effective tool. It is a key that can open many doors for you. For example, one of my students recounted her use of good speech in obtaining an apartment. Having read of an available apartment in a newspaper, she said that she telephoned to make an inquiry and asked to see the apartment. She was told that the apartment was not available, but was convinced that the voice on the telephone was not telling the truth. After she had hung up, she reflected that she had not used the standard of speech precision and dynamics demanded of her in class. So she practiced for a half an hour or so, and then put her practice to the test by calling again. This time she was told that there certainly was an available apartment and was invited to look it over. She went, and she got the apartment. Good speech increases your chances of getting what you want out of this life. Any healthy person with a sound speech structure can achieve effective speech if they will, and if they work.

In forming and linking sounds and words in connected speech, we employ the coordinated use of many muscles, just as with any other physical activity, and the speech muscles must be trained and maintained in optimal condition. The average person just going through a day's work generally doesn't need any additional muscle conditioning to sustain him. The golfer or tennis player, however, who sets out to perfect his game will find that this unaccustomed use of his muscles will require long hours of training. It is the same with the person who sets out to perfect his speech. Most every healthy, normal person can speak, and somehow manage to get through his day, but in the great majority of cases, the speech is careless and lacks impact. The person who desires to speak effectively, to be clearly heard and understood, will find that this activity requires long hours of training. Conscientious speech improvement requires conscientious speech practice. There is no other way. Desire alone won't do the trick. The muscles of the lips, the tongue, the velum, and the muscles that control the jaw must be trained to optimal tonicity and agility.

In performing any of the exercises for conditioning the articulators or when concentrating on specific sound production, you must remind your self that these activities are added to all that has gone before. You must constantly prepare for the exercises with full, comfortable breathing and an open, relaxed throat and neck. Monitor these two conditions throughout all of your work on articulation, to give sounds their proper support and resonances, and to keep body energy flowing. Warm up with some breathing exercises and use any of the exercises in the last chapter as conditioning for articulation. Yawning and chewing an *m* warm up the articulators; head drops and rolls are focused on the neck and throat and the area above it on which we concentrate for speech; and finger-tapping and massaging the head, neck, and face energize the articulation muscles, as does the act of moving the facial muscles around in making faces. Intersperse the narrower, more exacting work on speech with these exercises and with occasional arm swings and hip gyrations to relax you and loosen up body and feeling life.

In addition to establishing deep, easy breathing and an open throat before you start, be certain that your shoulder girdle is relaxed. Let your arms hang straight down at your sides and rotate your shoulders forward, up, over the top, down the back, and out to the front again. Do this vigorously with wide circles, but do it slowly. And after you've repeated the rotation in this direction three or four times, rotate the shoulders in the opposite direction. Rotate them back, up and over the top, down the front, and out to the back again. Repeat the rotation in direction three or four times, and then let them drop down.

Be aware now of just your right shoulder and its weight. Imagine that the weight of the shoulder is slowly dropping down into the upper arm, then into the elbow, the forearm, and the hands and fingers. And as the collective weight drops lower and lower, let it pull the trunk of the body to the right side, until you are bending over from the waist. For a long moment, experience the limpness in the relaxed right shoulder and arm. Now let your head float you back to an upright position, dragging the limp shoulder and arm after it. In the upright position, swing your limp right arm easily front and back a few times, concentrating on all the weight of the heavy right hand.

Now repeat the exercise with the left shoulder and arm, and when your head has floated you back up from bending to the left, swing both limp arms easily front and back a few times, concentrating on the weight of both heavy hands. The floating head and relaxed shoulders, combined with deep, easy breathing and an open throat should set you up for the following exercises.

In practicing articulation exercises, I suggest four tools that will aid you in reshaping your facial posture, in experiencing the sounds, and in isolating specific muscle functions.

The first is the continued use of the Ear-Stoppels. The explanation in chapter V should be read again.

The second suggested tool is the Tok-Back, which is a plastic voice reflector that encases the mouth and nose area and hooks over the ears. They can be obtained from Tok-Back, 2926 Avalon Avenue, Berkeley, California 94705. These can add remarkably to your achievement, especially when you are practicing alone and do not have the benefit of feedback from an instructor. Enclosing the front of the speech area where sounds are emitted, the Tok-Back helps you to keep your focus on the articulation process. It also, of course, encloses the energies and resonances of specific sounds and thus enables you to experience them. Further than this, the Tok-Back directs the warm breath back toward the facial muscles and lips and warms them up, which helps both your focus and your production of speech. In working over lines for a play, Tok-Backs are used to great advantage in discovering the threatricality of sounds, and the color and substance of words and phrases. Always remembering, of course, that, as with the Ear-Stoppels, the aim is to feel the sounds and not listen to them. Always be cautious of merely listening to your self, for this can breed an artificial and often limited vocal quality. Experiencing the energies and vibrations of sounds and words is an entirely different matter; this can connect you organically to newly discovered physical and psychological characterization. To set aside the sense of the words for short periods, and let the sounds play over and in your body, can trigger some amazing character discoveries and nuances.

The third tool that I recommend is the Bone-Prop. These should be from three-eighths to five-eighths inch in length, narrow enough in width to not interfere with tongue activity, and can be made of wood, cork, or plastic. I used to import Bone-Props from London, but now find that it is much simpler to buy narrow plastic rods from a hobby shop and have them cut into various sizes in the scene shop where I work. The three-eighths inch props are best for smaller mouths, and large mouths may need seven-eighths inch or one-inch props. The Bone-Prop is placed between the teeth in the front, straight up and down, and is used primarily to immobilize the jaw which forces you to exercise the muscles of the lips

and tongue. You are also forced to stretch the muscles in the lower face, which opens the oral cavity and throat cavity and improves the facial posture for better articulation.

The fourth tool used effectively in improving articulation consists of two Lip-Puffs. These are made from sheets of foam rubber, about three-fourths inch thick and are cut into pieces about three-fourths inch long and one-half inch wide. They are inserted between the lips and the gum ridge, top and bottom, and improve the tonicity and use of the orbicularis oris, which is the principal muscle that acts upon the lips. The orbicularis oris is an oval ring of muscle fibers which completely encircles the mouth slit, extending from just under the nose on top to the cleft of the chin at the bottom. It is a sphincter muscle which, when it contracts, closes the mouth and puckers the lips. Inserting the Lip-Puffs under the lips right in the center under the nose aids your focus on the experience of this ring of muscle fibers compressing against the teeth for the production of the *b-p-m-w* sounds; they also help the frontal placement of sounds and words; and the necessary pressure on the puffs to keep them from falling out increases the tonicity of the lip muscles and reinforces good facial posture.

As to how to use these tools, and in what combination, I find that each individual develops his own patterns. Most use the Tok-Backs throughout the entire practice period; a great many employ both Tok-Backs and Ear-Stoppels throughout the practice, since both of these tools aid in the focus and the experience of articulating specific sounds. The Bone-Props work well in the beginning of the practice period to get the mouth open and to exercise lip and tongue muscles, and this work seems to flow naturally into using the Lip-Puffs to further work on facial posture and lip tonicity and control. Throughout this chapter, it will be suggested where any or all of these tools might facilitate improvement.

FACIAL POSTURE

Just as body and neck posture is essential to effective breathing and phonation, so facial posture is essential to articulation and to well-resonated sounds. The Yogis, who are known for their strong, clear voices and who have taught us much about the art and skill of breathing, can also teach us much about the relation of facial muscles to the matter of voice and speech production. Combining the complete, deeply rooted breath with proper facial posture, they have produced flexible voices with great beauty and power. Prove it to your self. Observing your customary posture in a mirror, speak some words or lines; then close your eyes and be aware of the vocal quality of those words. Now open your eyes and observe your facial posture as you pucker your lips and whistle a short tune. Following this, loosen the pucker slightly so that the jaw doesn't move up and reduce the size of the oral cavity, and speak the same words or lines. Again close your eyes and be aware of the richer, fuller quality of the voice and the fact that the words seem to be right on the lips and the tip of the tongue and are articulated with more precision. Keep speaking, open your eyes and memorize the outside appearance as well as the inside experience of this essential posture so that you can more easily assume it as a permanent part of your equipment. Frequent observations in a mirror will help you to maintain the proper facial posture, as will the positioning and holding in place of the Lip-Puffs. Propping open the jaw with Bone-Props also helps posture, and we suggest their use on all of the practice on the vowel sounds to follow.

It is common practice to include exercises to relax the jaw, and, of course, the term "tight jaw" is a misnomer. The jaw is a bone and my research tells me that bones are incapable of tension. It is the muscles of the jaw and cheeks that are the problem and need to be freed of tension. Toward that end try the following.

Sit or stand upright, with head floating upward out of the shoulder girdle, and rib cage floating upward away from the pelvic girdle. Feel that all of you is soaring upward in defiance of gravity-pull, except your jaw. Let the jaw muscles completely relax and be the only part of you to respond to gravity-pull. Your lips will probably fall open.

Now with lips closed, easily inhale and puff out the cheeks. Then bounce the cheek muscles as you repeat *blubber-blubber-blubber* and *plop-plop-plop* over and over until the cheek and jaw muscles feel very relaxed. Bounce away easily, puffing out your cheeks before each *blubber* or *plop* and enjoy it. Try Bing Crosby's *b-b-b-boo*, along with your *blubber*s and *plop*s and bounce the cheek muscles until you are aware of reduced tension; then very gradually reduce the bounce, and imagine that all of the energy used in the bouncing is moving forward into the lips. When you continue your *blubber* and *plop*s without bouncing, you must experience all of that energy on the lips and the tip of the tongue. In this final step, forget your jaw and let the breath do most of the work, shaped by the lips and tongue. Wet the lips with the tip of the tongue to keep your frontal focus.

Now maintain the posture and say a few, slow *bo-bo-bo*s and *boo-boo-boo*s, rounding the lips and pushing them forward, and put your focus on the slight tension spot in the cheek hollows. Lay the tips of your forefingers on these spots on each side as you continue your *bo*s and *boo*s, and be certain that you feel no tension anywhere else but these spots in the cheek hollows. The throat should be open in the back, and the lips loosely puckered in the front.

Observe this posture in the mirror for it is one that will channel your voice forward, add resonance, and improve articulation. Your lowered jaw gives more room for precise tongue movement and placement, and your loosely puckered lips are in a flexible position for shaping words, as well as creating a smaller lip opening behind which voice can build intensity so that the words come out with greater impact. The pieces all fit, the dynamic of each being reinforced by the dynamic of all. Relaxed jaw and cheek muscles and a relaxed throat are mutually supportive, and in their turn reinforce the adequate degree of tension in the tongue and soft palate.

This facial posture is the one you must strive for and maintain in all of your practice in articulating sounds. As stated previously, Bone-Props and Lip-Puffs will help you to achieve this posture; and they can be put aside once you are able to maintain a permanent posture without them.

Repeat this sequence of exercises frequently, observing the outward appearance and experiencing the inner sensation. And if you do it correctly, that is, slowly with focus and awareness, it will be all you will need in relaxing the jaw muscles. I have never found any value in letting the jaw saw up and down or wiggling it from side to side. These activities require, and often induce, muscle tension, and in no way are an aid to facial posture. They can be said to open the mouth, but quite unnaturally, it seems to me. The proper posture for good speech is a mouth cavity opened as wide as possible with the lips meeting in front, and an open throat behind. This position causes sound to flow forward, like a reverse megaphone, and the lips are in the proper position to shape vowels and form consonants, as well as to be exercised.

LIP MUSCLES

To help you in focusing on your lip muscles and to warm them up, and to maintain your awareness that it is the breath that is supplying the major part of speech energy, try the following exercise.

Assume the correct facial posture as described above, and with lips closed, breathe fully and deeply two or three times, at the same time rubbing your tummy until it feels nice and warm. Remember that this area is the power center of breath and emotions that enrich the voice. Keep

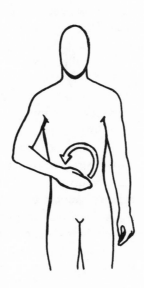

breathing easily and deeply as you rub this power center with your hand and imagine that the warmth is flowing upward onto your lips and facial muscles making you smile. Hum and chew and move the warmth around and feel it toning up the facial muscles and working its way in to add tonicity to the tongue and palate. Maintain a light, soft voice as you continue to hum-chew and move it up in pitch so that the warmth flows into the head resonators. Fill the head with warm, resonated sound, which will act like a cushion behind your words. And most of all, feel the warmth right on the lips as you chew your *m*. The use of Ear-Stoppels help you to experience this exercise, as will the use of the Tok-Back.

The combined use of the chewing movement and the image of warm breath flowing onto the lips and into the resonators will help you to connect the act of breathing with that of speech. Employ and enjoy this experience frequently and follow it immediately with words such as "bim, bam, bomb, boom, mean, mine, moan, moon, moonbeam, windy, green trees, bamboo; "How sweet the moonlight sleeps upon this bank," and then lines from any text.

The mobile lips, along with the tongue, and soft palate, make the mouth the most movable and adjustable of the cavities in the vocal tract. They act as modifiers of resonance and generators of speech sounds. The lips also mediate facial expression. The movements of the lips and other facial muscles provide cues which aid communication much more than most of us realize. Without being aware of it, most of us are lip readers and are fairly good at it, in spite of the fact that most persons' lips are lazy and don't help us a great deal. But mobility of the lips must be encouraged, since they are important in the process of articulation as well as being the external boundary of the oral cavity that shapes and resonates all of the vowel sounds and a great many of the consonants.

Another means of connecting the act of breathing with that of speech and channeling the warm breath from the tummy onto the lips is to use the lip-flutter, suggested in the previous chapter for vitalizing facial muscles. This begins with a full breath which is exhaled on blowing out the lips on a sustained *b*, or more exactly a series of fluttering *b*s. You did this as a child when you were imagining you were a car, and you probably still do it as part of a bodily shiver when you are cold. But whatever the image that motivates the lip-flutter, the increased energy and mobility of the lips as a result of the exercise make this most beneficial to your speech.

Following the above warming-up of the lips and facial muscles, you should maintain good facial posture and further exercise the lips by inserting the Bone-Prop between your teeth in the front. This, as we have said, will open the mouth and immobilize the jaw, and force the lips to accept their responsibility.

With your Bone-Prop in, say "Pompeii, Bombay, bamboo map, mama, Mimi," and "buy Bobby a peppy baby puppy." There are no consonants made with the tongue in these words, and it should lie quietly in the bottom of the mouth, with the tongue tip touching the bottom teeth. You will find, in fact, that all vowels and diphthongs, particularly in stress words, will improve by keeping the tongue in that position. Instead of just flopping loosely around in the mouth, this position of the tongue with the tongue tip anchored gives vowel sounds a firmness and enables you to sustain them. Prove this to your self by not tongue-tipping an *ah*. Just let the tongue do what it wants and you'll probably find that it drifts up and back, partially impeding sound from entering the mouth and the *ah* will be very weak and indefinite. Now tongue-tip the *ah*. Lay the tongue in the bottom of your mouth, touching (not pushing) the tip of the bottom teeth and do another sustained *ah*, and you will produce a full, firm, definite sound which you can sustain as long as you have breath, and which will project outward for you.

Now compress the lips against the teeth as you say: "wah, way, we, wo, woo, wow"; and "Wee Willie Winkle went away" or "Wee Willie Winkle wet his warm, winter woolies." Some of the consonants in the last two sentences are, of course, made with the tongue.

As with any muscle exercises, the above lip activities should not be done mindlessly. Putting on your Tok-Back helps your focus on the lip area, as does closing your eyes. Let your self experience the stretch of the facial muscles facilitated by the Bone-Prop, and imprint the facial posture in your sense memory, and when your jaw muscles feel relaxed remove the Bone-Prop and insert the Lip-Puffs and speak all of the words and sentences again, beginning with "bim-bam-bomb-boom," and try to maintain the facial posture with the open mouth and relaxed jaw, as you further pucker the lips to hold in the Lip-Puffs. After finishing the Wee Willie Winkle sentences, remove the Lip-Puffs and repeat it all again as conversationally as you can with good facial posture and precise lip movements.

As we have previously stated, this narrow speech activity can be exacting, and if this concentrated effort in one small area causes you to be uptight, blow out your lips and relieve body tension with a good stretch or other body exercise.

TONGUE MUSCLES

The tongue is unquestionably the most important articulator, as it is the most active, the most mobile part of the tongue being its tip. It modifies the shape of the mouth and thus the distinctive resonances of sounds, both in the mouth and its associated cavities. Together with the teeth, gum ridge, and palate, it generates sounds. The tongue is a remarkable facile organ, able to assume in rapid sequence a great variety of postures and movements. These are made possible by intricate arrangements of many muscle fibers, and extensive nerve distribution and impulses. The tongue is fastened in the back to the hyoid bone from which the larynx is suspended, to the epiglottis, the soft palate, and the pharynx. It is easy to see that tension in the larynx, soft palate, and pharynx can effect tongue tension, and the reverse is also true. Excessive tension in any of these muscle areas can affect both voice and speech production negatively.

The tongue can be exercised best by once again immobilizing the jaw and opening up the mouth with the Bone-Prop so that the tongue has room to move freely to points of articulation.

Repeat "handy, dandy, Canadian candy" a dozen or so times, then say as rapidly as you can, "the Canadian architect got hit in the head in Connecticut" over and over. Neither of these exercises requires the use of consonants made with the lips, and you can focus entirely on the rapid, precise movements and positions of the tongue. You can also "ticka-tocka" to good advantage, and then combine lips and tongue action in "typical-topical," and "uninhibitiable-uninhibitable," and "bippity-boppity-boo." And, once again, let your self fix the experience of the movements and posture in your mind and muscle memory, and then repeat them without the Bone-Prop, but maintaining the relaxed jaw and facial posture. The use of the Tok-Back, and frequently of the Ear-Stoppels will reinforce the experience and the focus of your practice.

You can further increase the flexibility of the tongue by pretending that you are lapping an ice cream cone with all kinds of vigorous swipes, or pretending that you are a kitten lapping milk and that if you don't lap it up quickly your brother and sister kittens will get it all.

Or you can move the tip up and down, from an *l* on the gum ridge above the top teeth to an *ah* with tongue tip behind the bottom teeth, as in *la-la-la*; then substitute an *n*, *t*, or *d* for the *l*, and say *na-na-na*, *ta-ta-ta*, *da-da-da*. Also you can swing the tongue from side to side, hitting the corners of the mouth opening.

All of these various movements will be of help because of the complex arrangement of the tongue muscles. Some of them go from front to back, some from side to side, and some from top to bottom, and probably other directions as well. So just about any form of exercise will strengthen muscles somewhere in the tongue. As a student, I was asked to pretend to clean my teeth with the tip of my tongue; first running it over the top teeth, in the front, on the cutting edges, and in the back; then running it over the bottom teeth, in the front, on the cutting edges, and in the back. This activity certainly provides a good tongue stretch.

THE SOFT PALATE

The palate extends from a fixed bony plate in the front, beginning with the alveolar arch above the top teeth, continuing with the hard palate, which is thick in the front and becomes thinner toward the top of the palatal arch, and ending in the muscular soft palate. The height of the palatal arch varies in individuals, and contributes to acoustic properties of the mouth as well as to individual characteristics of voice.

The soft palate is our direct concern in speech since it is the only part we can regulate. The soft palate may be raised, lowered, or tensed. In raising and lowering it we modify the shape and resonances of the vocal tract in the production of sounds. Normally, it is raised to produce vowels, and is lowered to produce nasal sounds. And since the soft palate is muscular, we are again concerned with tonicity and mobility. To that end, a few exercises are suggested, since soft palates can be lazy and sluggish if left to their own devices.

Once again use your Bone-Prop to open the mouth and immobilize the jaw and say *ka-ka-ka*, *ga-ga-ga*, and then combine the *ah* sound with the nasal sound in the word sing. These exercises also flex the back of the tongue, since it articulates with the soft palate in the production of these three consonants.

Say "Rangoon, Congo, and cockatoo"; and, of course, "typical-topical," and "ticka-tocka" exercise the soft palate as well as the tongue.

Now say the sentence "Coco couldn't get a cookie in the Congo," a few times, making precise consonants with the soft palate and the back of the tongue. And with consonants made in this position, be certain that there is energy expended only at the place of articulation. You must constantly monitor your throat muscles behind the soft palate and back of the tongue to be certain there is no excessive tension there, as this tension could extend into the soft palate and tongue and inhibit the free movement of the articulation process. It is important enough to repeat the fact that the throat muscles are constrictor muscles designed to aid in the passage of food from the mouth to the esophagus, and that they tense very quickly if not monitored.

Remove your Bone-Prop when you feel fairly sure of your open throat and crisp, easy production of the sounds made by the back of the tongue and the soft palate, and when you repeat them without the Bone-Prop, the Tok-Back or the Ear-Stoppels will aid you in experiencing the sounds. All of the tongue, lip, and soft palate exercises should be repeated daily for short periods and the permanent image of their production and sensations should be fixed in the mind and muscle memory.

Further, more precise descriptions of all of the sounds used in the above exercises will follow in our study of the International Phonetic Alphabet. In this study, it is strongly suggested that you use the four tools to help you experience the energies, positions, and movements of both isolated and connected sounds. Training your self to make the exact placements and rapid shifts is very necessary but is only part of the achievement of good speech.

The other necessary part is that you must feel the sounds. You must get inside them, and let them get inside you. You must explore their resonances and substance and connect to them physically if they are to become a permanent part of your speaking voice. You must allow yourself time to experience the rhythms of speech and the facility of the speech muscles. The sensory pleasures of tactile awareness and the relaxing, hypnotic elements of rhythm, repetition, assonance, and alliteration can alter your perceptions of speech and of your self speaking. The internal vibrations of sounds can relax you and increase your vocal energy, both as a break in rehearsals and as a way of getting feelings flowing at the start of the rehearsal or performance. As you pursue your study of individual sounds, keep in touch with their various physical sensations and be aware of how the sound energies engage all of the senses simultaneously.

THE INTERNATIONAL PHONETIC ALPHABET

The standard for the pronunciation of words for the average off-stage speaker is mainly to be able to communicate meanings intelligibly — be the speaker from Dallas, Boston, or Brooklyn. However, since some Dallas pronunciations might not be intelligible in Boston, and a Brooklyn dialect could certainly confuse some Dallas listeners, the implications for the actor are clear. For while the average off-stage speaker has the opportunity to pause and restate, the actor does not. Nor can the actor permit attention to be focused on him rather than the character he is playing. The actor must be immediately understood and must not allow a distracting regional dialect to limit either the range of roles to be played, or the areas of the country in which to play them.

In studying pronunciation we will use the International Phonetic Alphabet, since the Latin-based English alphabet is phonetically inadequate to bear the burden of English sounds, and is, therefore, not a reliable guide to pronunciation. Take, for example, the phenomenon of the "ou" combination of symbols in the six words *through*, *though*, *rough*, *cough*, *bough*, and *would*. The "ou" symbol combination represents a different sound in each of the six words, and by using the IPA, we can accurately transcribe the six sounds as [u] in *through*, [oʊ] in *though*, [ʌ] in *rough*, [ɔ] in *cough*, [aʊ] in *bough*, and [ʊ] in *would*.

Or to cite another example and imagine our three hypothetical speakers from Dallas, Boston, and Brooklyn discussing oil. The Dallas speaker probably would sound as if he were saying *all*, the Boston speaker as if he were saying *aisle*, and the Brooklyn speaker as if he were saying *earl*—and, of course, the standard vowel sound is similar to the vowel in *boy*.

Clearly, the International Phonetic Alphabet is an invaluable tool for anyone who wishes to learn a new dialect. It is a must for the acting student who needs to analyze and master the General American dialect that is intelligible and free of regional sounds, as well as to acquire such other stage dialects as American Southern, Standard British, Cockney, and Irish, to name just a few.

An individual could probably improve his speech without using the symbol of the International Phonetic Alphabet, generally referred to as the IPA, but by using these symbols the job is done more quickly and is more certain. Dictionaries can be helpful in pronunciation but only to a point, since different dictionaries use different diacritical markings, and some of the markings are ambiguous. The IPA uses one symbol, and one only, for each sound, be the sound in the English language or any other. The IPA can be used to study any language anywhere in the world. Somewhere I read that Sophia Loren learned her first English-speaking role by using the IPA.

Only those symbols needed for studying the English language will be included in this text. These IPA symbols will furnish you with a frame of reference for identifying, analyzing, and classifying specific sounds.

All of the sounds of the IPA are classified as either *vowels* or *consonants*. Vowels are resonated variations of the vocalized breath as it flows out through the open passageways of the throat and mouth. Their distinct qualities are formed by the resonance cavities, by the shape and tension of the tongue, and by the shape and tension of the lips. All vowels are voiced, that is they are produced by vibrations of the vocal folds. Consonants are produced by the articulators, i.e., the lips, teeth, tongue, palate, and glottis, as they variously impede or stop the vocalized or unvocalized breath.

The vowels could be thought of as the river of vocal power, constituting the substance and flow of the voice. The consonants, in turn, could be thought of as the banks of the river, which shape and define the flow of vocal power. Both vowels and consonants require careful attention to their production and function, and are equally important elements of clear, dynamic speech.

As you study the following IPA sounds, keep three things uppermost in your mind. Together they comprise my golden rule for speech, for as truly as you do unto your speech it will do unto you.

1. In the same way that your acting life must be more concentrated and larger than life, so must your speaking voice be more concentrated and larger than life. Dramatic speech must be the most expressive of all forms of speech, so it follows that sounds and words must undergo a change from everyday quanitites and qualities.

2. In the same way that you penetrate the inner experience of a character, so must you penetrate the inner experience of sounds and words. Sounds not associated with thoughts and feelings will not become a permanent part of your equipment. Sounds that are produced only mechanically will be forgotten in acting performance. Sounds must be welded to feelings and to auditory images, and approached through the imagination which conjures up a feeling and body condition for each sound.

3. In the same way that you use the controlled flow of vocalized breath in singing, so must you use the controlled flow of vocalized breath in speaking. Expressing means pressing out the combined energy and flow of full breathing and emotion, which gives the voice its carrying power.

VOWEL AND DIPHTHONG CHART

Front	Central	Back
[i]–beet		[u]–boot
[ɪ]–bit	[ɝ–ɜ]– her	ʊ–put
[eɪ]–bait–[e]	[ɚ–ə]	[o]–[oʊ]–boat
[ɛ]–bet	[ʌ]–but	[ɔ]–saw–[ɔɪ]–toy
[æ]–bat		[ɒ]–fog
[a]–bath		[ɑ]–hot

[aɪ]–buy   [aʊ]–now

VOWELS AND DIPHTHONGS

As seen in the accompanying diagrams, *front vowels* are those produced as the result of muscle activity bunched in the front of the tongue, *central vowels* are those produced as the result of muscle activity bunched in the middle of the tongue, and *back vowels* are the result of muscle activity bunched in the back of the tongue.

Vowels are also the result of tongue tension, which increases as the tongue is raised for the higher sounds, and decreases as the tongue is dropped for lower sounds. Lip tension is also a factor in vowel production, particularly for the back vowels, also known as "rounded" vowels. Diphthongs, of which there are five, are comprised of two vowel sounds, in which the first vowel is stressed and the second vowel is unstressed.

Use the Tok-Back, Ear-Stoppels, Lip-Puffs and Bone-Props, in any combination, to help you experience the inner life of the sounds. Frequent usage will dictate their individual or combined help. And also remember that whether the blade of the tongue is bunched for front, central, or back vowels, the tongue tip should be easily contacting the back of the bottom teeth in the front for firm, sustained sounds.

In the following drills, treat the pure vowels as just that. Don't weaken or distort vowels by adding an unstressed *uh* sound and turning them into diphthongs. Prepare for every sound by inhaling deeply as you assume the physical condition for it, then breathe sound into and feel it form inside you.

Front Vowels

[i]

Inhale, then breathe into and sustain the [i] sound in *mean, heed, grieve*. Shape it with unrounded lips and by holding the tongue high,

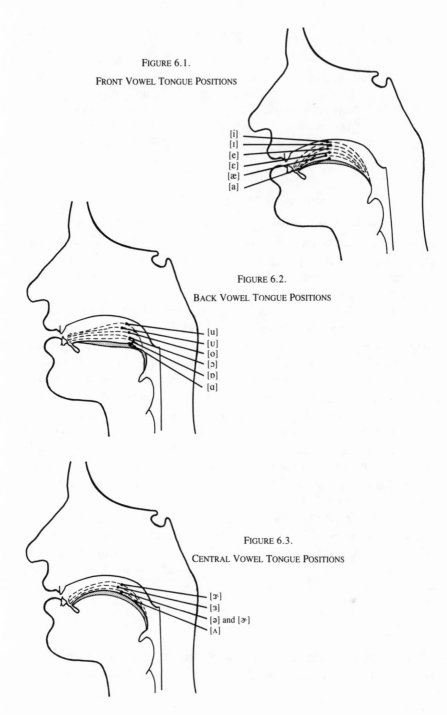

FIGURE 6.1.

FRONT VOWEL TONGUE POSITIONS

[i]
[ɪ]
[e]
[ɛ]
[æ]
[a]

FIGURE 6.2.

BACK VOWEL TONGUE POSITIONS

[u]
[ʊ]
[o]
[ɔ]
[ɒ]
[ɑ]

FIGURE 6.3.

CENTRAL VOWEL TONGUE POSITIONS

[ɝ]
[ɜ]
[ə] and [ɚ]
[ʌ]

124

tense, and forward. Don't let the tongue drop down toward [ɪ] or bunch back toward [ʊ] as it tends to do. Inhale, then breathe into the experience of the [i] sound in each of the single words in the lines below. Add to the intensity of that experience by massaging over the eyes and nose as you penetrate the inner experience of sound (see item 2 of the golden rule for speech). Use your Tok-Back and Ear-Stoppels to reinforce sound experience on the following phrases and sentences. (Lacking a Tok-Back, cup your hands over your nose and mouth.)

eat	easy	each	equal	ether	ego	even	east
steam	neat	cheat	deal	feast	least	beat	team
trustee	meek	teacher	believe	eastern	please	receive	eaten
mean	decree	theme	beam	seem	weaned	need	feel

free and easy	agree to teach	weak feet	need to agree
eat the cheese	see me ski	previous teacher	completely equal
mean trustee	steam heat	eager beaver	sweet peach
clean easel	meek leader	greasy key	green seas

deep feeling	complete relief	sweet grief	teaching machine
even teeth	supreme ego	these wheels	he kneels
please read	each meal	she peeked	feed the sheep
eat beans	mean edict	eastern team	free wheat

You need to keep your teeth clean.　　　　Please read me to sleep.
The leaves on the trees were green.　　　　Edith eagerly greeted the people.
Lee is keen on keeping sheep.　　　　Pete was seen feeding the weasel.
Each believed in seeking freedom.　　　　The deed was needed by Marie.

Phoebe was seen in *East of Eden*.　　　　Edie went skiing with her teacher.
Have either peas or beans to eat.　　　　The senior seized the fleeing thief.
Beatrice was meek but mean.　　　　Marie was weeping from being teased.
He vehemently agreed to the edict.　　　　The team's zeal brought needed prestige.

[ɪ]

Inhale, then breathe-into and sustain the [ɪ] sound in *into, big, hid*. Shape it with unrounded lips, and with the tongue high and forward, but a bit less tense than for the [i]. Don't let the tongue drop down toward [ɛ] or drop back toward [ʊ], and hold the tongue steady so the sound doesn't split into [ɪə]. Use Tok-Backs and Ear-Stoppels to reinforce the experience of the sounds.

The unstressed [i] in the second syllable of *city, lovely, many*, and in the first syllable of *elect, believe, pretend*, is closer to being an [ɪ]; practice this in the first two lines of phrases. Since several foreign dialects confuse [ɪ] and [i], practice making this distinction in the phrases below.

if	in	idiot	ignore	itch	it	into	ink
will	big	thin	still	thing	bill	elected	fish
began	decree	believe	receive	behalf	demand	been	prevented
dishes	kitchen	cabin	women	palace	chicken	wishes	chalice

demanded chicken	did the dishes	believed him	prevented it
will begin	elected him	protected her	pitiful behest
wishes to kill	spitted pig	bitter defeat	quickly needed
will decrease	prefer biscuits	beautiful baby	needed milk

deceived him	chases pigs	prepare dinner	will pretend
delightful swing	idiot declined	Bill returned	willing victim
ambitious women	foreign king	twin cabins	insulted him
decline the deal	mashes potatoes	will receive	unbelievable wit

spinning wheel	spitted veal	grisly theme	will decrease
wheat biscuits	need vinegar	three cities	itching feet
hid the geese	either issue	tricky decree	will grieve
pitiful people	needed milk	mixed feelings	three trips

tricky dealer	bitter defeat	clean stick	quick to agree
irritating siege	eastern women	equally quick	eager investor
bleeding lip	receive a tip	will meet	pretty leaves
prevent freezing	quit speeding	neat sister	witty scheme

He didn't wish to deceive.
His sister bought six peaches.
Will you eat biscuits with the fish?
The freezing wind chilled him.

She didn't receive the bill.
The Queen's decree came quickly.
Bill relieved him in Italy.
She insisted on freeing him.

The senior gave his sister a ring.
I believe Pete spilled the milk.
Edie and Phil pleaded sickness.
She developed skill in teaching.

Pete was defeated by Jim.
The significant issues increased.
We elected to lease the building.
The prince had three women.

[eɪ]

The pure vowel [e] is heard in many foreign dialects, but is heard in American English only rarely in such unstressed syllables as *cha*otic, *va*cation, *de*bris or Mon*day,* Tues*day,* and so on. We will consider the more commonly used diphthong [eɪ] in this position.

Inhale, then breathe into and sustain the [eɪ] sound in *aid, aim, hate.* Shape it with unrounded lips, and physically experience the energy of the two vowels as the tongue bunches forward for a firm [e], then relaxes for a shorter [ɪ]. Breathe into the experience of the [eɪ] sound in each of the single words in the lines below, and add to the intensity of the experience by massaging over the eyes and nose. Use your Tok-Back and Ear-Stoppels to reinforce sound experience on the phrases and sentences.

age	ache	ate	able	ape	aid	aim	alien
dame	plane	rain	station	lame	wait	sailor	aimless
stay	may	play	available	away	amiable	weigh	mail
fragrant	placate	railroad	say	ailment	day	train	place

rainy day	stay away	aging dame	same ailment
waiting train	delayed plane	great play	aimless tailor
aching face	swaying acorn	favorite place	bale of hay
gay apron	ate the cake	fragrant spray	sailed away

available date	alien face	great railroad	fate awaits
daily fray	eight sailors	available paper	pay day
rain and hail	rainy sail	pale raisin	eighty babies
fail to wait	nail the table	mail train	came to stay

It was a great day to sail.
Jane played her last ace.
May waited for the train.
He gave aid to the ailing baby.

Kate was frail for her age.
We hailed the mail train.
He told tales of great places.
Abe has been ailing for ages.

We bailed Ray out of jail.
Wait for James to open the gate.
Shakespeare wrote great plays.
Dale was late for his date.

Nate wailed when he saw the mail.
The sale was for eighty days.
We gave all available aid.
The sailor was an alien.

[ɛ]

Inhale, then breathe into and sustain the [ɛ] sound in *egg, head, wend*. Experience the shape and condition of the unrounded lips, and the tongue forward but lower and less tense than [eɪ]. Don't let the tongue bunch up to [ɪ] or down to [æ], and in such words as *very, merry, American,* don't let the tongue bunch back to the [ɝ] sound in *her*. Breathe into the experience of the [ɛ] sound in each of the single words in the lines below, massaging over the eyes and nose. Use your Tok-Back and Ear-Stoppels to help get inside the sound. Be aware that the first line of phrases contrasts [ɛ] and [eɪ], and that the second line of phrases contrasts [ɛ] and [ɪ].

effort	extrovert	expect	energy	end	any	elevator	elephant
went	echo	pencil	clever	heady	well	read	sent
epidemic	center	bread	says	shell	men	tension	estimate
exit	engine	them	egg	neck	bed	editor	felt

Eddie waited	tame epic	precious paper	plain red
devil came	never plain	better pray	daily bet
able retinue	wedding day	waiting men	insane error
ten planes	dress braid	plain vegetables	any place

met Ben	Fred went	sells pins	many dresses
thin men	get pins	send pills	thick pencil
wet milk	red lips	met Bill	will sell
Jim said	big echo	will lend	Jill's den

Red-headed Penny is my friend.
American men want health and wealth.
Seven against twenty is unfair.
Beverly engineered the session.

Ned brought bread and eggs.
Betty's dress was very red.
The General sent many men into battle.
Jerry entered the lead gates.

Jeff entertained at the wedding.
The twin engines were well made.
Jenny put a hem in the pink dress.
Ted put his pet hen in the pen.

The men helped to salvage the wreck.
Ben ate twelve eggs for breakfast.
Jerry's head ached from the tension.
The letter was sent on May tenth.

[æ]

Inhale, then breathe into the experience of the low, unrounded lips and low, front, lax tongue position of the [æ] in the words *and, half, man.* Hold the tongue steady and neither let the sound split into the diphthong [æ ə], nor let it become nasalized and bunched upward so that *Ann* sounds like *Ian.* Get inside the sound of the [æ] in each of the single words in the lines below, while massaging over the eyes and nose. Use your Tok-Back and Ear-Stoppels to reinforce the sound experience on the phrases and sentences.

and	answer	angry	action	ample	agony	anchor	ask
chance	hand	man	dance	ran	tan	fancy	frantic
past	fast	mast	glass	mass	mast	aghast	vast
bag	sag	nag	flag	bank	hand	thank	sank

mad man	bad habit	last chance	grab the hat
candid laughter	frantic manner	angry action	sad answer
grand manner	that rascal	Japanese fans	candied apple
rash banker	pack blankets	began to act	black hat

bank manager	camp land	lamp stand	Sam's ankle
thank Ann	candid language	agonizing tramp	angry man
hang the flag	ample bag	dancer ran	handy chance
Dan drank	Frank's glass	last plan	van sank

Jack had his hat in his hand.
Dan put his hand in the grab bag.
Jan sat on his back pack.
The candidate had a bad platform.

Sam spoke the Italian language.
The crackers came in wax-wrapped packs.
Nancy was glad to dance with Dan.
The agonizing rascal was avaricious.

Australia has vast expanses of land.
The hanging basket looked grand.
The land on which we anchored was sandy.
Allen and Sam went to France.

The actions of the man were frantic.
Dan examined the candy apple.
Sally sang the anthem on Saturday.
The tan cat ran down the path.

[a]

This is the front vowel with the lowest tongue position and the widest lip opening. In General American speech it is only heard as the first sound in the diphthongs [aɪ] as in *buy* and [aʊ] as in *mouth*. In New England speech it commonly replaces the [ɑ] sound in such words as *car*, and the [æ] sound in such words as *bath*. In Southern American speech it commonly replaces the [aɪ] diphthong in such words as *why, nice*. It replaces at least three sounds in the Irish dialect. Experience the [æ] in *hat* and the [ɑ] in *hot* and then aim for a vowel sound somewhere in the middle. Use your aids and tongue-tip the sound.

bath	last	chance	dance	France	half	calf	ask
castle	path	glass	mast	fast	pass	mask	cast

asked his aunt	last chance	dance master	pass the glass
grasped the raft	class answered	fast dance	vast ranch
half the castle	pastor's task	command the staff	wrathful reprimand
can't laugh	Lance can't	Frances laughed	Aunt Nancy

Front Vowel Drill

Use Ear-Stoppels, and lightly touch the tongue tip to the bottom teeth or gum ridge for the vowels and diphthongs in the following sentences so that you *feel* rather than listen, so that you penetrate the inner experience of sounds and words. Weld each sentence firmly to a deeply centered breath.

The wind was from the East that day.
Jim was left a handsome legacy.
Bill fastened the tack on the mare.
The Asian fish were interesting.

My friend agreed to play the villain.
Abe seized the heavy drill with his hands.
The prisoner schemed for his freedom.
The eastern team was easily defeated.

He believed what she said.
Ann received Bill with pleasure.
The teacher read about King Henry.
The children deceived their leader.

Peg demanded chicken for dinner.
Bea waited for Eddie at the station.
Freddie made errors on the test.
Birds sang and flitted in the trees.

The heaving seas were deep and green.
Kate and Sandy yelled for help.
The women declined to eat the meat.
The big hanger held ten planes.

Grace believed whatever Bill said.
The letter came three days late.
The brave men manned their stations.
Ben ate plain vegetables for dinner.

The leaves became green in the spring.
We waited for a better day to sail.
The Dean's expenses were paid.
He was an unbelievably clever wit.

The baby laughed at the kitten.
It was an excellent place to eat.
Nancy thanked him for the receipt.
They will begin to build in May.

Ray was anxious and tense.
The unbeaten team entered the race.
The seniors planned a trip to Japan.
The league established a precedent.

We had bacon and eggs for breakfast.
It was a compelling scheme.
The man raised rabbits and pigs.
Ben quickly initialed the decree.

The freezing wind chilled the people.
There were ashes in the grate.
The laughter was pleasing to hear.
The scheme advanced his prestige.

The elephant and the eagle were friends.
She created a splendid image.
Extra grants were made available.
The victims were freed by the police.

Back Vowels

[u]

Inhale, then breathe into and sustain the [u] sound in *coupe, goon, cooed*. Shape it firmly with rounded lips and the blade of the tongue high in the back. Preceding the sound with [k] or [g] helps to get the tongue back, so that the sound doesn't drift forward toward [ɪ]. Get inside the sound of the [u] in each of the single words in the lines below, while massaging over the eyes and nose. Use your aids and tongue-tip to reinforce the sound experience on the phrases and sentences, and tap your breast bone with your finger tips.

It is acceptable to use either [u] or [ju] in such words as *duty, new, endure, Tuesday, tune, during, opportunity, student, Duke,* and *produce*.

food	juice	through	tomb	blue	loose	clue	school
rule	lose	move	spoon	tooth	shoot	who	moon
tune	new	during	endure	opportunity	grew	duty	reduce
crew	soon	shoe	whose	excuse	Duke	true	booth

undo the shoe	blue shoes	new school	Ruth cooed
remove the spoons	whose tomb	true blue	unruly student
the tooth grew	loose clue	produce food	foolish rule
flew the coop	unique unit	whose pool	pursue the crew

hoot at the goose	Sue was rude	bamboo hoop	knew his duty
woo the recruit	chew your food	rumors endure	peculiar canoe
glue the boot	do tell Lew	choose a tool	beautiful tune
moody groom	too soon	salute the Duke	during the funeral

The newspaper had influence.
The two were usually feuding.
He knew who started the rumor.
Blue Moon is a nice tune.

The youth never chewed his food.
The Duke accused the group.
The tomb was gloomy and spooky.
It is humid during July.

Lew flew to New York.
Lucy grew moody and rude.
The troops moved on Tuesday.
The goose flew over the coop.

Blue light illuminated the room.
The fruit trees bloomed in June.
Hugh endured the foolish crew.
The group went to the zoo at noon.

[ʊ]

Inhale, then breathe into and sustain the [ʊ] sound in *could, good, cook*. Shape it firmly with rounded lips and the blade of the tongue high and back, with a bit less lip and tongue tension than for [u]. Maintain a steady tongue, so that the sound neither bunches forward toward the [ʌ] nor splits into [ʊə]. Get inside the sound of each of the single words in the lines below, while massaging over the eyes and nose. Use your aids and tongue-tip to reinforce the sound experience on the phrases and sentences, and tap your breast bone with your finger tips. [ʊ] and [u] words are combined in the phrases to enable you to contrast lip and tongue tension.

sugar	would	could	pull	cookie	wouldn't	look	wolf
should	put	shook	wood	push	fully	ambush	took
foot	look	cushion	cook	woman	stood	good	bushel
book	pudding	butcher	wool	bushes	crooked	brook	hook

pull the tooth	woolen suit
remove the roof	crude woman
the bullets flew	cooked a goose
moody cook	juvenile hood

good food	new book
full at noon	looks beautiful
crooked room	wooden canoe
chew the cookie	unique hook

shook it loose	looking through
blue cushion	fruit pudding
improve the cooking	beautiful brook
peculiar book	good music

amusing bulletin	bruised foot
took the cubes	look at the ruins
jeweled cushion	Brooklyn youth
who took it	cook the food

The lute was in the wooden nook.
The crook took the new bookcase.
The Duke was good looking.
Lucy pushed the broom.

Who pushed Ruth in the brook?
Lou took the footstool.
The woman wouldn't excuse him.
Look at the beautiful book.

The crook looked for the jewels.
The goose hid in the bushes.
Lucy is a good cook.
Put your foot in the shoe.

Sue's pudding was sugary.
They took a bushel of fruit.
He was pushed into the pool.
She shook the blue cushion.

[oʊ]

The pure vowel [o] is heard in many foreign dialects, but is heard in American English only rarely in such unstressed syllables as *o*bey, *ho*tel, *o*kay. We will consider the more commonly used diphthong [oʊ] in this position.

Inhale, then breathe into and sustain the [oʊ] sound in *own, open, be-low*. Physically experience the movement and energy of the two vowels as the tongue bunches back for a firm, well-rounded [o], then relaxes for a shorter [ʊ]. Preceding the sound with a [k] or [g] will help keep the tongue back and avoid the tendency to drift toward [ɛ]. Get inside the [oʊ] in each of the words in the lines below, while massaging over the eyes and nose. Use your aids and tongue-tip to reinforce the sound experience on the phrases and sentences, and tap your breast bone with your finger tips.

boat	bowl	oak	over	own	only	ocean	owner
robe	moan	those	wrote	toast	stroke	goat	known
phone	coat	open	snow	joke	don't	grow	pony
note	cold	scold	froze	though	yellow	follow	below

open slowly	go below	old soldier	grown cold
both poles	over and over	won't go	old goat
grown old	yellow tomato	going home	wrote an opus
throw snow	cold toast	sold the opal	moaning crows

broken tow	cold coke	sewed the coat	boat load
wrote a note	blow your nose	don't float	sold soap
growing old	yellow robe	opal stone	go alone
don't throw	don't know	old toad	don't phone

The soldier told old jokes.   Joan is going home on her pony.
It's too cold to open the window.   It was the only boat on the ocean.
Follow the swallow back home.   Joe grows potatoes and tobacco.
The old man sold coal and coke.   Only Flo knows who stole the opium.

Rose scolded the old stoker.   The snow froze his toes.
Don't use soap on that old cloak.   He showed the roan before he sold it.
He was told to blow his nose.   The old man went home slowly.
Don't use that tone to Joe.   The load of stones rolled over.

[ɔ]

Inhale, then breathe into and sustain the [ɔ] sound in *call, gone, caught*. The blade of the tongue is back, but is lower and less tense than [oʊ], the lips are foward and less puckered. Don't let the tongue drift forward to [ɛʊ] and hold it steady so it doesn't split into [ɔə]. Get inside the [ɔ] sound in each of the words in the lines below, while massaging over the eyes and nose. Use your aids and tongue-tip to reinforce the sound experience on the phrases and sentences, and tap your breast bone with your finger tips.

all	ought	almost	awning	organic	soft	author	cause
yawn	falter	ought	cough	wrong	guffaw	tall	small
saw	gnaw	raw	claw	jaw	always	law	water
talk	laundry	autumn	awkward	auction	pause	office	door

all wrong	audible yawn	caught the hawk	lauded the author
small chalk	long pause	wrong auction	awkward lawyer
water launch	autumn dawn	long hall	Albany outlaw
law office	almost gone	stalk the fawn	tossed the ball

saw a moth	long shorts	audience applauded	north shore
wrong door	more corn	often coughs	warn Paul
warn Maud	fall forward	awful storm	almost always
short form	gone north	coffee water	awful ordeal

Toss the ball on the lawn.
The dog caught the hawk in his paws.
Shaw is a thoughtful author.
It was a stormy morning in the fall.

The lawyer was a former outlaw.
Paul's daughter was born in Baltimore.
The call from the office was important.
Maud bought the horses at an auction.

George served sauce with the pork.
The launch headed for the north shore.
The orchard is often warm in the autumn.
There's an enormous board at the corner.

The dog walked Ross to the corner.
The foreman was offered a reward.
They applauded and called for more.
The outlaw's sword was drawn.

[ɔɪ]

This diphthong combines [ɔ] and [ɪ] and is frequently heard in Southern speech as [ɔ] and in New England speech as [aɪ]. Physically experience the movement and energy of the two sounds as the blade of the tongue bunches back for a firm [ɔ] then glides forward and relaxes for [ɪ]. Inhale, then breathe into and sustain the [ɔɪ] diphthong in *toy, poise, coin.* Massage over the eyes and nose as you get inside the sound in each of the words in the lines below. Reinforce the sound experience on the phrases and sentences by using your aids and tongue-tip, and tapping on your breast bone with your finger tips.

toil	boy	toy	joy	coy	enjoy	envoy	sirloin
poison	royalty	choice	noise	oyster	convoy	moist	joyous
joined	annoy	ointment	destroy	point	join	joint	poise
boil	broil	coin	foil	soil	voice	alloy	employ

pointed foil	noisy turmoil	poised envoy	oily ointment
noisy boys	moist oysters	convoy royalty	spoiled boy
anointed oil	loyal employees	enjoy the toy	Reuter's envoy
joyous voice	annoying point	voided appointment	coin alloy

corduroy doily	boiling point	moist sirloin	convoy destroyed
boys with coins	deploy the spoils	poisoned soil	soiled oilcloth
voiced annoyance	avoid the toil	annoy Lloyd	royal decoy
oyster broil	join Roy	boiled poi	loyally toiled

Roy was anointed with oil.
Boil the loin in soy sauce.

The noisy boys annoyed Lloyd.
Troy was adroitly destroyed.

The staff is poised and adroit.	Mr. Boyd annoyed the cowboy.
Mrs. Doyle soiled the oilcloth.	Doyle's choice was a Rolls-Royce.
The boys destroyed their toys.	She joined Floyd in Illinois.
She soiled her choice voile dress.	The loyal employees toiled.
Joyce pointed at the envoy.	The convoy was deployed to the point.
Roy had an appointment in Detroit.	Roy's voice was joyous.

[ɒ]

This is a vowel with slightly rounded lips and with the tongue in a low, back, lax position. In General American speech it is rarely heard; in New England speech it may replace the [ɔ] in *fog, dog, log*. It commonly replaces the [ɑ] in Standard British, in such words as *not, body, doctor*. Experience the [ɔ] in *naught* and the [ɑ] in *not* and then aim for a vowel sound somewhere in the middle.

off	froth	loss	not	horrid	often	cloth	watch
fog	dog	log	watch	cod	stop	swallow	draw

draw the dog	not quantity	odd lot	hot coffee
top notch	horrid fog	soft cloth	mop the spot
often gone	got a lot	toss the doll	bronze swan
got quality	drop the box	novel plot	got shot

[ɑ]

Inhale, then breathe into and sustain the [ɑ] sound in *honor, hot, calm*. Drop the jaw for this one, and be sure the tongue is relaxed and held low in the bottom of the mouth, with the tongue tip touching the inside of the bottom front teeth. Get inside the [ɑ] sound in each of the words in the lines below, while massaging over the eyes and nose. Use your aids to reinforce the sound experience on the phrases and sentences, and tap your breast bone with your finger tips.

optional	army	architect	option	almond	arctic	opera	optimum
father	calm	charm	drama	lock	starve	shot	bomb
arm	arch	honest	olive	honor	argue	onward	ominous
psalm	heart	barn	upon	farm	palm	car	doll

artistic commodity	ominous bomb	charming comedy	dark carpet
army marched	Doctor of Philosophy	father argued	opera and drama
park the car	martyr starved	shot the lock	suave architect
archaic opulence	hospital doctor	bizarre concept	hot sonata

harmful olives	solid opposition	ominous obstacle	marble arch
bronze arch	bourgeois novel	obstinate octopus	washes a lot

not operative	dock the yacht	Panama bar	Utah guard
calm robber	hollow spot	holly rotted	spotted shark

Honesty is the best policy.
The bomb hit the large dock.
The robber palmed the onyx.
The cod had rotted on the dock.

Polly played with the doll.
Tom is honorable but obstinate.
The doctor operated in the hospital.
The problem in the arbor was a fox.

The sergeant shot the guard.
Tom sent a card to his father.
The arcade was shockingly hot.
The farmer built a large barn.

The obsolete ark looked odd.
Father argued for quality not quantity.
The army pilot dropped the bombs.
The comedy had an opulent set.

Back Vowel Drill

Use Ear-Stoppels, Tok-Backs and lightly touch the tongue tip to the bottom teeth or gum ridge for the vowels and diphthongs in the following sentences so that you *feel* rather than listen, so that you penetrate the inner experience of sounds and words. And weld each sentence firmly to deeply centered breath.

Joe knew who stole the sword.
Dawn took the boat on the water.
Joey walked and talked at two.
The local gossip grew and grew.

Who started the rumor about Paul?
We will walk on the new board walk.
The poem was not at all good.
It was lost a long time ago.

The zoo got a boa and a mongoose.
Who told Maud that Don was home?
The ocean was beautifully calm.
By two o'clock he had gone home.

The road wandered to the cove.
It was Mo's duty to saw the wood.
Look thoughtful in this role.
The chauffeur drove much too slow.

The operator stopped at the wrong floor.
Go due north for forty-two miles.
He looked at the view a long time.
Don told Saul the whole story.

Tom knows all about the youth group.
We ought to have gone home sooner.
Joan was forty-two in July.
The horse's owner was tall and gaunt.

Sue bought an old copper coffee pot.
It was almost dark when Lew came home.
Who is knocking so softly at the door?
For a moment or two she stood alone.

It was too warm to walk that morning.
Prudence was tall and awfully haughty.
His new shoes were gone from the closet.
Rose was all alone in the huge room.

Volumes of books were lost that morning.
Hugh bought an opal for his daughter.
We saw no one walking in the woods.
The lawyer was amused by the goat.

There was no crew on board the launch.
Call me at home tomorrow morning.
No one knew where Paul's office was.
We saw Olive walking along the road.

They crawled ashore from the boat wreck.
The fog on the ocean was awful.
The route we took was shorter than yours.
No one knew the outlaw's motives.

The food was good but the room was warm.
Who put the overalls in the chowder?
The reporters were stupid and foolish.
Tony didn't approve of the eulogy.

[aʊ]

This diphthong combines [a] or [ɑ] with [ʊ], but since most General American speech does not contain the [a] sound, it is best to practice this with the [ɑ] at the beginning. Physically experience the movement and energy of the two sounds as the relaxed tongue drops low in the bottom of the mouth for the [ɑ] and then bunches up and back for the unstressed [ʊ]. Don't let the [ɑ] bunch up and forward toward an [æ]. Get inside the sound in the words in the lines below, while massaging over the eyes and nose. Use your aids and tongue-tip to reinforce the sound experience on the phrases and sentences, and tap your breast bone with your finger tips.

out	our	ounce	owl	outside	outer	outline	outlaw
allow	about	around	eyebrow	fountain	mountain	power	flower
down	town	tower	south	blouse	house	crowd	powder
bound	round	mouth	gown	clown	proud	vowel	cloud

down south	around the house	brown gown	proud mouse
loud crowd	doubtful prowess	proud outlaw	down the mountain
pronounce vowels	countdown	down and out	ounce of flour
brown blouse	crowd outside	our powder	down town

downy cloud	pouting clown	lousy cow	round flower
howling lout	shouted loudly	flower power	doubtful bout
south bower	our couch	hour by hour	rouse the town
mouse cowered	foul frown	shouted ouch	vow to endow

The crowd shouted outside the house.   Get the cow out of the flowers.
One rounds the mouth for back vowels.   The clown bowed to the shouting crowd.
Mound the flowers around the house.   The scout plowed the ground.
I doubt if he has the crown now.   The hound isn't allowed to growl.

The outlaw prowled around the house.   Somehow the owl got into the fountain.
He shouted loudly from the tower.   She was proud of her brown gown.
She bounced the ball up and down.   The scow bobbed around and around.
They found a mouse in the house.   They found the hound on the ground.

[aɪ]

This diphthong combines [a] or [ɑ] with [ɪ], but since most General American speech does not contain the [a] sound, it is best to practice this with the [ɑ] at the beginning. Physically experience the movement and energy of the two sounds as the relaxed tongue drops low in the bottom of the mouth for the [ɑ] and then bunches up and forward for the unstressed [ɪ]. Don't let the [ɑ] bunch up and forward toward an [ʌ], particularly before [p] as in *pipe*, [t] as in *night*, and [k] as in *bike*. Get inside the sound in the words in the lines below, while massaging over the eyes and nose. Use your aids and tongue-tip to reinforce the sound experience on the phrases and sentences, and tap your breast bone with your finger tips.

aisle	wife	eyes	idle	item	island	I	iris
fight	sight	strife	flight	quite	blight	bite	kite
nice	line	night	knife	kind	hike	high	hide
alike	ripe	pipe	tripe	swipe	tie	Mike	bike

try to comply	dry biography	sky high
tie your tie	blind eye	lime pie
tired wife	ironic reply	fine rhyme
irate sign	buy ivory	crying child

exciting night	quite a hike	buy a bike
fly a kite	five pipes	quite ripe
right side	write a denial	swipe the pie
might like it	buy the item	fine tripe

I've been invited for five nights.
Why did she hide the ivory?
His wife will fly to the island.
The kite was high in the sky.

What kind of pie shall we buy?
His height is five foot nine.
The spy spent an exciting night.
He wined and dined with his wife.

He tried rhyming as an exercise.
Hiram took only a tiny bite.
Eileen dried her eyes and sighed.
Cy might like to take a drive.

He cried over Ida's demise.
Mike got tired of trying.
He described the frightful crime.
Ira lied about the bite on his thigh.

Drill for [ɑ] [aɪ] and [aʊ]

Sign now for outbound flights.
The knight dropped the crown.
His pipe dropped out of his mouth.
Martha frowned at the crying child.

Tom climbed the mountain at night.
He sits five aisles down on the right.
Howard was proud of his civilized life.
The flower mound was quite a sight.

Why did Arthur hide the cow?
Bart found a pineapple pie.
Bob shouted loudly at his wife.
The mountain top was high.

Lottie put the ground ice in the icebox.
Dot's untidy gown was brown.
Giles plowed the ground on his farm.
The pilot was finally grounded.

A mouse and a fly were in the jar.
The child darted into the house.
The kite hit the ground very hard.
The guard found an outline.

The farmer's wife liked the cows.
The carpet in the aisle was brown.
The bike was found in the barn.
The car stood outside the armory.

Ida scowled and raised an eyebrow.
The vines arched downward.
The farm was far from the town lights.
There was a light in the south tower.

The old house was dark that night.
Giles has a large, loud mouth.
The guard put out his night light.
She took a swipe at Bob with a knife.

The white house was a bargain.   They found Martha's biography.
Father Michael was too stout.   He always buys a large amount.
Tom met some hardy mountain climbers.   The coward tried to hide in the barn.
St. Cloud is quite a large town.   It's a five-hour drive to Harlem.

Isaac devoured the pot pie.   The marble fountain was lighted.
Parker was found to be the right height. John idolized the Count.
The large sign fell to the ground.   Fire-fighters surrounded the park.
There was hardly any flour for the pie.   It's quite doubtful that Bob drowned.

Central Vowels

[ɝ–ɜ]

Inhale, then breathe into and sustain the [ɝ] sound in *first, word, earth*. The lips are rounded slightly and the blade of the tongue is bunched in the center and lightly touching the top molars. Don't let the tongue go too far back and press too hard on the molars, which makes the *r* coloring hard and prominent. Get inside the sound in each of the single words in the lines below, while massaging over the eyes and nose. Use your aids and tongue-tip to reinforce the sound experience on the phrases and sentences, while tapping your breast bone with your finger tips. The [ɜ] sound is the same sound with no *r* coloring and is not commonly heard in General American speech; it replaces the [ɝ] sound in American Southern and New England speech, as well as in the Standard British dialect. You should not feel the molars on this one.

early	earned	earnest	ermine	irk	urban	Irma	urge
birch	blur	bird	fir	curt	her	purse	sir
defer	curve	prefer	work	refer	worse	were	hurt
rehearse	turtle	adjourn	colonel	curtain	urchin	burn	first

early bird	perfect pearls	earth worms	ermine furs
third person	stirring words	return the urn	urgent words
first term	purple curtains	certain girl	virtuous verse
earnest work	dirty urchin	worst curve	worthy search

Irma smirked	urban church	Earl's journey	urged Erwin
working girl	nursing her	early rehearsal	heard it occur
purchased furs	earth's surface	irksome curses	early return
hurled a dirk	serve turkey	Herb turned	Bert turned

Bert took a turn for the worse.   They burned the church curtains.
Ernest wrote irksome verses.   She had slurring words for the colonel.
Herb worked on the furnace.   Turkey had a third earthquake.
Earl urged them to read Burke.   The Earl was earnest and virtuous.

The pert girl had an ermine fur.
The burden of the work fell on her.
First we turned on the furnace.
Erwin inferred the worst.

Erma's research was worthless.
The intern searched for germs.
Bertha smirked at the sermon.
We prefer the early service.

[ɚ]

Inhale, then breathe into and experience the unstressed [ɚ] sound in oth*er*, pap*er*, p*er*suade, oppo*r*tunity. This sound is the same as [ɝ] except that [ɝ] is stressed and [ɚ] is unstressed, as in the first and second syllables of *murder*. Use your aids to reinforce the sound experience on the words, phrases, and sentences.

other	better	letter	after	actor	driver	color	wonderful
surprise	lantern	mustard	perceive	persuade	curtail	survive	overtake
honor	humor	weather	glamour	picture	muttering	treasure	paper
darker	lighter	farther	fewer	waterfall	offer	calendar	summertime

brother and sister	better weather	father entered	better butter
over and over	mother and father	wonderful swimmer	shorter teacher
never offered	masterful actor	southern harbor	smoother water
fewer strangers	surprising offer	paper survived	glamorous hunter

hotter summer	sooner permit	better dancer	surprising picture
pillar of fire	silver treasure	bitter humor	pernicious rumor
new calendar	never remember	fewer murders	sooner perceive
offer curtailed	another letter	persuasive offer	ever undertake

[ə]

Like the sound above, this sound (called the *schwa*) is unstressed, as in *a*bove, *a*round, sod*a*. In the process of running words together in connected speech, the [ə] also occurs in unstressed words, as in th*e* book, bag *of* candy, ham *a*nd eggs. The [ə] replaces the [ɚ] (*schwar*) in the speech of American Southerners and Northeasterners, as well as in the Standard British dialect. Use your aids to reinforce the sound experience on the words, phrases, and sentences.

around	about	arrange	again	ahead	aware	assist	assume
telephone	emphasis	relative	necessary	syllable	alphabet	Mexico	terrible
data	mania	soda	vanilla	sofa	mama	dogma	cinema
remedy	privilege	magazine	delicate	advocate	universal	moment	dramatic

American advocate	comfortable sofa	convenient remedy	the parade
attach the telephone	the new territory	the syllable	amazed visitor

agreeable privilege	another postman	annoying editor	annoyed relative
excellent camera	adored from afar	papa's accident	Mexican dialect

a red balloon	audience agreed	a relative stanza	a circus gorilla
adores bananas	police accident	violent buffalo	another company
chocolate soda	abominable	complementary	considerable
commemorative	accommodation	beautification	communicable

Sooner or later the ballon will ascend.
The popular magazine has a new editor.
The pilot's parachute never opened.
They applauded the excellent performance.

The advocate handled the delicate matter.
Anita bought her sister a parasol.
The orchestra performed in the afternoon.
It was a terrible moment for the lawyer.

He fell asleep during the solemn lecture.
He was unaware of the accident.
Bertha and Anita were uncommunicative.
She suffered from claustrophobia.

The president visited Alaska.
The dancer had delicate features.
The accommodations were abominable.
His benevolence was unbelievable.

[ʌ]

Inhale, then breathe into and sustain the [ʌ] sound in *cup, just, one*. Drop the jaw for this one, and let the relaxed tongue lie flat in the bottom of the mouth with the tongue tip touching the bottom teeth. Hold the tongue steady, and don't let it drift up to [ɜ] or split into [ʌə]; and don't substitute [ɝ] in such words as *hurry, courage, stirring*. This sound turns up quite often, so improving it does a great deal for both your speech and your facial posture. Get inside the [ʌ] sound in each of the words in the lines below, while massaging over the eyes and nose. Use your aids to re-inforce the sound experience on the phrases and sentences, while tapping your breast bone with your finger tips.

other	under	uncle	oven	ultimate	umpire	upward	utmost
just	but	come	much	luck	blood	done	love
courage	nourish	borough	flourish	discourage	flurry	worry	current
hurry	encourage	surrey	furrow	burrow	worried	encouraged	hurried

another shovel	a dozen onions	dull subject	dumb luck
shut up	ugly bus	wonderful judge	humble nun
must consult	just one	upper crust	another governor
Dutch customs	study the results	corrupt brother	butter tub

plucky instructor	other usher	insulting son	lustrous sun
uncle worried	sudden flurry	current studies	hurried lunch
crumb buns	under the oven	truculent couple	just us
discouraging sum	begun to worry	Murray hurried	undernourished

Mother had buns and honey for lunch.
He worried about the unlucky bum.

Some try to shun Russian customs.
None of us were under the rug.

His beloved country was flooded.
My gloves and umbrella are in the pub.

My uncle had a dusty surrey.
Money encouraged the governor to run.

Her younger brother sucks his thumb.
Her son had much fun in London.
Multitudes were overcome by hunger.
There was a sudden flurry on Monday.

My cousin has wonderful courage.
The ugly monkey was unusually dumb.
Mother is coming for lunch.
The lovely plums were nourishing.

Central Vowel Drill

Use aids and tongue-tip vowels on the following sentences so that you *feel* rather than listen, so that you penetrate the inner experience of sounds and words. And weld each sentence firmly to a deeply centered breath.

Uncle muttered about Irma's curls.
None of us heard the bird chirping.
Ernest's cousin rehearsed in London.
The truculent girls huddled in a circle.

The turtle lurked under the oven.
Dudley was the first to wonder.
The curtain went up with a flurry.
The bird rushed to another perch.

Judge Bern preferred onions.
Only a certain number were returned.
Uncle worked for a southern firm.
The luncheon perch was done in butter.

My brother heard the thunder.
The third verse must be done.
Mother went to church on Sunday.
We discussed the research results.

Myrtle had company for supper.
Herbert had unusual courage.
She currently works for the governor.
The stirring words were encouraging.

The furs were too much money.
Earl worried about what he heard.
The nurse was summoned hurriedly.
Fern hurried to return the funds.

Drill for [ʌ] and [ɑ]

The hut had a cot and rug.
Wanda was fond of her lover.
The problem was not enough funds.
Nothing was promised to Uncle John.

The duck got stuck under the dock.
John dropped his gloves in the mud.
Donna touched the hot cup.
Tom had cod and buns for supper.

Huck followed the young mud hen.
The architect was overcome by hunger.
Father was struck dumb by the argument.
There was much opposition to the study.

He was not qualified to govern.
The doctor was a sullen suspect.
Olives are harmful to my uncle.
Not one couple went to the arctic.

The opera was done for a large sum.
The butler had a sudden shock.
The archaic opulence was stunning.
He parked the car in a muddy spot.

She flung the socks at Bobby.
Mother was a doll but father was dull.
Ron got an undesired number.
The plucky instructor shot the lock.

CONSONANTS

The degree to which we are understood when we speak is largely determined by the way we pronounce our consonants. As previously stated, the effect of the consonants on the free-flowing vowels is rather like the effect of the banks on a river. Or it could be thought of as the nozzle on the hose. In all instances, the stream of water or the flow of sounds is shaped and defined.

The firm, precise shaping of consonants is a significant factor in how well words carry to the back of the theater. Knowing the text and feeling the subtext are only the beginning. To project these intelligibly to an audience there must be the physical cooperation of increased breath pressure and of firm, meticulous muscle control. All of this applies to projecting vowels as well, of course, but generally it is the consonants that communicate the sense of the words.

The actor cannot afford the luxury of the lazy, off-stage speech of most individuals, which includes the errors of:

1. *Substitution,* such as the use of [d] for [t], so that a word like *matter* becomes *madder;*

2. *Omission,* such as leaving out the [t] in the word *gifts,* making it *gifs;*

3. *Addition,* which can make a word like *home* sound like *homuh;*

4. *Distortion,* as when the tongue tip for the [t], instead of being placed on the gum ridge above the upper teeth, is placed on the upper teeth and the [t] hisses;

5. *Reversal,* which can make a word like *ask* sound like *axe.*

The speech muscles must be trained to move instantly to the right position, and the perception of the position must be permanently imprinted.

Consonant sounds differ from open vowel sounds in that they are primarily the result of stopping or in some manner impeding the outgoing vocal sound. Consonants are classified as to how they are articulated, where they are articulated, and whether or not they are voiced or voiceless. *Affricates* are combined of two consonant sounds.

How Articulated

Plosive sounds are those produced as the result of stopping, then exploding, the exhaled breath as in

[p]–pie	[t]–toe	[k]–key
[b]–boy	[d]–do	[g]–go

Fricative sounds are those produced as a result of constriction and compression somewhere in the vocal tract as in

[f]–fee   [θ]–thaw   [s]–so   [ʃ]–shoe   [h]–how
[v]–vie   [ð]–though   [z]–zoo   [ʒ]–Gigi

Affricates are produced by combining a plosive and a fricative in a single consonant sound as in

[tʃ]–chain   [dʒ]–Jane

Nasal sounds are those produced as a result of the vocalized breath in the nasal cavity rather than the mouth as in

[m]–me   [n]–no   [ŋ]–sing

Glides, also called semi-vowels, are produced as the result of the movement of the tongue and lips from one position to another as in

[w]–we   [r]–raw
[hw]–when, which begins an [h]   [j]–you

The *Lateral* is produced by the phonated breath stream flowing over the sides of the tongue as in

[l]–lay

Where Articulated

Bilabial (two lips) sounds are made by the lips meeting as in

[p–b–m–w]

Labiodental (lip-teeth) sounds are produced by the lower lip contacting the upper teeth as in

[f–v]

Lingua-Dental (tongue-teeth) sounds are produced by touching the top of the tip of the tongue to the edge of the teeth as in

[θ–ð]

Lingua-Alveolor (tongue-gum ridge) sounds are produced by the tongue tip contacting the upper gum ridge as in

[t–d–n–l]

or approximating the ridge as in

[s–z]

CONSONANT AND AFFRICATE CHART

How Articulated							
		Plosives Voiceless-Voiced	Fricatives Voiceless-Voiced	Nasals	Glides	Lateral	Aff-ricates
Where Articu-lated	Bilabial	[p] [b]		[m]	[w–hw]		
	Labio-dental		[f] [v]				
	Lingua-dental		[θ] [ð]				
	Lingua-alveolar	[t] [d]	[s] [z]	[n]		[l]	
	Lingua-palatal		[ʃ] [ʒ]		[r] [j]		[tʃ–dʒ]
	Lingua-velar	[k] [g]		[ŋ]			
	Glottal		[h]				

Lingua-Palatal (Tongue-Hard Palate) sounds are produced by the tongue approximating the hard palate as in [ʃ–ʒ–r–j] and the two affricates

$$[tʃ–dʒ]$$

Lingua-Velar (Tongue-Soft Palate) sounds are produced by the back of the tongue and the soft palate as in

$$[k–g–ŋ]$$

The *Glottal* (glottis) sound is produced by the vocal folds constricting the breath as in

$$[h]$$

Voiced–Voiceless

Voiced consonants are produced by the breath stream vibrating the vocal folds. You can experience these vibrations if you place your fingers over the larynx (voice box) as you speak the following

[b–d–g–v–t̪–s–ʒ–dʒ–m–n–ŋ]

[w–j–n–1]

Voiceless consonants are produced on a whispered breath with the vocal folds not vibrating. You will feel no vibrations if you place your fingers over the larynx as you speak the following

[p–t–k–f–s–ʃ–tʃ–h–hw–θ]

The chart should help you to understand consonant production, as will the use of your aids. The Tok-Back and the Ear-Stoppels help you to both focus on your work and experience it. The Lip-Puffs will particularly help the necessary lip compression for the bilabial sounds, and the Bone-Prop should be used on all but the fricative sounds as it inhibits the necessary cooperation of the teeth on [f–v–θ–ð] and seems to somewhat inhibit the production of [s–z–ʃ–ʒ]. [h] is the only fricative that is produced comfortably with the Bone-Prop. It also helps focus and provides a brief moment of relaxation to frequently wet your lips with the tip of the tongue. Both the lips and the tongue are constantly working and need all the encouragement they can get.

Plosives

[p–b]

Keeping the lips closed, physically prepare to make a [p]. As you inhale through the nostrils and build up breath pressure behind the closed lips, be aware of the ready energy of the taut lip muscles. Now experience the lip muscle energy as you pop them open for *p-p-p, p-p-p, poo*. Repeat the same posture and breath preparation for [b], and experience *b-b-b, b-b-b, boo*. Repeat both sequences, including posture and breath preparation, and this time lay your fingers on your larynx, to experience and contrast the voiceless [p] and the voiced [b]. The sounds should be firm and precise — neither too lax nor exploded too violently. Pop them out easily in staccato fashion. Use your Tok-Back and Lip-Puffs to reinforce sound experience on the drill materials.

pack–back	mopping–mobbing	map–mab
peg–beg	ripper–ribber	pup–pub
Paul–ball	rapid–rabid	rip–rib
peer–beer	staple–stable	tap–tab
pate–bait	supping–subbing	fop–fob
pit–bit	roper–rober	gap–gab

peppy baby	blue bagpipe	bitter people	back pack
pesky brigand	proper top	bottomless pit	papa's bedtime
bamboo map	better stop	Barbary ape	bean prop
dapper Abe	snip ribbon	mobbing the fop	supping tab

purple cab	pitiful baboon	baby puppy	jumping bear
champion cub	bad pickles	beautiful pub	mop and scrub
bombastic Bob	powerful mob	step up	grab a cap
paper cap	robe the roper	big slab	jump rope

The people began buying in a panic.
They were scrubbing the baby in a tub.
Portly Abe is an apple keeper.
Bob put the soda pop under his robe.

The bear yelped at the bat bite.
Bob got a surprising new job.
Ben put the tape on the tabletop.
Nobby pleaded for a brown rabbit.

Please help to open the clamp.
Separate the capes and the robes.
Penelope was disturbed by the proverb.
The gullible boy grabbed the tab.

Pete reported that the tide had ebbed.
Pepi clasped the ship's rope.
Paul bought shrimp in the shop.
Paula took pictures of Pompeii.

[t–d]

Physically prepare to make a [t], by pressing the tongue tip against the upper gum ridge and lightly contacting the top teeth with the sides of your tongue. As you inhale through the nostrils and build up breath pressure, be aware of the ready energy of the taut tongue muscles. Now experience tongue muscle energy as you tap out [t-t-t, t-t-t] *too*. Repeat the same posture and breath preparation for [d], and experience [*d-d-d, d-d-d*] *doo*. Repeat both sequences, including posture and breath preparation, and this time lay your fingers on your larynx, to contrast the voiceless [t] and the voiced [d]. For a keener perception of the sound experience, use your Tok-Back or cup your hands over the nose and mouth area, as you proceed with the drill materials. Be certain to make short, staccato taps, using just the tongue tip.

[t–d] are not as fully exploded in the middle of a word as they are at the beginning or end. For the medial [t] especially, don't substitute [d] and tap the tongue tip so lightly that you hear an aspirated [h] after it. For instance, the word *letter* should sound like "let her," the stress, in both instances, being on let. Both [t] and [d] are exploded before vowels and pauses, and generally not exploded before other consonants.

tame–dame	writing–riding	bat–bad
time–dime	waiting–wading	hit–hid
ten–den	betting–bedding	bet–bed

tin–din	petal–pedal	pot–pod
teen–Dean	patting–padding	pat–pad
tier–dear	citing–siding	clot–clod

totally hidden	try to deride	bold attitude	dedicated tailor
loud talk	doomed kitten	old motto	dull testament
dirty bedding	tasty dinner	dull routine	delightful team
fading tune	notice of aid	tedious sitter	Betty's wedding

smart fad	heart of gold	leading court	quart of sand
old moat	first hand	handy partner	Daddy wept
first undertaking	dull paint	first reading	inept fiddler
thirty buildings	beautiful garden	notice Daddy	better caddy

The kitten hid under the cot.
We tried to get Addie's attention.
Tad had a British dialect.
The doctor solved the medical riddle.

Tad was sitting down when he heard it.
Marty's twins were identical.
The bottom of the boat needed painting.
Addie kept putting pods into the basket.

It was just a lot of idle chatter.
Better talk subtly to Eddie.
Betty's daddy had a soft heart.
Tweedledee and Tweedledum were twins.

Ned laughed and held the little cat.
Don't overdo the fact finding.
The widow pitied the pouting child.
Teddy was sliding down the door.

[k–g]

Physically prepare to make a [k] by raising the back of the tongue and lowering the soft palate. As you inhale through the nostrils and build up breath pressure, experience a firm, but comfortable posture, with none of the unnecessary tension that transmits itself to the throat and causes a harsh, unpleasant quality. Now pop out [k-k-k, k-k-k] koo. Repeat the same posture and breath preparation for [g], and experience [g-g-g, g-g-g] goo. Repeat both sequences, including posture and breath preparation, and lay your fingers on your larynx, to contrast the voiceless [k] and the voiced [g]. For a keener perception of sound experience, use your Tok-Back or cup your hands over the nose and mouth area, as you proceed with the drill materials. Work for a light, precise contact and constantly monitor and relax the throat muscles behind it.

cap–gap	lacking–lagging	tuck–tug
come–gum	tricker–trigger	brick–brig
cut–gut	bicker–bigger	peck–peg
cold–gold	meeker–meager	back–bag
call–gall	flocking–flogging	hock–hog
cot–got	tucking–tugging	knack–nag

good cake	staggering cat	stuck pig	wicket gate
big stick	sagging rack	current governor	leggy cat
frisky colt	sniggering cook	rigged a canoe	big oak
single actor	finger stuck	leaky organ	log cabin

meager cargo	bugging racket	frisky goat	garden basket
ask forgiveness	infected finger	hungry crew	bagged a skunk
exact language	give thanks	correct angle	single scheme
Pittsburgh Elk	ignorant prank	ugly duckling	rigging defect

The accident occurred in the bog.
The dog began to back track.
He flexed his trigger finger.
The organized election was rigged.

The banker thanked the organist.
Kate was ignorant of the occurrence.
We gaped at the curious figure.
The gambler was aghast at the scheme.

Ken had a nagging backache.
The cook began to make biscuits.
The Canadian geese honked.
Mike put the bike in the luggage rack.

Greg worked in Ankara, Turkey.
The pictures in the catalogue were big.
Gus went to Bangkok and Tokyo.
The burglar was dragging an anchor.

Plosive Drill

Use Ear Stoppels and Tok-Back on the following sentences so that you feel rather than listen, so that you penetrate the inner experience of sounds and words. And weld each sentence firmly to a deeply centered breath.

He didn't explain why he lagged.
Rick's report was fictitious.
Bobby played in the big league.
The Peking Duck was succulent.

My uncle was the bugler for the band.
The archaeologist crept into the crypt.
Enemy flack crippled the aircraft.
The cookout was a big success.

We had barbecued ribs for supper.
Connecticut is a beautiful state.
Eddie had a successful stag party.
The baby was contented in the crib.

Agnes went to Topeka, Kansas.
The ignoble act was significant.
His back was better after acupuncture.
It was the biggest crowd on record.

He couldn't fix the damper.
We expected it to be acceptable.
He promptly corrected the mistakes.
Eddie exploited his battle record.

The task of decoding was difficult.
The article was succinct and significant.
It was a tactical mistake by the captain.
Peg put it in her ample pocketbook.

His impracticability was exasperating.
The prestidigitator was systematic.
He was an opinionated hypochondriac.
It was an unprecedented opportunity.

The argument was calculated to succeed.
It was typical bureaucratic prodigality.
They underestimated his duplicity.
Ted bought a dietetic, decarbonated drink.

He was a benevolent philanthropist.
His catatonic state was inexplicable.
The dictator was quite diplomatic.
His dependability was repudiated.

He was a pacificatory demagogue.
It was tantamount to capitalism.
His was an indefatigable temperament.
He determinedly extirpated the plant.

He was characteristically peripatetic.
She was a dedicated palatinate.
He perpetuated his impermeability.
The pediatrist had a palpitating heart.

Their incompatibility was unexpected.
The vote was indubitably significant.
The statistician was indisputably creditable.
His procrastination was inexplicable.

Fricatives and Affricates

[f–v]

Physically prepare to make an [f] by pulling in the lower lip and pressing it easily against the edges of the upper front teeth. Inhale, and hold the posture firm as you force the breath out in a sustained, forceful [f]. Repeat the same posture and breath preparation for a firm [v]. Repeat both sequences, including posture and breath preparation, and lay your fingers on your larynx, to experience and contrast the voiceless [f] and the voiced [v]. For a keener perception of sound experience, use your Tok-Back as you proceed with the drill materials. Since these are commonly weak sounds, firm up the bottom lip by holding it taut in the [f–v] posture as you prepare the breath for every word pair, phrase, and sentence. And make certain that the outgoing breath is not exploded in one burst like a plosive sound.

fat–vat	wafer–waver	safe–save
file–vile	define–divine	leaf–leave
feel–veal	shuffle–shovel	proof–prove
few–view	infest–invest	waifs–waves
face–vase	effort–ever	beliefs–believes
fault–vault	after–average	surfed–served

famous voices	comforting wives	faltering provider	first hive
stiff driver	fat victim	frantic serve	safe dive
vivid fancy	vicious laughter	five puffs	rival staff
savage thief	never drives	careful visit	very rough

groovy gift	svelte gloves	fifth vowel	every shelf
have sulphur	very emphatic	five platefuls	triumphant rival
some value	comforting voice	give camphor	sulphurous fumes
spherical vault	never left	cupful of violets	comfortable cove

Fern braved the diving raven.
Such a variable friend deserves to fail.
Fred made twelve different discoveries.
Father grieves for his dead rival.

Vicious laughter revolved around Vivian.
Philadelphia was frosty in November.
The fanciful wife saw elves.
Fifteen vegetables is enough.

I should have driven faster.
Give me a cup of coffee.
I have the knives and forks.
The physician left camphor for Ralph.

I should have left before Vivian.
Hoover froze the roast of beef.
Van should have served breakfast.
He suffered from love of self.

[θ–ð]

Physically prepare to make a [θ] by lightly touching the top of the tip of the tongue to the edges of the upper front teeth. Inhale, and hold the posture firm as you force the breath out in a sustained, forceful [θ] in *thin, theme, think*. Repeat the same posture and breath preparation for a sustained, forceful [ð] in *then, though, this*. Repeat both sequences, including posture and breath preparation, and lay your fingers on your larynx, to experience and contrast the voiceless [θ] and the voiced [ð]. Use your Tok-Back as you proceed with the drill materials. Since these are commonly weak sounds, firm up the tongue muscles as you prepare the breath for every word pair, phrase, and sentence. Don't thrust the tongue too far out, and make certain that the outgoing breath is not exploded in one burst like a plosive sound.

thin–then	either–either	loath–loathe
throw–though	healthy–although	mouth–mouthed
thick–this	author–father	bath–bathe
thank–than	nothing–other	teeth–teethe
thread–them	method–lather	sooth–soothe
theme–these	frothy–bathing	breath–breathe

that month	thankful brother	rather uncouth	these teeth
thin clothing	writhing heathen	seething throng	neither cloth
either youth	Gothic theme	southern author	other thumb
they're athletes	scathing truth	thoughtful father	thy thigh

loathes Athens	soothing warmth	either length	Martha tithes
wealthy mother	further oaths	northern cathedral	earthy rhythm
everything mouthed	fourth or fifth	something pithy	sixth or seventh
these months	these growths	smooth paths	other births

Think about either the bath or the path.   Bertha thanked both of them.
Martha's was the seventh death.   Ruth arrived the sixth of the month.
The theme made thrilling theater.   That path has thick undergrowth.
Elizabeth's wealth is a myth.   Arthur sheathed his thick sword.

The cathedral is north of the theater.   They gathered the thirty feathers.
Throw the thread on the hearth.   It was the third Thursday in the month.
Both her brothers are healthy.   It was, nevertheless, rather thick.
He had strength and great warmth.   Thelma was sympathetic but apathetic.

[s–z]

Physically prepare to make an [s] by holding the sides of the tongue against the inner surfaces of the top molars. Generally the tongue tip will point toward the upper gum ridge. Inhale, and hold the posture firm as you vigorously channel the outgoing breath stream through the narrow groove in the tongue toward the gum ridge for a short, sharp [s]. Repeat the same posture and breath preparation for a short, sharp [z]. Repeat both sequences, including posture and breath preparation, and lay your fingers on your larynx, to experience and contrast the voiceless [s] and the voiced [z]. Use your Tok-Back as you proceed with the drill materials. If your [s] needs improvement, remember that it is a muscle-training job and experiment. Be certain that the sides of the tongue are firmly in place and that you have good breath support, then:

1. First make a good [t] which keeps the tongue high, then make an [s], then repeat *tzi-tzi fly;* and *mat, mast, mats.*

2. Make a good, firm [z] which has more strength and tension, then [s].

3. Spread the tongue for the final fricative sound in *fish,* and as you sustain it, bring up the sides of the tongue for an [s], and feel the difference, as in *fishsoup.*

4. Move the tongue tip up or down slightly, since this varies with individual production, but be careful not to let the tongue droop too much for a spread [s] or touch too much of the palate, which shuts off the sound, and don't aim toward the teeth and become hissy.

5. Don't prolong the sound; make short, sharp blasts.

sip–zip	lacy–lazy	advice–advise
seal–zeal	priced–prized	ice–eyes
Sue–zoo	bussed–buzzed	rice–rize
sag–zag	gracing–grazing	face–phase
sing–zing	bracing–braising	fleece–flees
sink–zinc	racing–razing	deuce–dues

lacy robes	six daisies	diced cheese	sweet raisins
small nose	nice music	pleasing dress	peaceful breeze
tubs of grapes	kills wasps	graceful sails	busy place
impressive tombs	certain flights	easy does it	sells coats

does deceive	is necessary	was loose	is classic
carries caps	lacks furs	easy laughs	has boats
dozen flasks	surprising casts	doesn't enhance	was first
inspiring zeal	hazardous risks	is sleepy	small weeds

It was the last of the minstrel shows.   Sandy did an analysis of Brazil zoos.
Sam said he needs all sorts of foods.   The council bans the use of guns.

Sue's party gags included bags of eggs.   The crazed mobs seized the labs.
Rose didn't realize it was Tuesday.   Seth gives gazelles to his wives.

His task was to sell masks and casks.   The spray splashed on the masts.
He lisps and gasps around wasps.   Romance is best, east or west.
Sally's stove was smoking furiously.   The starving cats ran after the rats.
Saul fits the nets on the pots.   They saved six quarts of soda.

[ʃ – ʒ]

Physically prepare to make a [ʃ] with a tongue posture that is similar to
the [s], except that the tongue is flatter and a bit farther back in the
mouth. Inhale, and hold the posture firm as you direct the outgoing breath
between the tongue and hard palate for a firm [ʃ] in *shoe, show, she*. Repeat the posture and breath preparation for a firm [ʒ] *Zsa-Zsa, Gigi,
beige*. Repeat both sequences, including posture and breath preparation,
and lay your fingers on your larynx, to experience and contrast the voiceless [ʃ] and the voiced [ʒ]. Use your Tok-Back as you proceed with the
drill materials, and neither let the tongue touch too much of the palate and
shut off the sound nor let the breath escape over the sides of the tongue.

sure – usual	dilution – delusion	push – garage
shall – vision	glacier – glazier	cash – beige
shame – casual	Aleutian – allusion	flesh – massage
shop – visual	Confucian – confusion	plush – rouge
sheep – seizure	notion – evasion	wash – prestige
shawl – intrusion	national – treasure	leash – camouflage

additional leisure	facial massage	unleashed confusion	shiny garage
machine erosion	azure shroud	usual threshold	fresh seizure
slashed version	lush mirage	Sheila's rouge	Gigi blushed
rash decision	treasured dish	Shah's entourage	Danish intrusion

Fisher's treasure	legion's lesions	Confucian confusion	fish sauce
use rouge	last clash	Hutch hushed	fresh lecture
nice shad	blushing Gus	thin shin	shattering vision
leisure hours	unusual shop	obnoxious regime	passionate seizure

The rash composer had no composure.   It was a shameful occasion.
Zsa-Zsa wore a flashy negligee.   Sheila had a shack at the seashore.
Division weakens national prestige.   Shawn was subjected to derision.
The Persian legions saw a mirage.   Charlotte had a facial massage.

She washed her casual cushions.   The ship's motion shook Shirley.
The shiny Chevrolet was in the garage.   The English shawl was azure and beige.
She had shad, squash, and radishes.   The mesh camouflage caused confusion.
Shakespeare wrote *Measure for Measure*.   Asher spoke on the Russian invasion.

[h]

An [h] is made by partially closing the vocal folds and then exhaling the breath stream through this opening (called the glottis). Inhale, and feel how the [h] sound takes on the posture and quality of whatever vowel sound follows it, as in *heel, whom, hide.* For a keener perception of sound production, use the Tok-Back as you proceed with the drill materials. Be aware that, while the [h] sound is heard in stressed syllables and words, it is generally not heard in ongoing speech in such unstressed words as *him, her, have, has.*

hand	have	heavy	hardware	perhaps	rehearse	behold	unhappy
hold	home	hit	happening	ahead	inhale	inhabit	uphold
happy	hide	horse	hospital	anyhow	exhale	inhuman	prohibit
heart	hello	had	human	behind	behave	somehow	mahogany

his home	her house	who has	huge highboy
he has	heavy handed	Helen hid	has humor
how high	has help	high hill	head of hair
hear him	horse's head	Hello, Hugh	helpful Hannah

rehearsed Hamlet	Herbert behaved	unheated playhouse	behind the house
high lighthouse	overhaul the house	disheartening hit	ahead of him
heard foghorn	hiding perhaps	happily unhurt	prohibit help
he exhaled	her behalf	happened anyhow	inhuman history

Hugh hurried Harry to the hospital.	Hubert hit his horse on the head.
Harriet hid behind the bathhouse.	Hard-hearted Hannah had a mishap.
Herbert put his helmet on his head.	Henry had a handsome head of hair.
Hal hollered hello from the hill.	Hugh headed down the highway.

It ill behooves Hilda to misbehave.	Hal is in cahoots with Horace.
He had mahogany and mohair furniture.	Perhaps we will rehearse anyhow.
Hugh hurried to help the grasshopper.	Herbert inhaled and then exhaled.
Hans saw the lighthouse just ahead.	Hy was too inhibited to be happy.

[tʃ–dʒ]

This pair of affricates combines a plosive and a fricative. Put the tongue up in a firm [t] position, inhale, and then explode the plosive [t] into the fricative [ʃ], as in *chin, chap, chase.* Repeat the same posture and breath preparation, inhale, and then explode the plosive [d] into the fricative [ʒ]. Repeat both sequences, including posture and breath preparation, and lay your fingers on your larynx, to experience and contrast the voiceless [tʃ] and the voiced [dʒ]. Use your Tok-Back as you proceed with the drill materials. There are usually no problems with these sounds if the [t] and [d] are firm to start.

cheap–jeep	perches–purges	etch–edge
chip–gyp	searching–surging	catch–cage
chain–Jane	britches–bridges	march–Marge
chin–gin	matches–Madge's	batch–badge
chump–jump	etched–edged	riches–ridges
choking–joking	lunched–lunged	lecher–ledger

choice ridge	rich manager	jolly etching	edgy justice
chilly cage	jumping chimp	gentle questions	large coach
strange church	cheap cabbage	mature judge	cheap gesture
urgent march	champion image	courageous bunch	charming genius

chocolate fudge	genuine approach	matching hinge	which lodging
average exchange	orchard damaged	cordial merchant	bulging chin
charming chap	matching swatches	rich match	baggage coach
gentle judge	George's joke	such oranges	cheap joke

Gin ran down Jim's chin.   Jane adjusted the chain.
Jack bought the jeep cheap.   I was gypped on that diamond chip.
The chump jumped off the bridge.   He choked laughing at the joke.
We searched the surging water.   Madge gave George a match.

The edge of the etching was beige.   They searched for the rich ridge of coal.
Roger judged the large pictures.   Jim and Marge jogged after the lecture.
Charlie's gesture was courageous.   He kept his badge with his chest patches.
The cage was at the lodge's edge.   John adjusted the engine on the bridge.

Fricative and Affricate Drill

Use Ear-Stoppels on the following drill so that you *feel* rather than listen, so that you penetrate the inner experience of sounds and words. And weld each sentence firmly to a deeply centered breath.

Janet chose a large velvet pouch.   Charlie filled the hampers with flags.
Massachusetts charmed the visitors.   The judge's agent has a small paunch.
The birches stood against the azure sky.   The actor's manager was unjust.
The scientist was assured of his facts.   George always exaggerated the truth.

Harry was in a dangerous situation.   The grasshopper beheaded the wasp.
The elevator stopped at the sixth floor.   Ashley sailed in the English Channel.
Smith had the wealthiest family in Kansas. We saved the swallows from starving.
The brief vision of success was heady.   Shirley used the Shavian quotation.

The chicken was flavored with sage.   Catherine suffered a third seizure.
The tourists were injured on the bridge.   She dived into the surging waves.
Elizabeth marched onto the huge stage.   They polished the leather on Thursday.
Smith lunged at the large coach.   Do the fifth and sixth exercises.

We rehearsed Chekov's play.
Ava enjoyed the Japanese villages.
The captives had few privileges.
He quenched his thirst with fresh cherries.

Harry hid the Spanish themes.
Los Angeles smog can be dangerous.
The Chinese children laughed at the chimp.
He believes the treasure still exists.

Somehow the mist encompassed him.
Fay pushed the chair near the hearth.
They improved the existing systems.
Their past conversations were pleasant.

His life breeds vulgar mayhem.
Vivian loathed the officious teacher.
The usual results were dismal.
Jesse reached the refuge safely.

The mischievous children hid the toys.
Helen strives to accomplish results.
James is noisy, selfish, and harsh.
It was an unusual reason to leave home.

They hopefully revived the peace talks.
Susan assists the British officer.
The Egyptian excursion was opposed.
Shawn has the latest magazines.

Nasals

[m]

Physically prepare to make an [m] by firmly closing the lips. Inhale, and hold the posture firm, experiencing the ready energy of the taut lip muscles. Now breathe out the vocalized breath through the nostrils and feel the vibrations on the lips. Get inside the [m] sound in the single words below, while massaging over the eyes and nose. Use your Tok-Back, Lip-Puffs, and Ear-Stoppels to reinforce the sound experience on the phrases and sentences, and tap your breastbone with your finger tips. There is a great deal of musical resonance in this continuant consonant, so strengthen the lips and velum by holding them firm as you sustain the [m] sound. This is one of three consonant sounds that, without benefit of a vowel, stand alone as a syllable, as in *spasm, schism, patriotism.*

mine	mob	sometime	almost	memory	home	names	champ
may	mean	company	stormy	hymnal	seem	climbed	prism
more	made	simply	aimless	number	dime	primp	trump
meet	many	triumph	extremely	shambles	helm	jammed	symptom

hometown team	champion tomcat	some homework	famous company
crimson umbrella	seems calm	something grim	dumb animal
aimless rhythm	simmering shrimp	male organism	timid lamb
humming hymns	come home	seemly criticism	Tom's witticism

pompous patriotism	simple clamp	random example	milky foam
doomed elm	overwhelming film	same arm	many firms
tomato blossoms	shameful schism	museum smashed	maple cream
handsome man	alarming mumps	whimsical scream	rambling campus

The mob smashed the team's room.
The comely miss murmured her name.

Jim makes marvelous plum jam.
Milton was extremely promiscuous.

Tom made a criticism of her campus.   Mary was uncomfortable with Sam.
Pam chased the ram around the farm.   Her dreams were alarmingly somber.

They scrambled into the empty dorm.   Minnie moved from Mobile to Tampa.
Kim has optimism and enthusiasm.   Tom was impressed by Mark's memory.
The roomful of farmers grumbled.   The ambling mammal climbed the mound.
The Major commanded the men to march.   Some crimes were committed in Miami.

[n]

Physically prepare to make an [n] by putting the tongue tip against the upper gum ridge, as in [t–d]. Inhale, and experience the ready energy of the taut tongue muscles. Now breathe out the vocalized breath through the nostrils and feel the [n] vibrations in the back of the nose and eyes. Get inside the [n] sound in the single words below, while massaging over the eyes and nose. Use your Tok-Back and Ear-Stoppels to reinforce the sound experience on the phrases and sentences, while tapping your breastbone with your finger tips. As with the [m], there is musical resonance in this sound, so hold the posture firm and give it its full value as you get inside. Along with [m], this is a consonant sound that, without the benefit of a vowel, stands alone as a syllable, as in *cotton, garden, kitten*.

night	nine	dinner	morning	window	tent	can't	won't
noon	noun	penthouse	wonder	candy	govern	pinch	sooner
knowledge	neutral	many	only	under	owned	then	tin
nimble	nominate	senses	lunch	tension	maiden	wooden	harden

found money	Chinese print	never learn	nice present
brown kitten	ungainly tent	green paint	lemon skin
round can	monthly dinner	union dance	didn't pinch
fine lounge	moon's glint	train window	another inmate

down town	nimble infielder	Grand Canyon	stony mountain
canny invalid	unbroken branch	government fund	no tension
dancing hen	only lunch	never knew	ran downward
winter season	considered opinion	unmanly notion	none went

The kitten ran into the barn.   The inmate was proven to be insane.
Nine inches of fence were broken.   The bunch of bananas was rotten.
Nancy couldn't endure the noise.   We had chicken seasoned with wine.
His den was unguarded at noon.   Norma's mind was unbalanced by the tension.

The ranch was considerably changed.   Ann went into the lounge with Dan.
John went downtown with his friend.   Ben wanted to get inside the fence.
The old man and woman lived alone.   The opening was a wonderful occasion.
We had champagne and danced till one.   Ben was keen on sun-dried raisins.

[ŋ]

Physically prepare to make an [ŋ] by lowering the soft palate to meet the back of the tongue, as with [k–g]. Experience the firm, but comfortable posture as you inhale. Now breathe out the vocalized breath through the nostrils and feel the [ŋ] vibrations in back of the nose and eyes. Get inside the sound in the single words below, while massaging over the eyes and nose. Use your Tok-Back and Ear-Stoppels to reinforce the sound experience on the phrases and sentences, while tapping your breastbone with your finger tips. As with [m] and [n], there is musical resonance in this sound, so give it its full value. As you firm up the muscles by holding the posture steady, constantly monitor and relax the throat muscles behind it. If you intrude a [k] or [g] click after [ŋ] in words where it doesn't belong, get some guidelines from your instructor. It helps to realize that [ŋ] and [k] are two sounds, just as [m] and [p], and [n] and [d] are. Say *trump,* then *hand,* then *hunk;* now say *hung,* which has only the [ŋ] sound at the end of the word.

swing	coming	singing	gangster	sing	thing	uncle	English
hang	going	belonging	youngster	sink	think	length	hunger
tongue	riding	ringing	jingle	bank	rang	anxious	finger
wrong	eating	banging	kingdom	bang	rank	instinct	anguish

sing a song	ping pong	hungry uncle	longer length
saying things	thronging gang	English monk	drunken minx
spring cleaning	strong tongue	yankee banks	single ankle
something wrong	amazing hanger	anchor sunk	cranky banker

leaving England	anxious gangster	wrong instinct	distinct longing
bankrupt singer	amazing angle	Lincoln longed	pink hanger
finger stung	young monkey	strong drink	anxious king
beginning angle	strong language	tangled string	being hungry

The young kangaroo was hungry.
His tongue tingled from singing.
They were stung in the Congo jungle.
He sang in Washington and Binghamton.

Angus languished in the hanger.
She lingered among the English throng.
She flung the hanger at the banker.
He's spending Thanksgiving in Rangoon.

Thank you for bringing me a drink.
He put the wrong ring on her finger.
We went sailing off Long Island.
The linguist longed to be working.

There were milling throngs in Hong Kong.
Frank visited Congress in Washington.
Hang the gingham on the long string.
In the spring evenings we would swing.

Nasal Consonant Drill

Use Ear-Stoppels and Tok-Back on the following drill so that you feel rather than listen, so that you penetrate the inner experience of sounds and words. And weld each sentence firmly to a deeply centered breath.

He flung his strong arms around Kim.
Sometime he wants to plant an elm tree.
He hammered the nail in an angry manner.
Mini's chrysanthemum blossomed.

The victims were alarmed by his anger.
Nancy never comes in time for dinner.
The King of England had pneumonia.
Frank's telephone number is unlisted.

The magazine lampooned his stammer.
The insurance company was confident.
The mean man grumbled in his bunk.
He anchored his launch in Miami.

Manny was playing ping pong with Pam.
The Danish Ambassador had influence.
Linda flung her dungarees on the line.
The singer hummed for his warm-up.

I answered his questions succinctly.
The distinguished musician conducted.
Janet wouldn't fasten her buttons.
She winked at him behind her fan.

Ann was young but Kim was younger.
The singer won't sing in the summer.
It was a long day but a longer night.
Angus was swinging and singing.

The children were playing in the sand.
The English kingdom is dwindling.
Amy was timid around Ann.
They increased the monthly treatment.

The new milking machine is in the barn.
The bungalow was burned to the ground.
Nathan conducted scintillating meetings.
Sam painted the new fence brown.

The monstrous museum was made of cement.
The chimney beams were burning.
The moon beamed and the stars twinkled.
The onions were hanging by a string.

A sitting was arranged for the Queen.
The harangue was against the government.
The Senator's language was influential.
The twins danced in the conga line.

The Lieutenant is too cranky to command.
Tom interviewed the chamber of commerce.
The drunk stumbled clumsily over the bunk.
The criminals strangled their victims.

My uncle has no strength to swim.
He was no longer a longer after fun.
Pam put tincture of iodine on her ankle.
The communication influenced Ben.

Glides

[w]

Physically make a silent [w] by rounding the lips in a pucker. Experience the taut muscle position as you inhale, and feel how the sound takes on the quality of whatever vowel sound follows it as you breathe voice into *we, why, woe.* Since the [w] sound appears only in initial position, a firm production will help to project words. Get inside the sound in the single words below, with posture and breath preparation, and massage over the eyes and nose. Use your Tok-Back to reinforce the sound experience on the phrases and sentences, while tapping your breastbone with your finger tips. The [w–hw] distinction is disappearing from everyday usage and for the actor would only be a consideration in classic plays, particularly in a comedy of manners. Be careful of an intrusive [w] in the middle of a word like *showing;* this is a mark of uneducated speech. [w–hw] contrasts are in the last two columns of the first group.

we	want	anyone	quiet	witch – which	wear – where
were	was	between	awake	wail – whale	wile – while
water	would	language	backward	wine – whine	weather – whether
will	work	dwell	reward	were – whir	watt – what

we want	will wait	always thwarted	which reward
twelve women	quick swim	wayward quest	went where
everyone went	windy squall	quick swindle	while awake
twelve sandwiches	one language	quite unwise	whether unwind

wayward wind	wait elsewhere	meanwhile work	unworthy whispers
quite well	quaint woman	somewhat quickly	why wonder
wash water	was warped	bewhiskered whale	was qualified
went between	wonderful reward	wishing well	went backward

The twins twirled the twine on the wheel.
Everyone in the choir waited quietly.
The dwarf walked quietly forward.
Twelve swans were swimming languidly.

Wally watched Wanda make sandwiches.
The white whale whizzed through the water.
He swears he wanted to watch the squire.
Willie spoke the Welsh language well.

Stalwart Wilbur washed the windows.
The quintet wove backward and forward.
The swindler had sandwiches and wine.
Waltzing with Wanda was unwise.

Wilfred wove the tweed for the Queen.
We always did homework in the quad.
We will always wait for Willie.
Why does Wilma always whine?

[j]

Physically make a silent [j] by arching the front of the tongue near the hard palate. Experience the ready tongue energy as you inhale, then feel the movement of the tongue to the following vowel sound as you breathe voice into *you, your, yell*. This sound occurs only before vowels and is generally not difficult to articulate. Get inside the single words below, with posture and breath preparation, and massage over the eyes and nose. Use your Tok-Back to reinforce the sound experience on the phrases and sentences, while tapping your breastbone with your finger tips. [j] sometimes precedes [u] in words like *news, tune, duke*. See preceding material on [u] sound.

yes	yell	yard	unit	few	onion	abuse	value
yearn	year	yeast	usual	amuse	million	volume	stallion
you	your	yawn	unite	canyon	junior	civilian	amuse
yam	yacht	yet	Europe	familiar	companion	fuel	humid

beautiful music	viewed Europe	yellow yarn	pure genius
pupil argued	usual few	familiar review	Yale junior
united opinion	your opinion	senior refused	million years
yearly volume	valuable yacht	accusing youth	unique views

yesterday's news	pure dew	amusing platitude	Duke's yacht
young student	useful gratuity	accusing steward	Yankee knew
usual duty	amuse few	new argument	stupid review
refused Tuesday	confused producer	resume yelling	induced unity

The seniors and juniors abused him.
The new pupils were amusing.
It was the youth's duty to review.
The Duke's retinue was in uniform.

Her musings of William were futile.
Eunice had youthful enthusiasm.
The huge yacht was beautiful.
She used onions in the stew.

His opinions were useless and confusing.
The tutor's accusations were astute.
The union feuded with the newspaper.
The European yachtsman was unique.

The future holds few opportunities.
He used new tunes in his reviews.
The young genius was a nuisance.
We viewed the canyon in Utah.

[r]

Physically make a silent [r] by raising the entire tongue toward the palate and letting the sides of the tongue lightly contact the inside edges of the upper molars. Experience the ready energy in the muscles as you inhale, and then breathe voice into *rut, ran, red*. Be certain that the sound is not too hard and tense, and that it does not stop the breath like a plosive. Feel the vibrations first on [ʒ], then on [r]. Say [ʒi–ri, ʒi–ri], feeling vibrations on both of the initial consonants, and be certain that the lips are relaxed and the tongue is doing the work. For a keener perception of sound experience, use your Tok-Back and Ear-Stoppels as you proceed with the drill materials below. When preceded by other consonants, [r] performs rather like an affricate as in [tʃɛs–dʒɛs–drɛs].

read	around	story	worry	brush	ground	scratch	scream
ran	erase	arrange	every	cream	preach	spray	strong
wrap	sorry	very	arrest	drug	cruise	strike	sprung
routine	terrible	orange	errand	frantic	brandy	sprinkle	stride

proud beating	more trunks	mere brag	every group
raises fruit	straw spread	fried shrimp	shrill shriek
barn door	proud girl	starving guard	divorce George
marvelous farce	marching strikers	strange scream	drug arrest

rugged ride	straight road	snarling swarm	creamed shrimp
worry Harry	overcome fear	Martha sputtered	strict scrutiny
never heard	carry brandy	orange stripe	charming scroll
parched form	spraying room	strenuous cruise	terrible script

Robert rode around the ranch.
Randy's friend was wrong.

Ruby was frantic about the strike.
Roberta struck the snarling raccoon.

She would rather run rapidly.	Ron repaired the wrecked cruiser.
Ryan reached the train before Rob.	Rita was arrested on the third of February.
The trout thrashed in the water.	The throng was thrilled by the performance.
Artie carried the dress on her arm.	The trek over the bridge was a treat.
Ross threatened Carla with divorce.	Every story berated tyranny and greed.
Where did you store the large shrimp?	Mary will marry Harry tomorrow.

The Lateral

[l]

Physically make a silent [l] by placing the tip of the tongue against the upper gum ridge. Experience the taut muscles as you inhale, then breathe vocal life into the sound and feel it flowing laterally over the sides of the tongue. Following another consonant and before a vowel, the back of the tongue is low, only the front spreads, and it is called a light [l], as in *let, slip*. In final position and before another final consonant, the back of the tongue is slightly high and spreads and it is called a dark [l], as in *all, told*. The [l] will be low and dental only before "th." When [l] is preceded by front vowel sounds, particularly [i] and [eɪ], as in *feel, fail*, there is a see-sawing motion caused by the energy being in the front of the tongue for the vowels and in the back of the tongue for the [l]. This can be minimized for a cleaner pronunciation by energizing the entire tongue for both sounds. This is called "sympathetic spread" and works fine if you go after it easily. Along with [m] and [n], this is a consonant sound that, without benefit of a vowel, stands alone as a syllable, as in *table, medal, battle*. Get inside the [l] sound in the single words below, while massaging over the eyes and nose. Use your Tok-Back and Ear-Stoppels to reinforce the sound experience on the phrases and sentences, while tapping your breastbone with your finger tips. Be certain to touch the tongue tip to the ridge and exaggerate the length to firm up the sound. As you hold the position, feel the sides of the tongue spreading toward the cheeks. This sound is too often lost altogether and replaced by something that sounds like an [ʊ].

live	pull	lean	still	heel	steal	coil	spoiled
laugh	tell	lint	fell	kill	spilled	smile	miles
light	call	late	ball	gale	sales	foul	growled
letter	hill	lost	cool	yell	help	goal	holes
large bowl		little girl		land fall		let's pull	
feels ill		leaky pool		long hall		last ball	

late fall	unlike Bill	bluebell	lost soul
false plot	will reply	gold plume	sells glass
feels ill	steel mill	child beguiles	smile awhile
conceal the keel	steals a reel	boiled oil	broil spoiled
twelve pills	sells nails	spoiled eel	steel coil
daily mail	males and females	mild gale	while sailing

Nell's film of the elk was pleasing.
Lance concealed his frail colt.
Twelve pills were stolen from the table.
He yielded his shield and kneeled.

Bill blamed his poor health on Ralph.
The old sailboat hulk still floated.
The small children were really thrilled.
The daily mailboat failed to sail.

The old lady sold silken shawls.
Alfred lost twelve golf balls.
Phil told wild tales of Australia.
Helen disliked filing the filthy valve.

The wild bull clawed at the kettle.
The elk concealed himself on the hill.
Lee welded the steel rails to the logs.
Lily will help solve Milly's problem.

Glides and Lateral Drill

Use Ear-Stoppels and Tok-Back on the following drill so that you *feel* rather than listen, so that you penetrate the inner experience of sounds and words. And weld each sentence firmly to a deeply centered breath.

Arnie's pupils worked quietly.
The twins had lots of young friends.
Wally was confused about the course.
Lord Nelson is a British hero.

Throw your uniform on the table.
Randy will not tolerate fools.
The young woman sells oranges.
Summer lingered late last year.

William won't listen to reason.
Wally spread manure on the field.
Rita wondered daily about Will.
The blue dress looked well on Mary.

The Duke wanted a million dollars.
Yancy worried about his health.
Larry yielded the right of way.
The warm quiet laughter lingered.

Quantity is less desirable than quality.
The old woman dreamed of her youth.
The straw strap held very well.
The huge barbecue was held on
    Wednesday.

Wilma knew where to strike the nail.
Force the scorched barge into the water.
Hugh was abusing the small twins.
The student yelled at everyone.

Useful work is unlikely to hurt anyone.
The workers swarmed into the vineyards.
Wilma travels to Europe every year.
Twelve billion dollars were lost.

Ron was willing to learn a new language.
Wilbert has a working ranch in Utah.
Everyone in the yard was thwarted.
The large reward was very welcome.

We lunched frequently on the yacht.
Eunice performed the role awkwardly.
Why did Lars put the wheat in the barn?
The curfew was awkward for the seniors.

Harry inquired about the young student.
The play was unworthy of the artists.
We went to all the New York plays.
The warbler whistled beautifully.

Wally's duty was to carry the harp.
We swam awhile in the cool river.
Walter reviewed the daily mail.
The soldiers went forward into battle.

We all felt that Roberta was a witch.
The valiant yeoman was very astute.
Arthur wended his way to the dwelling.
Warner settled himself on the camel's back.

Linking Words Together

One of the keys to smooth, intelligible speech is the way we link our words together. Unless you are pausing for a logical and/or a psychological reason, language should flow and the consonants are the pulses that give it force and rhythm. Generally a final consonant is pronounced and linked to the following word, as in the following phrases.

stop over	strap hanger	home team	keep them
bad end	it will	was grand	match stick
come in	have you	leave me	watch him
good apple	head home	pack this	was furious

The exceptions to this rule are when the final consonant of one word and the initial consonant of the following word are *identical,* or are *cognate sounds* (made in the same way and in the same position, except that one sound is voiced and the other is voiceless, such as t and d), or are *related* as to position (such as p and m). In all of these instances, you simply take the position for the first sound and release the second, being certain to allow time for both. You do not break the linkage by exploding the final sound on *don't* before saying *try,* nor releasing the final sound on *help* before saying *Bob,* nor the final sound on *eating* before saying *good.* This would be overarticulating and would call attention to itself. Wherever possible words must be linked so that the words and ideas flow.

Identical Sounds

don't try	rob Bill	one night	lush shore
bag groceries	pick cotton	less said	path through
help Peter	feed Doris	are rich	hit Chan
some money	half full	will linger	had gin

In the word *hit* the final sound is a [t], as is the first sound in the affricate [tʃ], which begins *Chan.* In the word *had* the final sound is [d] as is the first sound in the affricate [dʒ], which begins *gin.*

Cognate Sounds

help Bob	of faith	bath then	back gate
hot dog	dog kennel	this zoo	beige shoes
has seen	was sent	not just	Ralph verified
live fully	drab place	bad chain	had time

Related Sounds

eating good	writing cramp	red shoes	stop making
good night	home plate	truth didn't	one left
will talk	stop Martha	he'll never	bad thought
hot zinc	bet Lillie	good soup	grab money

The final sound in the word *truth* and the initial sound in *didn't* are both tongue tip sounds, although the final [θ] is made on the edge of the top teeth and the [d] is made on the gum ridge, and you link them by sliding from one to the other. The words *bad thought* present the same sliding factor, but in reverse.

Word Ends

Most speakers invest their energy in the sounds at the beginning of words and, as a consequence, sounds at the ends of words are often weakened or dropped altogether. This dropping of energy at the ends also happens with phrases and sentences. After the first stressed word, the volume and pitch drop lower and lower and many last words are completely unintelligible. We will deal with phrases and sentences in the following chapter, but first we need to focus on the words with which we build them.

As you work on the following sentences, let your self get inside the sounds of the words and realize their potential power. Use Ear-Stoppels and/or Tok-Backs so that you feel rather than listen, so that you penetrate the inner experience of the words. Anchor your tongue tip behind your bottom teeth on the vowels and diphthongs in the stress words, weld each sentence firmly to a full breath so that it does the work for you, link the words easily, and project your mind and energy to the ends of the words and the sentences. Following are further aids to your pronunciation.

General Rules for Voiceless or Voiced Endings are as follows:

• When "s" follows a vowel, diphthongs, or voiced consonant, it is pronounced [z], as in *sees, nose, owns.*

- When "s" follows a voiceless consonant, it is pronounced [s], as in *hits, helps, packs*.
- When "es" follows [s−z−ʃ−ʒ−tʃ or dʒ], it is pronounced [ɪz], as in *chases, poses, rushes, garages, clutches, surges*.

- When the verb ending "ed" follows a vowel, diphthong or voiced consonant, it is pronounced [d] as in *sawed, tried, grabbed*.
- When the verb ending "ed" follows a voiceless consonant, it is pronounced [t], as in *raced, picked, pushed*.
- When the verb ending "ed" follows a "t" or "d," it is pronounced [ɪd], as in *shifted, folded, handed*.

Word Ends — Mostly Plosives

Bob ripped his best shirt.
Art won't rib Albert about a part.
Don't ask Ann to take a risk.
We'd like a bag of old rags.

He backed up and bagged the varmint.
Al helped rope the huge herd.
We padded the packed wigs.
Bob ran and tagged Herbert.

Kit was masked for the part.
The guest actor was gifted.
He wouldn't risk a bit of it.
We gasped at the crushed craft.

She stacked her figs in a box.
He threw big rocks at the pigs.
He shouldn't have grabbed that rope.
They hollered and hunted for the cat.

The dog in the trunk wore a tag.
Ted forgot to thank her for the robe.
Pete hit him over the head.
Pat wanted only bread and milk.

Put the potted plant in the yard.
Webb always rips his best robes.
He laughed every day he lived.
It was a fact we all suspected.

She clasped Abe's right hand.
The potatoes were mashed at last.
He rouged and brushed his wig.
We risked an all-out attack.

She was made-up and robed at eight.
Ask for just a bag of cookies.
The child cried and asked for help.
Dick handled the cowed bandit.

Word Ends — Mostly Fricatives and Affricates

He served martinis before he surfed.
He saves his tennis prizes.
He managed to save part of his wages.
He dislodged and washed the chips.

He waved the loaves in their faces.
The youths believed in miracles.
The colleges offer arts and crafts.
He dived into the waves in his shorts.

His performance rivals his father's.
She always dries the dishes.

The judges have the proofs in the safe.
He works in the fourth and fifth zones.
In his rage he smashed the cages.
He wished he had observed the services.

The savages refused to save their lives.
The mists lasted for six weeks.
He advised the traders to leave.
He seized the lioness by the jaws.

He misses the cows and chickens.
He believed he had reached the ledge.

He urges her to save the gauze.
He proved his case about the leagues.

He fixed the boat's crushed mast.
He lunged at the masses of wasps.

The actress refused to use an asp.
He endured the baths for his health.
He grieves over his wife's death.
The cover crops improved the fields.

He judged his losses to be cash.
He disagrees with the widths and lengths.
The fast vessels arrived first.
He loved and missed his olive groves.

Word Ends—Mostly Nasals

The champion took an extended vacation.
The band played an enchanting tune.
Sandy scampered around the farm.
He was exempt from the examination.

Randy can't understand him.
Don was the quintessence of excellence.
Ann ran in front of the home team.
The plane left the ground in the rain.

He planned in advance to return home.
His amended application was sent.
Don't ascend the mountain without him.
The salmon was tainted with poison.

The alliance took action against him.
The king's abdication was demanded.
His hands are brown and strong.
It didn't happen in my apartment.

The corporation founded a bank.
The opposition demanded abolition.
Stand up and announce the program.
The system underwent fragmentation.

Don't offend our excellent accountant.
Sam can't imagine how it happened.
My intention remains the same.
It was a fragrant mound of mums.

We want a compartment on the train.
The warmth of the room was welcome.
I can't and I won't make a demand.
The alliance took action against him.

Tom's pencil point was broken.
We noted the change with excitement.
I want to rent my apartment.
I had ample trump in my hand.

Word Ends—Mostly "l"

Bill always bowls with Al.
The field was full of wild bulls.
Phil's health improved in April.
The principal was difficult to fault.

The milling crowd filled the aisles.
The pupil was extremely versatile.
Will you help to solve the problem?
The people in the hall were joyful.

The couple was unable to handle him.
The beautiful opal was valuable.
He travels to Australia in the fall.
The bottle of pills is on the shelf.

The gold was a remarkable spectacle.
Al had the principal role in the play.
He finally wrote an article on gold.
The federal building was finally sold.

They filled the well themselves.
His angle was unusual and irregular.
His uncle mumbles about trifles.
The stealthy owl is a noble rebel.

Bill followed April to the hospital.
Only simple people came to the chapel.
The yodel startled the camels.
Gold sparkles and silver twinkles.

He sold automobiles in Philadelphia.
The middle of the table was filled.
The plants on the shelf were wilted.
We saw an additional film on elves.

That building holds felt or silk.
A single bolt held the cable.
The pole was twelve feet tall.
The bell tolled for the old couple.

Keep reviewing the energy and function of the various sounds defined above by recreating in your mind and muscle memory the body conditions that produce them. Imagine a sound first, then say it. Feel the sounds form inside you. Taste them in your mouth. Assume the body condition for a [k], then say it. Feel an [u] form inside you, then say it. Experience the overall image for an [l], then say it. Now put them together and say *cool*. Frequently review key word sounds while rehearsing lines. Experience their muscularity and substance, individually and then linked. And contrast them, one with the other. Contrast [k] with [u], [u] with [l], and [l] with [k].

Practice the physical postures and movement of sounds without voice, known as "lip-syncing" in which you simply mouth the words. Then whisper them to feel their resonances. Whispering lines for short periods of time can do wonders for your speech. It puts the focus on the articulators and vitalizes the speech muscles. Without the vocal power to project what you are saying you tend to overuse and energetically project the words with speech alone, and for short periods that's just great. Fifteen or twenty minutes at a time would be long enough, however, since prolonged whispering will put a strain on the vocal folds. A very fine Canadian actor, Donald Davis, once told me that he always whispers the words of a new script to ferret out its muscularity and help determine its meaning. He said that his vocal power tended to get in the way of meaning, and, also, that it lulled him into a false sense of security about his speech.

Turn your self onto vowels by singing them, which alters breathing and increases vibrations. If you have trouble getting your mouth and throat open for the vowels, think an 'h' in front of them. And watch for glottal harshness or clicks when you initiate vowels; thinking an 'h' will help this too.

Shape the sounds as emotion gestures to let the self come through. Feel sounds and words with every nerve-end of your skin. Find the basic reasons to sustain a sound; emphasize important things. The alliance between sounds and meaning is manifest in about four-fifths of all words.

Don't bend over backward and overarticulate. You can make it all sound too important. Keep speech moving with rhythm. Project your energy to the ends of words, particularly key words, link words smoothly, and watch for unvoiced endings. To correct for a final [ə] (schwa), which can make a word like *home* sound like *homuh*, a two-syllable word, release the sound before you release the posture for the final sound.

Whenever possible, precede articulation practice with relaxation exercises, so that the suggestions of the sounds can penetrate your inner life

like those of a hypnotist. And practice with your eyes closed. There is
nothing that gives one so strong a sense of the inner dynamics of sounds
and words as experiencing invisible movement and action. And keep in
mind that the breath is the power for sounds, not the jaw and lips. Use the
breath consciously, until the response becomes strongly physical and automatic. Let the breath do the work.

SOUNDS AND WORDS

Remember that sounds and words are alive, the extension of all that
you are. Sounds and words are the combined energy of your muscle
movement, your breathing, your emotions, and your mind. Sounds and
words are a product of your entire body, by the integration of all its tissues. It is calculated that there are some seven hundred muscle patterns
that are involved in the production of consonant sounds in the English
language. Your voice and speech are diagnostic signs of your body condition. Speech is dynamic, ever changing, just like the body that produces
it. Speech sounds are different, because body conditions are different,
and, in reality, no one sound is ever produced the same way twice. This is
particularly true of connected speech, where sounds are influenced by
whatever sounds precede or follow them. The pulses and energy of your
speech are a reflection of the pulses and energy of your total self. Use the
physical techniques to condition the body and use the mind and imagination to alter your perceptions of speech.

Analogize your speech in as many different ways as you can. Think of
the speech as the skeleton and the voice as the meat on the skeleton. Like
a skeleton, each speech sound is attached to, and dependent on, the connecting sounds. If the skeleton sags or has weak spots, the whole structure is weakened. Think of speech as music, as an art which must have
form and patterns, and yet have room for improvisation and creative
melody. And, just as a musician must know where and how the sounds of
his instrument are made, so must the speaker. The music of speech can be
light and lilting, like the delicate sounds of a flute, or rich and deep like
the resonant sounds of a cello. Think of voice and speech in terms of
sculpture; of the voice as the piece of clay, and the speech as molding and
defining the clarity of the design. Think of speech in terms of the atmosphere it can create, atmosphere as tangible as elements of nature. Dull,
unintelligible speech can create the oppressiveness of a sultry, summer
afternoon. Clear, crisp speech can create the cool crispness of an autumn
morning. Good speech should flow like leaves on a breezy, fall day, a
pattern of movement and color.

A smart person has an intimate relationship with the life of the body, the life of the mind, and the life of sounds and words. He cherishes their power and engulfs their energy. He penetrates the body experience of words, assimilates their sense and emotions, and they reward his devotion by dynamically interpreting every nuance of his expression. It is reported that the only direction Dylan Thomas gave the readers who first performed *Under Milkwood* was "love the words."

Using the Ear-Stoppels and Tok-Back, read the following selection: the opening passage of *Under Milkwood* by Dylan Thomas. Slowly whisper it first, to experience the resonances, and energetically shape the sounds with the articulators. Then, just as slowly, speak it with full voice, experiencing the vibrations of the sounds in the resonators of the body. Taste the sounds on your tongue and lips. Let them communicate their color and substance, their theatricality. And finally, remove the Ear-Stoppels and Tok-Back and read it more conversationally, in your natural speech rhythm. Let your self respond to the mood established by the alliterative and onomatopoetic elements, to the imagery and rhythms.

To begin at the beginning:

> It is Spring, moonless night in the small town, starless and bible-black, the cobblestreet silent and the hunched, courters'-and rabbits' wood limping invisible down to the sloeblack, slow, black, crowblack, fishingboat-bobbing sea. The houses are blind as moles (though moles see fine tonight in the snouting, velvet dingles) or blind as Captain Cat there in the muffled middle by the pump and the town clock, the shops in mourning, the Welfare Hall in widows' weeds. And all the people of the lulled and dumbfound town are sleeping now.[1]

Dylan Thomas provides the very best of physical language, of experiential sounds and words. The mental images and sounds feed each other to establish a mood in which all of you is involved. Sound and word production requires the combined energy of breath and muscle movement and if you allow your self to experience the different muscle movements in shaping the words you will find that they trigger different feelings. Thus the physical involvement in pronouncing a word is a significant part of the word's identity. The words "fishingboat-bobbing sea" feel different from "lulled and dumbfound town." Let your self experience how the body and feeling life, the mental energy, and the senses are all expressed

---

[1]Dylan Thomas, *Under Milkwood*. Copyright 1954 by New Directions Publishing Corp. Reprinted by permission of New Directions and David Higham Associates, Ltd.

simultaneously in the shaping and texture of the words "moonless," "cobblestreet," "hunched," "limping," "dingles," "muffled," "muffled," and "pump." Every word has a different feel as well as a different sound, one triggering and reinforcing the other.

The repetition of sounds, the *alliteration*, is of interest in this piece as well, and should be experienced as part of its performance: the repetition of the sounds and words "begin at the beginning," in which the [b] and [g] plosives are the pulses that start us off; the [t] plosive which quickly projects us into the two sustained [s] sounds and the sustained [ŋ] of "It is Spring"; the predominant nasals and liquid l's in "moonless night in the small town"; the contrast of fricative [s] and the [b] and [k] plosives in "starless and bible-black"; the titillating blend of plosives, sustained l's and fricatives which seem to emphasize the single [n] in "cobblestreets silent"; the pulses of the dominant plosives that punctuate "hunched, courters'-and rabbits' wood"; the [p] and [b] plosives which interrupt the flow of the continuant nasals, fricatives, and l's, and reinforce the action of "limping invisible"; the muscular play of repeated sounds and words with varying stresses in "sloeblack, slow, black, crowblack"; how the repeated [b] sounds make it truly a "fishingboat-bobbing sea"; the sustained fricatives, nasals and l's which unify the words "houses are blind as moles"; another provocative blend of fricatives, nasals, l's and plosives in "snouting velvet dingles"; the alliterative "Captain Cat" of plosive production and one nasal, and the "muffled middle" triggered by [m's] and sustained by [l's]; the pulses of plosives in "pump and the town clock"; the sustained fricatives and nasal sounds in "shops in mourning"; the alliteration of the [w] glide in "Welfare Hall in widows' weeds" and the repetition of l's in "Welfare Hall" and of the [d] and [s] in "widows' weeds"; the expansive sound of the l's in "all the people"; the muscular activity and blend of nasals and l's in "lulled and dumbfound town"; and the contrast of the constricted sounds in "sleeping" and the open sound of "now."

Consonants are generally more fun because they are easier to feel. The physical movements and contacts of the articulators in forming consonants provide a greater tactile awareness and sensuous pleasure than the forming of vowels. However, consonants must never be overemphasized to the detriment of vowel production. Both are equally important, and there must always be a balance. It is just as important to read through a selection concentrating on the use of vowels and diphthongs, on their energies and functions.

There are not as many repetitions of vowel sounds, called *assonances*, as there are repetitions of consonants in *Under Milkwood*, but there are a few. The [ɪ] sound dominates the opening line, "To begin at the beginning" and is repeated in the following phrase, "It is Spring," and again in the words "limping invisible." There is the assonance of the [oʊ] and [æ] sounds in "slowblack, slow, black, crowblack"; of the [aɪ] diphthong in "fine to-night"; of the [æ] sound in "Captain Cat"; of the [ʌ] sound in "lulled and dumbfound"; and of the [au] sound in "dumbfound town."

The [ɪ] sound, which dominates the first two phrases of the piece, is a vowel of short duration and serves to move us quickly to the first image and the longer vowels and diphthongs in "moonless night . . . small town", the [u–aɪ] and [ɔ–aʊ]. In both of these pairs of words the tongue moves from a back vowel to a diphthong which begins with the tongue in low position: [u] to [aɪ], and [ɔ] to [aʊ]. This movement is reversed in the next phrase, in which the tongue is low for the [ɑ] in "starless" and for the first vowel in the diphthong [aɪ] in "bible" then moves up for the front vowel [æ] in "black." In "cobblestreets silent" the tongue moves from the lowest back vowel [ɑ] up to the highest front vowel [i] and down again to the diphthong [aɪ]. The phrase "hunched, courters'-and rabbits" woods is dominated by the short vowels [ʌ–æ] and [ʊ], as "limping invisible" is dominated by the short vowel [ɪ]. The rounded back diphthong [oʊ] contrasted with the front vowel [æ] adds to the feel of the image in "sloeblack, slow, black, crowblack," as does the movement from the short front vowel [ɪ], to the longer back diphthong [oʊ] in "fishing boat" and the movement from the lowest back vowel [ɑ] to the highest front vowel [i] in "bobbing sea." There is also a great deal of movement required for the shaping of the diphthongs [aʊ], [aɪ] and [oʊ] in "houses . . . blind . . . moles" and "though moles . . . fine tonight." The diphthong [aʊ] contrasts effectively with the shorter vowel sounds [ɛ] and [ɪ] in "snouting velvet dingles" as does the diphthong [aɪ] with the shorter vowel [æ] in "blind . . . Captain Cat." Another interesting feeling is produced by the short vowels [ʌ] and [ɪ] in "muffled middle . . . pump" and the longer sounds [aʊ] and [ɑ] in "town clock." The image "shops . . . mourning" requires energetic tongue and lip movement from [ɑ] to [ɔ], both back vowels, but with the tongue and lip muscles open and relaxed for the [ɑ] and then the tongue tensing and moving up and back and the lips tensing and rounding for the [ɔ]. In "Welfare Hall" the tongue moves forward for the stressed, front vowel [ɛ] and then back again for the rounded [ɔ]. The [ɪ] and [i] high, front vowels are close to producing an assonance in "widows' weeds," the longer [i] sound neatly stressing the noun "weeds." The long back vowel [ɔ] and the long front vowel [i] reinforce the expansive image of "all the people" and the short central vowel [ʌ] reinforces the "lulled . . . dumbfound" image and contrasts effectively with the diphthong [aʊ] in "found town." The energy and muscular feeling of the piece continues through the final words "sleeping now" in which the tongue moves from the highest, front vowel [i] to the low, rounded diphthong [aʊ].

I can recommend nothing better than that you get a copy of *Under Milkwood* and work your way through it. This meticulous experiencing of the muscular activity of the vowels and consonants puts you in touch with the piece and in touch with your self performing it. Concentrating first on consonants and then on vowels (although there is no prescribed order for this and you can work on vowels first if you prefer to do so) will make you aware of the alliterative elements of consonants, the assonances of vowels, and of how the muscular feel of the sounds support, and often trigger, the images and mood of a selection.

Notice too the *onomatopoetic* words and phrases, which are imitative of the thing they denote — such as "cobblestreets," "limping," "fishingboat-bobbing sea," "snouting," and "lulled." There is a tendency, of course, to interpret many words as onomatopoetic when the sounds do not clearly echo the meaning; this is particularly true of language such as that of Dylan Thomas which contains so many words that have sounds suggestive of a familiar meaning. You may have trouble with this distinction; I do myself. But I don't think it matters for us, since we are not literary specialists in the strict sense. We are simply seeking as many ways as possible to involve ourselves with words, with their combined physical, emotional, and mental energy. So that if we feel that the sound of the words "lulled and dumbfound town" are onomatopoetic in imitating the thing they denote, and this feeling serves to further involve us in sounding the words, then we are that much closer to a total self-expression.

When you finally blend the vowels and consonants together in the total expression of the piece you will discover that your delivery will be enriched by these various analyses. In your final performance, make certain that your facial and body posture and deep, full breathing all support your production, and that you extravagantly enjoy the physical feel of the words, on your lips and tongue, and in your entire body.

An interesting distinction can be made between the Dylan Thomas selection and the following poem of William Wordsworth. Where the excerpt from *Under Milkwood* is dominated by the constrictions and explosions of consonants, "It Is a Beauteous Evening" is dominated by the sustained sounds of vowels and continuant consonants, sometimes called semivowels. Using the Ear-Stoppels and Tok-Back, read the following lines, and experience the free flow of open, sustained sounds. Whisper it first to experience the resonances and the shape of the sounds, then add voice to let it communicate its entire feel and substance.

> It is a beauteous evening, calm and free
> The holy time is quiet as a Nun
> Breathless with adoration: the broad sun
> In sinking down in its tranquility;
> The gentleness of heaven broods o'er the Sea:
> Listen! the mighty Being is awake,
> And doth with his eternal motion make
> A sound like thunder—everlastingly.

The stress words "beauteous evening" contain the long vowels [u] and [i] and their effective sustention is supported by the continuant [s] and [v] fricatives and the [ŋ] nasal sound. The phrase "calm and free" flows easily on the open [ɑ] and [i], and on the sustained [m].

In the second line, the key words "holy time . . . quiet . . . Nun" are projected by the diphthongs [oʊ] and [aɪ] and the continuant [m] and [n].

In the phrase "Breathless . . . adoration" the short vowel [ɛ] is followed by the sustained [θ], the liquid [l], and the continuant [s]; "adoration" is projected by the [eɪ]. The key words "broad sun" are dominated by the long back vowel [ɔ] and the sustained [n]; and the key words "sinking down . . . tranquility" are dominated by the repetition of the [ɪŋ] combination, the [aʊ] and [æ] open vowel sounds, and the sustained [n].

In the fifth line, the continuant [n] effectively sustains the mood and flow of the image, as does the [u] in "broods" and the [i] in "sea."

Even the sudden, one-word exclamation "Listen!" is projected by the continuant [l], [s], and [n] sounds; and the key words "mighty Being . . . awake" flow freely on the [aɪ], [i], and [eɪ] sounds, supported by the [ŋ] in "Being" and the [w] glide in "awake."

In the seventh line, the key word "doth" is sustained once again by a short vowel [ʌ] linking neatly to the sustained [θ] fricative; the phrase "eternal motion" flows outward easily on the dominant [ɝ] and [oʊ], the continuant [l], and [m and n], the nasals.

The final phrase, with the key words "make . . . sound . . . thunder," is emphasized by the diphthongs [eɪ] and [aʊ] and the nasal consonant [n]; and the final word "everlastingly" flows on the sustained [æ], [l] and [ŋ].

The predominant use of words with long vowels and diphthongs, supported by the predominance of nasal sounds, l's and a few sustained fricatives will cause this poem to flow "calm and free" in support of its mood and image.

Taking the time to establish an intimate relationship with the life of sounds and words cannot help but enrich their performance. Sounds and words all have specific experiential qualities which should be heard, and which should be felt, by both the speaker and the listeners. Only through these sorts of careful analyses can you establish with assurance the moods, energies, and rhythms of words and phrases.

In furthering the sensation of physically feeling sounds and words, as well as developing precision and flexibility of the articulators, rhythmic poems and jingles are very helpful. They also contain the element of fun, combining as they do the relaxing factors of rhythm and rhyme and the tactile awareness of articulatory movement, all of which produce a relaxed feeling of well-being.

In the following ten lines from "The Dream Song" from Iolanthe, by W. S. Gilbert, let the rhythm sweep you along. Support the long phrases with full, deep breathing and a facial posture that places the resonated words well forward in the mouth, both of which reinforce the image that you are popping the words out with the tip of the tongue and the lips. Respond to the feel of the words, and let your self enjoy them. The Tok-Back and/or Ear-Stoppels will aid your focus, and your enjoyment.

Don't try for too much speed on the first reading. This will only reinforce bad habits and can leave you feeling very frustrated if you are stumbling along out of control. Start slowly, first concentrating on the vowels, and then on the consonants. Then slowly repeat the piece, blending vowels and consonants together and smoothly linking the words.

Make sure the tongue is back for the back vowels and that the lips are rounded, and that the tongue is well forward for the front vowels. Left to its own devices, the tongue will tend to drift toward the central position, particularly in rapid speech. Feel every consonant, firmly and precisely.

When you're lying awake with a dismal headache, and repose is tabooed by anxiety,

I conceive you may use any language you choose to indulge in without impropriety.

For your brain is on fire, the bedclothes conspire of usual slumber to plunder you;

First your counterpane goes and uncovers your toes, and your sheet slips demurely from under you.

Then the blanketing tickles, you feel like mixed pickles, so terribly sharp is the pricking,

And you're hot and you're cross, and you tumble and toss 'till there's nothing 'twixt you and the ticking;
Then your bedclothes all creep to the floor in a heap, and you pick 'em all
   up in a tangle,
Next your pillow resigns and politely declines to remain at its usual angle.
Well, you get some repose in the form of a doze, with hot eyeballs and
   head ever aching,
But your slumbering teems with such horrible dreams that you'd very
   much better be waking.

W. S. Gilbert writes very physical language which demands clarity and
agility. Meticulous attention must be given to the production of individual
sounds, to the blending of sounds into words, and to the linking of words
into meaningful phrases. And the fun, of course, is related not only to the
rhythm and rhyme, but to the rate of speed at which it is delivered. You
must practice all together until you can speak it "trippingly on the
tongue." This means very gradually increasing the speed rate, as well as
determining where you will need quick breaths to sustain your effort. And
this means that you may occasionally need to blow out your lips and
move your tongue from side to side for purposes of relaxation. Frequently
wetting your lips with the tip of your tongue also is relaxing, and helps
maintain your frontal focus. Bouncing the cheek muscles in the "blubber-
blubber-blubber" exercise also makes for a relaxing break, as does
chewing an *m,* in which you imagine that you are really chewing on some
food in your mouth so that the tongue moves around as well in pushing
the food into the teeth to be masticated.

There are many W. S. Gilbert patter poems that are excellent for the
purposes of getting the feel of words and developing the ability of the
speech muscles. There are also many simple jingles that focus on specific
sounds, as in the following. These are three of the best, I think, for the
first jingle focuses on correct tongue placement for the [t] sound and on
rounding the lips and pulling the blade of the tongue back for the [u]
vowel. The second jingle concentrates on good lip compression for the
[w] glide and on keeping the tongue well forward for the [ð]. And the
third jingle focuses on the crisp precision of the [b] and the production of
the medial [t].

> A tutor who tooted a flute
> Tried to tooter two tooters to toot.
> Said the two to the tutor, "Is it harder to toot,
> Or to tutor two tooters to toot?"

Whether the weather be fair or whether the weather be not,
Whether the weather be cold or whether the weather be hot,
We'll weather the weather whatever the weather,
Whether we like it or not.

Betty Boata bought some butter
"But," she said, "this butter's bitter.
If I put it in my batter
It will make my batter bitter."
So she bought some better butter
And it made her batter better.

·7·

SELF-EXPRESSION:
Elements of Interpretation

To BE ABLE TO PRODUCE and project clear, well resonated speech sounds and perfectly shaped words is a laudable achievement. In fact, it is an achievement of such rarity as to be remarkable when it does happen and it quite sets apart and elevates individual effort and discipline. This remarkable achievement, however, is meaningless to everyone but the individual unless it has a loftier purpose than self-glorification. A Lady Macbeth who is concentrating on shaping her words while performing the "Come you spirits . . . unsex me here" speech is projecting neither the fearful images nor the dreadful mood of the lines. And a Tom Wingfield who is concentrating on how well he is sustaining his vowels and defining his consonants in the "Across the alley was the Paradise Dance Hall" speech is projecting neither his own frustration nor the helplessness of the "unsuspecting kids" who "danced" in a world "that was really waiting for bombardments."

There is certainly a need and a time for perfecting the clarity of speech sounds. Developing the precise use of speech muscles is as necessary for the speaker as practicing scales for the precise use of finger muscles is for the pianist and practicing bar exercises for the precise use of body muscles for the ballet dancer. In fact, if speakers practiced as diligently as first-rate pianists and ballet dancers we would have more first-rate speakers. The scales for the pianist and the bar exercises for the ballet dancer are the muscle preparation that enables the artist to freely express his interpretation in performance. Just so, well-pronounced speech sounds and words are not an end in themselves. They are part of the preparation for performance. They are building blocks and, as such, they must be firm and true. Their primary function is to help define the structure of ideas—to build bridges of experience between people. Speech sounds are properly applied to the universal purpose of communicating meaning and, therefore, their use must be integrated with the interpretive elements of stress and phrasing, of pauses, and of expressive intonation.

Far too many people have speaking patterns which are relatively meaningless and certainly uninteresting. Words and phrases are carelessly run together with no definitions and no emphases. It is often impossible to hear perceptions of meaning when people speak. There are several reasons for these careless speaking habits.

One of the main reasons is that in these times when buttons are pushed for answers, words have lost their value. Language has become too lean and sparse. We communicate less and less and let things do it for us. Individual thought and speech are stultified by the daily bombardment of words through the airwaves and by the continuing explosion of printed words that crosses our desks. We live in the midst of a word fallout of repetitious, trite, meaningless phrases—a fallout of such devastating effect that language has become stale and lifeless. If "language is the leading edge of the human personality," as Jonathan Miller says in Judith Cook's book *Director's Theatre*,[1] then it must also be said that most personalities, based on their language, come across as uninteresting, ambiguous, and evasive. Instead of extending the self through the art and skill of language, the self is hidden behind a meaningless spate of words. Language has become a barrier to communication rather than being used, in Miller's words, as "the only form of communication in which we can express the subtle discriminations which make us different from animals, and different from savages."

Another reason for today's careless speaking habits is that speaking is not emphasized in most courses of study as the most important and immediate form of human communication, even though most people will speak and listen in the course of a lifetime far more than they will ever read and write.

---

[1]Judith Cook, ed., *Director's Theatre* (London: George C. Harrap and Co. Ltd, 1974), p. 107.

A third reason is that the process of speaking anesthetizes and dulls our senses so that we are often neither aware of what we are saying nor of how we are saying it.

And a fourth reason is that most people in our speech community speak the way we do, so why bother? The professional speaker, particularly the actor or broadcaster, must either bother or get a different profession. The professional speaker must audibly and intelligibly project the sense of what he is saying — and for the actor this means reaching everyone in the theater.

Projection, of course, involves a great many more factors than sheer vocal volume. Text that is projected by the expedient of simply getting louder becomes unnatural, unbelievable, and generally unintelligible. Specific meaning can be entirely lost in the generalized excitement of im-passioned shouting. The subtleties and nuances of meaning can be found only in grouping the right words together into phrases and stressing the key words within each phrase, in determining the relationship of phrases to each other and to the whole idea structure, in orchestrating the idea structure with meaningful intonation patterns, and in supporting these factors with full, deep breathing and clear articulation.

Certainly the most sensitive exponent of language should be the actor, who must accept responsibility for the language of his script and find the varied human experiences in it. And this applies from the first run-through to the closing night performance. The factors that prohibit an ac-tor from effectively communicating off-stage are the same factors that prohibit him from communicating on-stage. Far too many actors just hear their voices and do not hear the words they are saying. This frequently happens as the result of repeating the same lines night after night in the re-hearsal period and for a long run of performances, when the words are spoken by rote from the memory level instead of being actively recreated on the conscious level.

There needs to be a regaining of contact with words and there needs to be a full response to their inner fibre. For any good playwright sets down the definitions of character and motivation in the very precise language of his text. Words must be used with thought and feeling for the power they are expressing and for the significant fact that words are the audible ex-pression of inner action. Words are alive. They are viable, living entities formed of muscle, breath, and emotion and are part of the character's dy-namic as set down by the playwright. The resonances of the sounds that make up words are part of the performance that should be felt and heard.

To ignore this fact implies ignorance — or laziness — or both. It also indicates an appalling disregard of the playwright's intentions.

The same actor who will, without question, scour his textual blueprint for meaningful physical gestures to energize his character will completely disregard the potential energy of the speech gesture of the words — which is also indicated in the textual blueprint. And to not fully use the dynamic energy of living words in character portrayal makes about as much sense as to not fully use the dynamic energy of the living body. "Anything which refines and makes language more accurate is a better form of theatre," says Jonathan Miller, "and it's the duty of everyone who works in the theatre to honour language first and foremost."[2]

A virtuoso performer uses it all — revealing character through the movement of the mind as well as the movement of the body. The mind must concentrate intensely at all times to actively recreate the words as they are being spoken. The words must vibrate. Each successive thought unit should arrive intensively, the words energized with the movement of thought. This linkage is positive and active at every sound and syllable, adding sharpness and clarity that is riveting.

Only immediate experience is real and alive, and it is the business of the actor to be fully alive in the present moment. This means the active involvement of the mind and the emotions. It means the immediacy of thought as well as of feeling. Simply reciting memorized lines means that the mind is not fully alive in the present moment. It means that the mind is merely an audience to the emotions and the acting dynamic is, therefore, considerably weakened. It's exciting to experience the energy of an actor's emotion. It's equally exciting to experience the energy of his mind. And when you find the total emotional and mental energy combined in a technically skilled actor, you have high art and a quite extraordinary experience. In such an instance, we find that we are thinking, feeling, even breathing, with the actor, for the reason that he is totally into his words.

History has been defined as a series of accidents. I think it could also be defined as a series of events which were brought about, in large measure, by the effect of words. A study of the influential men and women of history is a study of the words they spoke and wrote; words that not only shaped the minds and actions of the people of their own times, but words

---

[2]Cook, *Director's Theatre*, p. 108.

which, in many cases, so disordered the existing social and political structure that the effect of their words exists today. As evidence of the power of words, reflect on Hitler on one side of the English Channel, whose verbal blasts armed his nation and embroiled the Western world in the slaughter and enslavement of millions, and then reflect on Churchill on the other side of the Channel who, in the words of John F. Kennedy, "marshaled the English language and sent it into battle," fortifying his own nation and ultimately, with the help of the Allies, defeating the Nazi horror. To read aloud the words of the Declaration of Independence; Lincoln's Gettysburg Address; the fifth, sixth, and seventh chapters of St. Matthew; or any other words that have influenced and shaped history is to experience dynamic instruments of great power.

As J. Donald Adams has said, words "are one of the most living things of man's creation. They possess more vitality than anything else the race has fashioned," for "what else is there that man has made which leads an independent life? Words do."[3] And, indeed, they do. Words have the power to create beauty, to lift the spirit, to open the heart, to unite, to generate energy, to release tensions, or to manipulate, to terrify, to generate hatred, to maintain control, and to keep people in bondage.

Words are a nuclei of thoughts, emotions, and imagination, of all the inner connotations that form their subtext and give them their life. It is with the expression of this life and subtext that we now concern ourselves.

An intelligent actor will have a lifelong love affair with words. He will learn everything he possibly can about the words and constructions of his language. An actor has only two ways to convey the inner life of his character—the way he moves and the way he speaks his words. Words are nowhere more glaringly apparent than on the stage. Words are the actor's tools, the means through which he expresses the inner meanings of the character and play, and through which he involves his audience.

DETERMINING THE MEANING

Effective expression means knowing the text. It means understanding what you are saying and why you are saying it. Knowing the text means learning everything you can about the words, knowing which words need

---

[3]J. Donald Adams, *Literary Frontiers* (New York: Duell, Sloan and Pearce, 1951), p. 97.

emphasis and which words do not, knowing how the words should be grouped together into phrases and phrase-groups. Knowing the text means understanding the inner content of attitudes, thoughts, and feelings that are inherent in the words—the subtext. If an actor doesn't understand what he is saying neither will the audience. An audience comes to the theater expecting to be moved by the meanings and rhythms of the words and this can only happen if the actor is moved by them. It is the actor's job to impregnate his words with the total humanity of his character and to be able to involve his audience in the felt expression of his impregnation. For this reason we must consider the techniques of interpretation. An actor's expression can never exceed his understanding of his text and his grasp of the means to express it.

Finding the meaning of the words a character is to speak requires, first of all, that the entire play be read. An isolated line or speech of a character can be understood only in its relationship to all the rest of the words the character speaks, to the words of the other characters in the play, and to the overall meaning of the play's theme, plot, mood, and other effects. The words must be understood in relation to the playwright's ordering and interpretation of human experience; understood as the expression of the intensifications, changes, and revelations of an inner life; understood in terms of attitudes and actions to which an audience can respond. In referring to the necessity for understanding the language of a play, William L. Sharp writes in *Language in Drama* that "A good playwright uses contrasting scenes, contrasting characters, even contrasting actions as well. But he creates his scenes, his actions, and his characters with language. If he is good, with very precise language."[4] And, of course, the playwright's precise words must be clearly understood and interpreted. Although it may sound paradoxical, it is a fact that the ability to appreciate good plays is both a means and an end in their study. This ability is dependent on knowing what to look for in a play.

A literary analyst would say that the factors inherent in a good piece of writing are its *individuality*; that is, the uniqueness and originality that distinguishes it, not only from bad writing, but from other writings on the same subject; its *universality*: that is, its reference to the human experiences and motives common to all people; and its *suggestion*: that is, what is left unsaid or is merely implied or hinted at, and which stimulates indi-

---

[4]William L. Sharp, *Language in Drama* (Scranton, Penn.: Chandler Pub. Co., 1970), p. 3.

vidual thought. It is stating the obvious to say that all three factors are vividly apparent in a first-rate play.

Other factors inherent in good plays are their *structure*, that is, the overall organization of the plot, its complications and resolutions; their *unity*, that is, the way in which every element of the play contributes to its underlying theme or purpose; and their *aesthetic experience*, that is, the basic emotional effect that is produced through the actualization of the play in performance, using language as its central means.

It is with the language that this chapter is primarily concerned, with key words, with combinations of words, and with the rhythm, flow, and melody of words as they relate to the above-mentioned factors in expressing meaning.

Words may be defined by an explicit, direct dictionary meaning, known as *denotation*, or by the associations or suggestions they excite, known as *connotation*. For instance, the denotation of "violin" and "fiddle" is the same, both being explicitly defined as an "instrument of the modern string instruments played with a bow." However, "fiddle" has a more humorous and deprecatory connotation than that of the "violin" which connotes the associations of classical music, symphony orchestras, and formality. In the same way, "fiddler" and "violinist" both refer to a person but arouse different connotations or associated qualities of a person.

The *emotive* meaning of words may also be contrasted with their *cognitive* meaning. Emotive meanings are the emotive associations of words present in their usage, while cognitive meanings are assertions about a reality and which do not express attitude or emotion. For instance, a violinist might make the purely cognitive assertion, "I am not a fiddler, I am a violinist." However, if the idea of being thought a fiddler was offensive, the same statement might be spoken with a purely emotional meaning. It is generally accepted that poetic language has emotive meaning rather than cognitive since it does not make realistic assertions but expresses and excites emotions.

In any case, meaning is determined by the response to words in terms of individual experience. A comprehension of the playwright's words and his motivations for their spoken performance must guide your interpretation of meaning, but your choices and expression of meaning can only be in terms of your own experience, which suggests several things. It suggests that without experiences there can be neither understanding nor meaning. It suggests that complete understanding and expression requires a great breadth and depth of experiences. It suggests that the same word or words hold different meanings for different people. And it also suggests, considered in terms of individual experience, that spoken words may be categorized by more than one of the above-named terms. The statement, "I am not a fiddler, I am a violinist," could be a cognitive assertion and, based on the speaker's connotative associations, the words could also contain an emotive meaning. It must be kept in mind that meaning is determined by the response to words in terms of individual experience.

The implications for the actor are very clear. The actor needs a wide variety of experiences to extend his scope of understanding. Also, since the words he speaks represent another experience than his own, he needs to learn as much as he can about the playwright and the period of time in which he wrote. He needs to understand how the words express the playwright's response to his experience and also to determine the playwright's purpose in writing them. The tenets of rhetoric, which is the art and science of using words effectively, hold that words are used to inform, to persuade, to convince, and to entertain. These are broad categories. There are other varied and distinctive reasons that motivate a playwright. The actor should learn as much as he can about the playwright's experience and purpose in writing his play. And with these factors as his guide, he should then interpret the playwright's words in terms of his own knowledge and experience.

The denotative, or dictionary, meaning of every word must be clear in the actor's mind, which is not as easy as it sounds if the words were written during the sixteenth and early part of the seventeenth centuries, as in the following Shakespeare sonnet, number 30. However, the attempt must be made, and most good Shakespeare anthologies supply a helpful definition for an unfamiliar word or for an unfamiliar usage of a word. For instance, the word *sessions* in line one is defined as "the sittings of a law court"; the word *dateless* in line six as meaning "everlasting"; the word *expense* in line eight as meaning "waste"; and the word *foregone* in line nine as meaning "past". It would be impossible to intelligently express these words, or any other, without understanding their defined meaning. Every word that is not understood, or about which you have the slightest doubt, should be checked.

> When to the sessions of sweet silent thought
> I summon up remembrance of things past,
> I sigh the lack of many a thing I sought,

And with old woes new wail my dear time's waste.
Then can I drown an eye, unused to flow,
For precious friends hid in death's dateless night,
And weep afresh love's long since canceled woe,
And moan the expense of many a vanished sight.
Then can I grieve at grievances foregone,
And heavily from woe to woe tell o'er
The sad account of forebemoanèd moan,
Which I new-pay as if not paid before.
But if the while I think on thee, dear friend,
All losses are restored and sorrows end.

The particular connotative associations and suggestions also need the actor's consideration as do the emotive meanings of the words. What, for instance, do the following groups of words mean to you: "sweet silent thought," "dear time's waste," "death's dateless night," "long since canceled woe," "vanished sight," and "forebemoanèd moan." The best words have connotative, experiential, and emotive content and are, therefore, the most effective and dramatic.

Another element used by a playwright and which must be understood by an actor, is that of the allusion to something outside the work itself. For instance, Horatio in the first act of *Hamlet* says, "In the most high and palmy state of Rome, A little ere the mightiest Julius fell, The graves stood tenantless, and the sheeted dead Did squeak and gibber in the Roman streets." And Tom Wingfield in his opening narration in *The Glass Menagerie* says, "In Spain there was revolution. Here there was only shouting and confusion. In Spain there was Guernica. Here there were disturbances of labor, sometimes pretty violent, in otherwise peaceful cities such as Chicago, Cleveland, St. Louis."

The background for the references in both of these instances is easily recognized and can excite relevant and comparative associations. Many allusions, however, are much more obscure, and impossible to understand unless the interpreter has an extensive background in mythology, literature, and history. Wherever possible, the background for all references outside the text should be understood to effectively illuminate and speak the words.

Another element which should be appreciated and understood is figurative language, for it provides a way of saying one thing in terms of something else. For instance, when Romeo says, "Juliet is the sun!" it is a literal absurdity, for Juliet is certainly not an incandescent heavenly body that is the center of a solar system about which planets revolve and which furnishes light, heat, and energy; but in employing indirect, figurative language Romeo can most vividly describe Juliet and also indicate his degree of emotional involvement. It is essential that the actor appreciate the value of figurative language, that what is impossible to effectively express in an unimaginative, literal manner is highly possible by using imaginative figures of speech.

There are many types of figurative language such as the metaphor, of which "Juliet is the sun" is an example; and an understanding of their function is another excellent tool for understanding a character. Toward this end, Jill Taft-Kaufman has written an article in the May 1980 *Communication Education* journal that every actor should study. In the article entitled "A Rhetorical Perspective for Teaching the Solo Performance of Shakespearean Dramatic Literature," Taft-Kaufman discusses the interpretation of a character in terms of what he or she says, the style and content of the verbal expression. This is particularly helpful in Shakespeare's earlier plays, for as Taft-Kaufman states, these were characterized by "their general lack of character development" and that "he learned how to control audience perception of character and event as he matured."[5] The author makes the point, however, that with any of Shakespeare's plays a study of the verbal expression of a character can provide helpful insights into what the character is all about.

The character of Romeo, for instance, who is described by Taft-Kaufman as being "guided only by extreme passion in carrying out the dictates of love" uses the "stylishly consistent" figurative language of *hyperbole*, which is overstatement or exaggeration; *personification*, which is the attribution of human qualities or feelings to inanimate things or ideas; and *oxymoron*, a figure of speech in which opposite or contradictory ideas or terms are combined. These figures of speech are all present in Romeo's speech about Rosaline.

Alas that love, whose view is muffled still,
Should without eyes see pathways to his will!
Where shall we dine? Oh me! What fray was here?
Yet tell me not, for I have heard it all.
Here's much to do with hate, but more with love.
Why then, O brawling love! O loving hate!

---

[5]Jill Taft-Kaufman, "A Rhetorical Perspective for Teaching Solo Performance of Shakespearean Dramatic Literature," *Communication Education*, 29 (May 1980), pp. 114-15.

O anything, of nothing first create!
O heavy lightness! Serious vanity!
Misshapen chaos of well-seeming forms!
Feather of lead, bright smoke, cold fire, sick health!
Still-waking sleep, that is not what it is!
This love feel I, that feel no love in this.
Dost thou not laugh?   (I, ii)

It would probably be difficult to find a speech of Romeo's that did not contain one or all of these figures of speech defining its style and content, and in turn defining the consistently passionate character of Romeo.

Romeo's flamboyant speech, suggests Taft-Kaufman, seems all the more "immoderate when viewed next to the rational Benvolio," whose "relatively simple" and "thoughtful choices" are demonstrated in the following speech to Lady Montague.[6]

Madam, an hour before the worshiped sun
Peered forth the golden window of the east,
A troubled mind drave me to walk abroad,
Where, underneath the grove of sycamore
That westward rooteth from the city's side,
So early walking did I see your son.
Towards him I made; but he was ware of me,
And stole into the covert of the wood.
I, measuring his affections by my own,
That most are busied when they're most alone,
Being one too many by my weary self,
Pursued my humor, not pursuing his,
And gladly shunned who gladly fled from me.   (I, i)

In defining Benvolio's diction as moderate and thoughtful, and containing less exaggerated figures of speech, we are once again defining the character himself. In this example of Shakespeare's earlier plays the characters are clearly distinguished by their idiosyncratic use of words, and these patterns remain relatively consistent throughout the extent of the play.

In Shakespeare's later plays, however, the style and content of the characters' verbal expression are neither as obvious nor as consistent. Taft-Kaufman's article contains many examples to demonstrate this change in writing style, from the use of distinctive verbal expression to distinguish individual characters one from the other, to the use of the

---

[6]Ibid., p. 115.

varying diction of one character to indicate that character's changes of attitude. The author cites the diction changes of *King Lear*, among others, as an example of the shift from "the highly florid and indirect language of royalty to the simple utterances of a man who has learned what matters in life"; she also demonstrates how changes in attitude may fluctuate, as seen in the utterances of Marc Antony, whose "flashes of self-awareness alternate with his attitudes of indifference for his image and his passion for Cleopatra." There are other examples, all concerned, of course, with the delineation of Shakespearean characters. But it is obvious that an understanding of the terms and uses of figurative language, indeed of all literary devices, can tell an actor a great deal about his character, his motivations, and his actions.

One final literary element to which we should give consideration is that of imagery, usually defined as the sensory content of words, involving the sensations of sight, hearing, taste, smell, and touch, as well as those of pressure, pain, temperature, movement, hunger, and thirst. To put it another way, certain words have the power to make us see, hear, smell, feel, and so on. It is the sensory content of language that most intimately involves us for our brains and nerves receive and react to its stimuli. Imagery is a significant part of the meaning of certain words for both speaker and listener and the audible expression of words can be greatly enriched for both if it is invested with the personal experience of the speaker's senses.

Let your self experience the images of hearing, sight, movement, and touch in the following excerpt from the prologue to *Henry V*, Act IV, and be aware of how the sensations illuminate and personalize the words for you.

> Now entertain conjecture of a time
> When creeping murmur and the poring dark
> Fills the wide vessel of the universe.
> From camp to camp, through the foul womb of night,
> The hum of either army stilly sounds,
> That the fixed sentinels almost receive
> The secret whispers of each other's watch.
> Fire answers fire, and through their paly flames
> Each battle sees the other's umber'd face.
> Steed threatens steed, in high and boastful neighs,
> Piercing the night's dull ear; and from the tents
> The armourers, accomplishing the knights,
> With busy hammers closing rivets up,
> Give dreadful note of preparation.

Let your self experience and thus animate the words of Clarence, from *Richard III*, as you realize the images of pain, pressure, hearing, movement, touch, and sight.

> Lord, Lord! Methought what pain it was to drown!
> What dreadful noise of waters in mine ears!
> What ugly sights of death within mine eyes!
> Methought I saw a thousand fearful wrecks,
> Ten thousand men that fishes gnawed upon,
> Wedges of gold, great anchors, heaps of pearl,
> Inestimable stones, unvalued jewels,
> All scattered in the bottom of the sea.   (I, iv)

Letting your self respond to the imagery of words is an important factor in determining their meaning and in bringing them to life. An actor can vivify his words only in proportion to his ability to let the images feed him, to let them capture his emotions.

It is the actor's obligation to reproduce, as nearly as possible, the playwright's intention, to understand the denotative meanings of the words, to enrich the words with personal connotative and emotive meanings, to comprehend the use of allusions, and to recapture the figures of speech and imagery. Words are not static; they have a life which must be realized. Words are the audible expression of human thought, senses, and emotions. Understanding the various terms and functions of literary devices can help enrich this expression.

Problems are not solved by being named, of course; but being able to name them isolates them from their allies, unreasoning insecurity and anxiety. An understanding of how words function provides the actor with a type of support. Lacking that understanding and support, the actor's situation is analogous to the cartoon character who looks down to discover that he is not standing on anything, and then falls. So if you find your self "up in the air" about what the words are asking you to do, look to your support. And enjoy it. Put your mind and imagination to work and browse in the words as though they were a meadow, enmeshing your physical-spiritual-feeling self; and you will emerge from your browsing with new insights and awareness of your character, your self, indeed of all humanity.

EXPRESSING THE MEANING

In addition to knowing everything he or she possibly can about the inner content of the words to be spoken, the actor must also be familiar with the techniques to clarify the meaning of the words for the listening audience. The sense and feelings of words must be communicated by the actor's speaking voice, by the way he or she groups words together into meaningful phrases, emphasizes key words and subordinates unimportant words, and reinforces meaning with the use of pauses and intonation. The actor's ability to employ these techniques is greatly dependent on his grasp of the elements of language discussed in the first part of this chapter.

Phrasing

The first thing the actor must do to understand the sense of his words is to separate them into meaningful phrases. A phrase is defined grammatically as a part of a sentence not containing a subject and a predicate. This text uses the word "phrase" as meaning a single thought unit, which is generally expressed in a group of words — although an idea existing in the mind might be expressed in a single word.

For example, the single word *you* might be spoken to express an entire unit of thought, such as "How dare you come here after all that has passed between us!" or, "What a delightful surprise!" or, "Can't you see that I need help!"

In the final scene of Albee's play, *Who's Afraid of Virginia Woolf*, the characters Martha and George express their thoughts in many single word responses.

GEORGE: Do you want anything, Martha?
MARTHA: No . . . nothing.
GEORGE: It's late.
MARTHA: Yes.
MARTHA: Just . . . us?
GEORGE: Yes.
GEORGE: Are you all right?
MARTHA: Yes. No.

These single word responses are generally spoken in a mood of stillness and utter exhaustion, but in terms of all that has gone before between George and Martha, none of them could be said to be meaningless. Each single response is weighted with an image existing in the mind of the speaker.

The repetition of single-word units of thought throughout an entire scene is somewhat rare in dramatic literature. Generally thoughts are expressed in groups of words, as in the following lines from *Romeo and Juliet*.

1. BENVOLIO: *Come//* he hath *hid* himself/ among these *trees//* To be *consorted/* with the humorous *night://* *Blind/* is his *love//* and best *befits* the dark.///
2. TYBALT: *This* by his *voice* should be a *Montague.* *Fetch* me my *rapier* *boy.*
3. NURSE: *Marry* *bachelor* Her *mother* is the lady-of-the-*house* And a *good* lady and a *wise* and *virtuous:*
4. CAPULET: *Welcome* *gentlemen* *ladies* that-have-their-toes-unplagu'd-with-*corns* will walk *about* with you.
5. ROMEO: But *soft* what *light* through yonder *window* *breaks*? It is the *East* and *Juliet* is the *sun.*

The possible phrases in each line have been indicated by a space; some are more obvious than others, and within the prescribed limits of phrasing, someone else might phrase them differently. Phrasing is very much a factor of individual interpretation. Listening to the various recorded versions of *Hamlet* will easily prove this point. Just select one of the Hamlet soliloquies and compare the various ways it is phrased, and remember that you are listening to well-known, professional actors.

For the purposes of studying a technique, however, let us accept the arbitrary phrasing as set down in the lines above, and let us also consider other elements of phrasing. We have defined a phrase as being a single thought unit. We are further defining a phrase as having one key word that receives primary stress. There may be one or two, or sometimes more, secondary-stressed words, but there is only one primary-stressed word in each phrase. The whole area of stress will be dealt with later in this chapter, but for now, and in order that you may better grasp the technique of phrasing, let us also accept the italicized words as receiving primary stress in each phrase. As you read aloud the five lines above, emphasize the primary-stressed word in each and don't, for the present, concern your self with secondary stresses.

Pauses

Another element of present concern is the use of pauses. Pauses, and by this we mean logical pauses, help to clarify meaning by uniting sense-groups and by separating the sense-groups from one another. Pauses are also needed to take an occasional breath. For instance, in line one you will probably take a breath after the word *night*, thus combining five phrases into one breath-group. Or if you needed it, you could take a breath after the word *trees*, combining three phrases into one breath-group. There are really only two principles at work here; one is that you take a breath at a logical pause and do not break up a sense-group; the other principle is that, generally speaking, language must flow. Sense-groups, separated by logical pauses, are joined into complete ideas by long sustained breaths.

Read the five lines aloud, separating the sense-groups with logical pauses and be aware, first of all, of how the use of logical pauses clarifies meaning. Also be aware of how the natural component of rhythm involved in the use of pauses, plus the fact that the mind must be constantly focused on the meaning, involve you with the content of the words. You both feel and understand them. The technique of phrasing is still another way to work your way into a role.

You will notice too as you read that not all the pauses between the phrases are the same in length. Phrases that are closely related in content have a shorter pause between them, such as the pause between "he hath hid himself/ among these trees." Just as words combine logically into sense-groups or phrases, so do phrases combine logically into phrase-groups. In the first line, the end of a phrase is indicated by one slash mark (/) and the end of a phrase-group is indicated by two slash marks (//). Three slash marks (///) always indicate that the idea is complete. Go through the other four lines and, with a pencil, mark the phrases and phrase-groups. Then read the lines aloud and see if you have judged correctly.

The slash marks are also an indication of another element of phrasing known as intonation. In fact, phrases are sometimes referred to as intonation groups, since every phrase ends with a glide of the voice signifying whether the idea is complete or incomplete. If a phrase does not complete an idea, it must be indicated that there is more to come by the use of a rising intonation or by a level intonation. If a phrase does complete an idea, it must be indicated by a falling intonation (the obvious exception being some types of questions that will be discussed in a later in-depth discussion of intonation).

For a demonstration of how these three intonations function, look at the line "It is the East / and Juliet / is the sun." The voice flows naturally forward in a level intonation on "East," glides upward in a rising intonation on the last syllable of "Ju-li-*et*," and glides downward in a falling intonation on the last word, "sun." Read aloud all five lines and let your self experience the logical intonations at the end of each phrase, being certain that your intonation signifies that there is more to come until you reach the concluding phrase of the idea.

In summary, a phrase is defined:

- as containing a single thought unit, which can be a single word or a group of words;
- as having one primary-stressed word, and possibly one or more secondary-stressed words;
- as being separated from other phrases by a pause, by an intonation glide, and sometimes by a breath;
- as sometimes being related to other phrases in a phrase group.

We have considered pauses as a necessary factor in clarifying meaning by unifying groups of words into logical phrases and by separating the phrases from one another. Pauses deserve further consideration.

Vocal sound may be present in a pause, such as that between the phrases "It is the East / and Juliet / is the sun," or vocal sound may be absent in a pause, such as that after "sun"; but it should be clearly understood that meaning should always be present in a pause. In the mind of the speaker the pause must be redefined. For the speaker, the pause must be divorced from its dictionary definition, for it is not to be thought of as "a short period of inaction; temporary stop, break, or rest." On the contrary, the speaker's pause must be active, significant, full and rich in meaning, prolific of feeling and thought. Pauses are not breaks in the flow of meaning; rather are they an important part of meaning's flow, binding phrases together into whole ideas, furnishing points of assimilation for listeners, and thrusting meaning forward. Pauses are the glue that reinforces meaning. Pauses can intensify meaning by creating anticipation and suspense. Logical pauses in creating intense moods of suspense, are thus converted into psychological pauses, and as such are alive with meaning and activity. Consider how psychological pauses intensify Iago's meaning in *Othello* in his "I hate the Moor" speech (Act I, sc. iii).

> He holds me   well.
> The better   shall my purpose   work on him.
> Cassio's   a proper man.   Let me   see now.
> To get   his place   and to plume up   my will
> In double   knavery——— How   how?——— Let's see.
> After some time   to abuse   Othello's ear
> That he is too familiar   with his wife.

The lines after "knavery" and "how?" are included in the text and meant to be used as pregnant pauses. I have also heard this speech delivered with slight psychological pauses before "purpose," before "proper," and before "familiar," which subtly enriches Iago's spoken intent and pro-vokes interest and excitement in the listening audience. Psychological pauses can be very powerful and can be as eloquent as spoken words, sometimes more so, for they can communicate the part of the subtext not easily expressed in words, such as in a Chekhov or Pinter play.

The actor must learn to use both logical and psychological pauses in conveying the meaning of his words. Pausing is an important skill and must be mastered. However, and this is equally important, the skill of pausing must be used judiciously. Pauses are employed to enhance mean-ing and keep it moving forward, not to slow it up. Pauses are not an end in themselves and should not be held just for an effect, nor should every logical pause be converted into a psychological pause. They are an impor-tant part, but only a part, of meaning. But when their proper function is understood, and pauses are used properly to sustain the concentrated ef-fort of mind and emotion, the spoken words are energized and connected, and there is less danger that the last word in a phrase will not be heard.

Last words are lost far too often, and part of the reason is that the en-ergy of the subtext is not projected into and through the pauses. When the combined effort of thought and feeling is not carried on into the pauses, phrases come out in spurts, with all of the energy expended in the first couple of words and gradually diminishing into weak endings. This is a common failing among actors, indeed among all speakers, and is proba-bly related to the whole concept of phrasing. We, in fact, conceive a thought in the mind all at once; a sense-group, of whatever number of words, springs into the consciousness as a single unit, on a single burst of mental effort, which having been expended in the initial burst, leaves words trailing off at the end with no conscious support. And if there is no conscious effort there will be no breath support, and the last words will just lie there where they were dropped. This produces a curious stopping and starting kind of delivery which breaks the rhythm and flow of intelli-gible speech.

It is hoped that you will rethink and revalue the pause and its uses. Pauses, together with intonation, play an active role in communication. In his book, *Building a Character*, Stanislavsky says that "intonations and pauses in themselves possess the power to produce a powerful emo-tional effect on the listener."[7] Stanislavsky tells in the book of an instance

---

[7]Constantin Stanislavski, *Building a Character* (New York: Theatre Arts Books, 1949), p. 137.

when his acting coach recited for the class in a foreign language and yet he involved them in the meaning that was conveyed through the use of the sounds, enhanced by pauses and intonations. It is reported that Sarah Bernhardt could, in like manner, completely enrapture English speaking audiences who didn't understand a word of the French language. You should try it for yourself, and prove the point that pauses and intonation should not be neglected, that they have the power to stir an audience even when they are not connected to meaningful words.

Using just single vowels and consonants, or combining vowels and consonants into nonsense words and phrases, communicate an imagined subtext of thought and feeling by the use of vocal sound, intonations, and pauses. Enrich the sounds with the subtext and let the meaning flow into and through the pauses and intonation glides. If you have difficulty structuring nonsense words, then take a simple sequence such as [wɑ - weɪ - wi - woʊ - wu] and play with it, as follows: [wɑ] - [wɑ - weɪ - wi] - [wi - woʊ - wu] - [wɑ - wei - woʊ - wu] - [wɑ - woʊ] - [weɪ] - [wɑ - wi - wu]. The point is, of course, to imagine that you are speaking meaningful phrases, so that your delivery has a conversational rhythm. This exercise can be done as a monologue or as a dialogue with a partner, and if done properly, it can be an amazing experience, for both you and your listeners. In separating the communication from recognizable words and their associations, you are able to focus on the remarkable effects achieved by intonations and pauses.

As a follow-up to the exercise, go back and read aloud the five lines from *Romeo and Juliet* and use the pauses and intonation to bind the phrases together and thrust the meaning forward until each separate idea is completely expressed and indicated by a falling intonation. Try intensifying the meaning on a few phrases and converting them into psychological pauses. Then apply this technique to lines from a scene you may be working on and you may be sure that you will discover new levels of meaning in the words and in your character.

Before concluding our discussion of phrasing we must consider the fact that not all phrases are of equal importance. The speaker is often confronted with subordinate phrases, those that are less important in that they are either dependent upon or in some way qualify another phrase and are not part of the main idea. These less important phrases must be subordinated so that the main idea comes through clearly. For instance, in the simple sentence "His oldest sister (who has blond hair) has gone to Europe," the main idea is that "his oldest sister has gone to Europe."

Clearly, the phrase "who has blond hair" is extraneous information and should be subordinated. Techniques for stressing key words and phrases and subordinating less important words and phrases will be discussed in the forthcoming section on stress. But for the present, consider some of the following passages and try to decide on which phrases carry the main idea and which simply furnish explanatory or qualifying information.

1. HELENA, *Midsummer Night's Dream*: And sleep, that sometimes shuts up sorrow's eye, Steal me awhile from mine own company.

2. DUKE OF AUMERLE, *Richard II*: I brought high Hereford, if you call him so, But to the next highway, and there I left him.

3. SILVIUS, *As You Like It*: But if thy love were ever like mine — As sure I think did never man love so — How many actions most ridiculous Hast thou been drawn to by thy fantasy?

4. TITANIA, *Midsummer Night's Dream*: These are the forgeries of jealousy. And never, since the middle summer's spring, Met we on hill, in dale, forest, or mead, By paved fountain or by rushy brook, Or in the beachèd margent of the sea, To dance our ringlets to the whistling wind, But with thy brawls thou hast disturbed our sport.

5. SHYLOCK, *Merchant of Venice*: You knew, none so well, none so well as you, of my daughter's flight.

Obviously the main ideas in the lines are these:

1. And sleep Steal me awhile from mine own company.

2. I brought high Hereford But to the next highway, and there I left him.

3. But if thy love were ever like mine How many actions most ridiculous Hast thou been drawn to by thy fantasy?

4. These are the forgeries of jealousy. And never Met we, But with thy brawls thou hast disturbed our sport.

5. You knew of my daughter's flight.

And, just as obviously, the subordinate phrases are of varying importance. Their importance is dependent on the relationship of characters to each other, on the specific action of the scene in which they are spoken, on the underlying subtext and theme of the entire play. In line one, Helena is speaking to herself, so we might say that the subordinate phrase group "that sometimes shuts up / sorrow's eye" is not as important in qualifying the main idea as that of the Duke of Aumerle, who is speaking to King Richard, and therefore the "you" in the phrase-group "if you / call him so" has more significance and gives the phrase-group more weight. In line three, Silvius is speaking to Corin, a shepherd like himself and older, so the situation does not demand deference nor does the youthful ego in the words "As sure I think did never man love so" suggest empathy or understanding. In fact, the subordinate phrase-group is more like that of Helena, spoken to oneself. In line four, Titania's subordinate phrase-groups furnish a great deal of explanatory information which reinforces the main idea, but which also must not be allowed to fog the clarity of that idea. In line five, Shylock, in speaking to Salarino, uses two phrase-groups to emphasize his main idea, so these subordinate phrase-groups are relatively important, but once again must not be permitted to dim our perception that Shylock is referring to his "daughter's flight."

There are some speeches in which phrases and phrase-groups are all equally important, the main idea being further established by each successive sense-group, such as the speech of Macbeth when he is told that the Queen is dead (Act V, sc. v).

> She should have died hereafter,
> There would have been a time for such a word.
> Tomorrow, and tomorrow, and tomorrow
> Creeps in this petty pace from day to day,
> To the last syllable of recorded time,
> And all our yesterdays have lighted fools
> The way to dusty death. Out, out, brief candle!
> Life's but a walking shadow, a poor player
> That struts and frets his hour upon the stage
> And then is heard no more. It is a tale
> Told by an idiot, full of sound and fury,
> Signifying nothing.

There is not one subordinate phrase or phrase-group in this entire speech. Each phrase is part of the main idea, continuing from the phrase that preceded it and leading directly into the phrase that follows. Where the tension of the preceding lines requires the balance of emphasis and subordination, the lines of Macbeth require a sustained tension, broken only once by the necessary emphasis on the four words in the exclamation "Out, out, brief candle!" It is interesting, too, how the tension tends to wind down in the shortening of phrases at the end; from the three phrases and eight words in the phrase-group "It is a tale / told / by an idiot," the two phrases and five words of "full of sound / and fury," to the last two phrases and two words, "Signifying / nothing."

Read Macbeth's lines aloud and realize the sustained tension and flow of the ideas. Then read the other five lines aloud and realize the balance of emphasis and subordination and the varying tensions. Delivering the lines of Macbeth is rather like the act of swimming, in which you push off and maintain your stroke and forward thrust until you reach your goal. Delivering the other five lines is like the act of juggling balls, in which they must all be kept in motion and aloft but where one ball is given prominence by being periodically tossed higher than the others. And if you allow your self to enjoy the act of phrasing, as swimmers and jugglers seem to enjoy what they do, you will more quickly master the skill. As we said in Chapter II of this text, a playful attitude is infinitely more creative and productive than the tension produced by the hard-driven, hard-driving, "make-it-at-all-costs" attitude. So structure your phrases to make sense out of your words, and then play with them, juggle them if a speech calls for this, and enjoy the activity. Balance phrases and phrase-groups against each other; feel and sense their tensions.

Since we all speak naturally in phrases, or sense-groups, it should be a simple matter to project the main ideas of a script. The key, of course, is that the words must be actively recreated in the mind as if they were a first occurrence. This type of delivery has energy and believability, and will be heard and understood. Maintaining the concentrative mental and emotional effort on one phrase or phrase-group means that you know where you are and where you are heading, that you will see the final word in the group even as you speak the first, and that the delivery will have a firm, forward flow that sweeps listeners along with it. Don't let your attention lag on any phrase. If you attend to what you are saying, so will an audience. Let the breathing, thinking, sensing, feeling life of the subtext and the details of the words sustain your attention and motivation so that the immediate intention of the character comes through.

I know of no better way to get at the meaning of a text than taking a pencil and the time to structure and balance the phrases and phrase-groups. You will understand what you are saying and, more important, so will the audience. That more of this kind of attention is not lavished on scripts is evident from the disconnected, illogical, and incoherent delivery that flourishes on our stages. If you know what you are saying you will be correct, only if your habits are correct. Themes, relationships, and motivations must be understood. End words, phrases, lines, and speeches must be perceived as the development of the beginning. Lines should not be run together; there must be attention given to each phrase. There are natural pauses in all lines for greater clarity and for breathing. If these factors are observed, then in the greatest freedom of playing there will be a secure, underlying structure. Freedom of playing comes from knowing the text.

Stress

In addition to learning how to structure and balance phrases, it is necessary to learn how to structure and balance words. Within each phrase are words of varying importance. As already stated, a phrase is defined as having one primary-stressed word, and possibly one or more secondary-stressed words. There will probably be other words of lesser importance that serve as a link for the important words. We must learn how to distinguish the important words and how to emphasize them with the techniques of stressing.

Stress is defined as the relative force of utterance given a syllable or word. Stress can also be thought of as intensifications of mental, physical, and emotional energy, of pulses of meaning which penetrate and rhythmically stimulate listeners. These pulses of energy are perceived as pressures by the breathing muscles on the exhaled breath. It is also perceived that extreme degrees of stress affect other body muscles.

There are basically two different patterns of stressing words for all languages. The stress pattern of the English language is characterized by rhythmic pulses, which are fairly regularly spaced in most sentences no matter how many words or syllables may come between them. Consider, for instance, the following three sentences.

1. *Tom* went *bowl*ing with *Bob*.
2. *George* left his *books* at *school*.
3. *Ma*ry went to the *thea*ter to see the new *play*.

Each of the three sentences would generally be spoken with three major stresses, as marked. This stress pattern would cause all the sentences to be spoken with the same general rhythm and within the same relative time-space, even though the word-syllable count in between the major stresses varies in all three sentences.

In the first sentence, the word-syllable count between the first and second major stresses is one, and between the second and third major stresses it is two.

In the second sentence, the word-syllable count between the first and second major stresses is two, and between the second and third major stresses it is one.

In the third sentence, the word-syllable count between the first and second major stresses is four, and between the second and third major stresses it is five.

The second basic pattern for stressing words can best be understood by listening to a native speaker of Spanish or French. In both cases, it is noticeable that every word and syllable receives relatively equal stress. This differing stress pattern is most clearly noted when a native Spanish or French speaker speaks English as a second language. The use of English grammar and vocabulary may be quite correct, but when the pattern of stressing every word and syllable is imposed on the English language, it calls attention to itself. Conversely, when a native English speaker speaks Spanish or French and imposes on them the stress pattern of the English language, it also calls attention to itself.

Underlying physiological processes, particularly the rhythm of breathing, make these two speech patterns possible, but do not dictate which stress pattern a speaker will use. Stress patterns, along with languages, are learned. A child born into a speech community will imitate the speech patterns of that community. It is curious, however, that while this child may later in life master a language other than his own, sometimes more than one, he is not always able to master a different pattern of stress. It is probably owing to their dependence on basic physiological processes that stress patterns are difficult, and often impossible, to change. A native English speaker talking in French or a native French speaker talking in English, albeit they have both mastered their second language, will generally give themselves away every time, particularly to the trained speech person, by their pattern of stress.

Mastering a different pattern of stress presents similar problems for the actor in learning stage dialects. Those who have the least problems are usually those who have the best understanding and control of the breathing process.

To restate, the stress pattern of the English language is characterized by rhythmic pulses, which are fairly regularly spaced in most sentences. These rhythmic pulses are defined as the relative force of utterance given a syllable or word. In the English language there are considered to be *primary* or strong stress which international phonetic transcription would indicate by the mark (') placed in front of the stressed syllable or word;

secondary or light stress indicated by the mark (ˌ) placed in front of the stressed syllable or word; and zero or reduced stress which is generally not marked.

Two-syllable words generally have one primary stress. The exceptions to the rule are the double-stressed words which receive relatively equal stress on both syllables, such as the words in columns four and five. Read the following words aloud and consciously emphasize the stressed syllables.

a-'bout	fa-'cade	'no-tion	'em-'pire	'school-'house
de-'mand	'ha-bit	pa-'rade	'vi-'brate	'un-'known
'ea-ger	'may-be	re-'ward	'en-'core	'Ju-'ly
'guil-ty	ob-'serve	'u-nit	'broad-'cast	'dash-'board

'bla-tant 'com-ment	'stun-ning ef-'fect	'sin-gle 'en-try	'ear-thy 'hu-mor
'ne-ver con-'firmed	'ba-by 'gar-ment	'to-tal e-'clipse	'ea-ger de-'fense
com-'plete de-'fense	ig-'nore 'ru-mor	with-'out 'war-ning	de-'mand re-'ward
'qui-et 'um-'pire	'du-al 'en-'core	'hea-vy 'suit-'case	'Ju-'ly 'six-'teenth

Three-syllable words generally have one primary stress, as in the first two columns, or one primary and one secondary stress, as in the second two columns. Read the following words aloud and consciously emphasize the stressed syllables.

a-'ban-don	'he-mis-phere	ˌcon-de-'scend	'ex-tro-ˌvert
'bi-cy-cle	re-'por-ted	'va-ga-ˌbond	'yes-ter-ˌday
de-'fi-ance	'co-lum-nist	ˌquin-'tes-sence	ˌgi-'gan-tic
'e-di-fy	o-'pin-ions	'kins-ˌwo-man	ˌjam-bo-'ree

a-'ban-doned 're-si-dence	com-'mer-cial 'car-pen-ter	'ter-ri-ble 'ac-ci-dent
de-'ci-ded o-'pin-ions	'na-tion-al 'ca-pi-tol	'ju-ven-ile de-'lin-quent
ec-'sta-tic 'de-bu-ˌtante	ˌdog-'ma-tic pro-'fes-sor	'se-pa-rate 'he-mis-ˌphere
ˌfan-'tas-tic ca-'the-dral	'moun-tain-ous 'a-re-as	ca-'pri-cious be-'ha-vior

Four-syllable words generally have one primary stress, as in the first two columns, or one primary and one secondary stress, as in the second two columns. Read the following words aloud and consciously emphasize the stressed syllables.

a-ber-'ra-tion	'ra-tion-al-ize	'en-ter-ˌpri-sing	ˌsci-en-'ti-fic
be-'ne-vo-lent	tu-'to-ri-al	'dic-ta-tor-ˌship	ˌmag-'ni-fi-cent
ca-ta-'clys-mic	op-po-'si-tion	ˌin-'tel-li-gent	ˌha-bi-'ta-tion
de-'plo-ra-ble	'qua-la-ta-tive	ˌcom-pe-'ti-tion	ˌcon-'ser-va-tive

'fa-shio-na-ble   il-lus-'tration   'en-ter-,pri-sing   op-por-'tun-ist
'cham-pi-on-,ship   a-'bi-li-ty   me-'ti-cu-lous   ,sta-tis-'ti-cian
'ne-gli-gi-ble   ,dis-tri-'bu-tion   'cal-cu-,la-ted   du-'pli-ci-ty
,ab-so-'lute-ly   de-'plo-ra-ble   ,un-'oc-cu-pied   'dor-mi-to-ry

Five-syllable words, like three and four syllable words, generally have one primary stress, as in the first two columns, or one primary and one secondary stress, as in the third column. Read the following words aloud and consciously emphasize the stressed syllables.

a-'bo-mi-na-ble   fe-li-ci-'ta-tion   'dis-ci-pli-,na-ry
ca-pa-'bi-li-ty   op-por-'tu-ni-ty   ,un-'pre-ce-den-ted
de-ter-mi-'na-tion   re-'pu-di-a-ted   ,com-pre-'hen-si-ble
de-nun-ci-'a-tion   ma-'te-ri-a-lize   ,ec-cen-'tri-ci-ty

in-dis-'pu-ta-bly   dic-ta-'to-ri-al   un-'pre-ce-den-ted   fra-ter-ni-'za-tion
con-'si-de-ra-ble   de-li-be-'ra-tion   e-cu-'men-i-cal   col-lec-'ti-vi-ty
a-'bo-mi-na-ble   ac-com-mo-'da-tions   com-'pan-ion-a-ble   ,con-ser-'va-tion-ist
'dis-ci-pli-,na-ry   ca-pa-'bi-li-ty   ob-'jec-tion-a-ble   ,dis-cri-mi-'na-tion

It is not necessary to continue this study into six, seven, or eight syllable words — few play scripts contain these multisyllable words. However, it is necessary to begin a study of stress by practicing the emphasis of primary and secondary stressed syllables within words. Words are, after all, the basic units of phrases and sentences. Read the following sentences aloud and, wherever appropriate, use the initial consonants of syllables to aid you in emphasizing the primary and secondary stresses. Read each sentence aloud once at a deliberate pace, determining the stressed syllables and the vowels and consonants used in stressing the syllables. Be certain that you pronounce the subordinated syllables just as precisely, even though they are given less prominence. Then read the same sentence two or three more times, getting faster each time. This exercise will develop both your skill in stressing and your flexibility in articulation.

1. The deplorable documentation of the ecumenical editorials caused considerable emotionalism among the conscientious representatives.

2. Such claustrophobic aberrations are absolutely unprecedented and totally inexplicable.

3. Motivated by commendable felicitation, her benevolence and empathic consideration assuaged her rebellious constituency.

4. It was a creditable and astonishingly comprehensive study of the decentralization of decadent colonialism.

5. It is imperative to particularize a characteristically conservative conciliation immediately.

6. The commemorative proceedings were completely incomprehensible to the bewildered congregation.

7. The conspiratorial consortium completely underestimated the degree of bureaucratic entrenchment and departmentalization.

8. In addition to his incivility and avariciousness, he purposely cultivated a despicable degree of uncommunicativeness.

9. His compatibility, dependability, and competitiveness were substantiated by extensive uncontrovertible evidence.

10. The nondenominational organization was magnanimous in its distribution of the considerable inheritance from the octogenarian philanthropist.

11. The intellectual delegation evidenced enthusiasm for the edifying deliberations of the dispassionate diagnostician.

12. His effervescent egotism and fascinating eccentricities guaranteed his domination of the nonconformist conglomeration of individuals.

13. Her incalculable changeability and incorrigible kleptomania were insufferable and humiliating to her puritanical bibliographer.

14. The consolidation of the capitalistic bureaucracies accentuated the conspiratorial compulsions of the reactionaries.

15. The administration of the Commemorative Conservationist Corporation particularized their negotiations with the competitive Constituency for Enlightenment.

16. Such subversive commercialization suggests a misrepresentation that is characteristically incomprehensible.

17. The negotiator's nonintervention into the reprehensible machinations of the municipality was inexplicable and indefensible.

18. The manifestations of gravitation and electricity are known, but to know what gravitation and electricity are is to know the varied infinitude of eternity, inexhaustibility, and cosmical essence.

19. The entire phenomenal world is under the compulsion and inexorable sway of inherent, polarized opposite and contrasted principles.

20. The simple inadmissible and undignified prayers of the people were replaced by the monotony of canonical invocations and intellectual petitions.

Individual sound stress can also be significant in intelligibility. Our inability to distinguish one word from another or to grasp the sense of a phrase is frequently due to some mispronunciation of a single sound. As previously stated, the primary function of sounds is to construct the words that define the ideas to be communicated. Speech sounds are properly applied to the purpose of projecting the meaning. As an exercise in sound discrimination, read the following sentences twice. Read them aloud, once with the first word enclosed in the parentheses, and again with the second word, and precisely distinguish between the two different sounds.

1. You cannot (taunt/daunt) me.
2. That couple has no (poise/boys).
3. The (coat/goat) was in the yard.
4. The child would not go near the (store/shore).
5. We expect a (reference/reverence) for the minister.
6. She (wondered/wandered) about the house.
7. She covered her (knees/niece) with a blanket.
8. I insist that they are not (sheep/cheap).
9. He has a small (mouth/mouse).
10. They praised the (wine/vine).
11. (Either/ether) was acceptable to the patient.
12. Let's do some (writing/riding) today.
13. She liked his (chin/gin).
14. He was told to (wash/watch) the dog.
15. She was upset by her father's (death/debt).
16. There were no (bricks/breaks) in the wall.
17. They (bought/fought) him off.
18. The (vat/fat) was in the fire.
19. The English (team/theme) was amusing.
20. She (mothered/muttered) strange things.

For purposes of sharpening listening ability as well as sound discrimination, the above exercise is effective done with two people, or even with a group. Participants will turn so that their backs are to each other so that lips cannot be read. In the interests of projecting in a large theater, it is also advisable for participants to be separated as much as possible, with one person or one group of people at each end of the room. One person will then read the first sentence twice, using the two different words, and a person will then repeat them as he thought he heard them, and then ask if he heard correctly. For instance, the person repeating the sentences could say, "You said 'You cannot taunt me' and 'You cannot daunt me.' Is that correct?" This procedure is continued until each member of the group has had a turn at reading the initial two sentences and at repeating them. Everyone participating has to listen very attentively. And, of course, the two contrasting words do not have to be read in the order in which they appear on the page. In fact, if everyone has a copy of the sentences in hand it should be understood that they may not be read in the order written.

It is, of course, understood that most of our comprehension of meaning comes from the context in which individual words are used. But it is not at all uncommon for one mispronounced sound to obscure the meaning of an entire thought unit, so that increasing the precision with which we pronounce individual sounds can be a useful experience.

The actor's problems with stress vary from not stressing enough to stressing too much. The actor who does not use enough stress sounds like a monotonous drone as he forges ahead with no variations in pitch, volume, or rate. The actor who stresses too much sounds like a peevish boor as he hammers away at every word. Both types of speech are barriers to intelligibility. If every word gets the same emphasis, be it too little or too much, then none of the words stands out.

Improper use of stress may be due to any one or any combination of the following reasons.

1. The speaker may not have studied the text sufficiently to really understand what he is saying, or why he is saying it.

2. The speaker's delivery may be dominated by habitual idiosyncratic tune patterns which do not support the textual patterns and, therefore, obscure meaning.

3. The sense of the lines may be completely obliterated by the raucous clamor of underlying passion.

4. The speaker may be simply reciting memorized lines without actively recreating them in the mind—much as most people recite the Pledge of Allegiance to the flag or the Lord's Prayer.

All of these factors need consideration, as does the actual performance of stressing. The act of stressing too often has a curious up-and-down motion, a bludgeoning effect which causes speakers to come down so heavily on words that they literally drive them right into the floor. This means that they are constantly stopping and starting, stopping and starting, like a mid-city bus. And, like the mid-city bus, such speakers move forward very slowly. There's another similarity which can be drawn from the bus analogy; the similarity being that every time the bus stops and has to labor for a fresh start, the accompanying traffic moves off and leaves the bus behind. Likewise, every time a speaker stops and has to labor for a fresh start, the attending audience moves off to its individual thoughts and leaves the speaker behind. In both cases, contact is lost. In the speaker-audience situation this means a loss in communication, and that the speaker has been completely ineffective.

Words are not external objects that have to be hammered down out of the way before forward progress can be made. Words are the evocation of inner images; they are a pervading substance in which we exist and through which we express the self. Expressing means to reveal, to let the self out into words. The words on the page are nothing in themselves. We animate the words by involving ourselves with their dramatic values. Stressing should be thought of as a way of breathing and feeling words, of experiencing the rhythm of the text. Stressing is adding persuasive buoyancy to words; it is a heightened awareness of the power of words. Stressing means emphasizing the important words; it also means maintaining the drive to where these places of meaning are.

Within every phrase are key words which must be given emphasis since they carry the meaning. The term "key" will be used throughout, since it is, by Webster's definition, "something that completes or holds together the parts of another thing — a controlling, or essential thing that explains or solves something else." Not every word in a phrase is a key word. There are nearly always some words in a phrase that are more important than others, that are key words, and should be stressed. The most important words are generally the nouns, verbs, demonstrative pronouns, adjectives, and adverbs. The words of lesser importance, and therefore not stressed, are generally those which serve as connecting links between the key words — the articles, conjunctions, auxiliary verbs, prepositions, and personal pronouns. It is impossible, however, to set down an absolute rule on this. Any word can be important which supplies needed information. For instance, the following six-word sentence could have six different meanings, depending on which word is stressed:

I have a letter from Helen.

As the sentence stands, the meaning is clear. The six words used are simple, familiar, and therefore easily understood. Read the sentence aloud, without any strong emphasis, and be aware of the meaning you are communicating. Now read aloud the following six variations and be aware of the different meanings.

- *I* have a letter from Helen. (Helen wrote to you, not someone else.)

- I *have* a letter from Helen. (In spite of what someone else says, you do have a letter from Helen.)
- I have *a* letter from Helen. (You have one letter, not more.)
- I have a *letter* from Helen. (You have a letter, not a postcard or package.)
- I have a letter *from* Helen. (The letter you have is from Helen, not one you have written to her.)
- I have a letter from *Helen*. (The letter is from Helen, not someone else.)

When you read the sentence aloud for the first time, you probably gave slight stresses to "letter" and "Helen," since they are the key words that carry the meaning in the original sentence. And, generally speaking, nouns are important and should be stressed, since they name the things that are talked about. If the nouns "letter" and "Helen" were removed from the sentence, it would be meaningless.

In reading the sentence aloud the first time, you probably did not stress the personal pronoun "I," the auxiliary verb "have," the article "a," and the preposition "from." And you would have been quite correct, for these words are not normally stressed. In fact, the first three words, "I have a," could be removed from the sentence and the meaning could still be communicated with the remaining three words "letter from Helen" and *any word that can be removed without interfering with the meaning does not need stress*. Using the proper vocal inflections, you could probably communicate the message with just the two words "letter . . . Helen." This is what is known as "telegraphing" the message, sending just the important words. It's rather like the "Me Tarzan, you Jane" phenomenon. The same thing happens when you speak entire sentences, in that you telegraph the key words, and the less important words are treated as a pathway of syllables to get you to the key words.

To gain fluency in speaking, it is of value to find the weak words in the script and practice subordinating them. Following are categories of words not generally stressed. Read the sentences aloud, stressing the important words and de-emphasizing the weak words, and never losing your drive to stress the words of meaning.

Articles (a, an, the)

It was a good book.	He's an old man.	Give him an apple.
She ate an orange.	Put it on the table.	Did you peel the potatoes?

| He got the part. | Give me a peach. | It was an awful experience. |
| Take a chance. | Have a good time. | Who took the paint? |

Auxiliary Verbs (am, are, can, could, do, does, had, has, have, must, shall, should, was, were, will, would—all verbs that help form tenses, aspects, moods, or voices of other verbs)

I am going home.	When do we leave?	You must have known.
We are rehearsing.	Does she care?	You should tell him.
He can write plays.	He had already gone.	They would arrive late.
She could go tonight.	He has practiced.	I would like to go.

Conjunctions (and, as, but, or, nor, if, when, because, though, either, than, that)

We ate bacon and eggs.	Come early if you can.	He had more than we did.
It was almost as good.	I left when he did.	He told of all that he did.
I want to but I can't.	He went because she did.	Neither he nor I want it.
Either Tom or Bob will go.	It was nice, though expen-sive.	Take only one or two.

Prepositions (at, by, for, from, into, of, to, with, under, about, over, in)

They are not at home.	Put it in the box.	She stood under the tree.
She traveled by boat.	It's the best of the lot.	He didn't care about Tim.
He stayed for a week.	Give it to the children.	Tell us about your trip.
I had a letter from Pat.	He went along with Bob.	Hang it over the mantle.

Pronouns (I, me, he, her, him, his, she, some, that, them, us, we, you, your)

Tell me about it.	She held his hand.	He gave us our cue.
Where did he go?	He gave some to Eva.	We will go by bus.
He gave her the box.	He knew his lines.	Have you eaten yet?
Tell him to be quiet.	Give them to Alice.	You dropped your pen.

The lists of words following each category are not all inclusive. There are others. This particular consideration of generally unstressed words was done to make you aware that the factor of stressing has two sides, equally important. Just as you must learn to give more prominence to key words, so you must learn to give less prominence to the words that connect the key words. The connecting words must not be slurred or run together so that they become unintelligible, but they must be given less space so that the key words will stand out.

As previously stated, key words are generally nouns, which name the things talked about, and verbs, which express the action, occurrence, or existence. Adjectives, which describe nouns, and adverbs, which modify verbs and other modifiers, can also be significant and require stress. All of the key words are italicized in the following selections. Read the selections aloud and stress the italicized words.

SHYLOCK: He hath *disgraced* me, and *hindered* me *half a million*, *laughed* at my *losses, mocked* at my *gains, scorned* my *nation, thwarted* my *bargains, cooled* my *friends, heated* mine *enemies*. And *what's* his *reason?* I am a *Jew.* Hath not a Jew *eyes?* Hath not a Jew *hands, organs, dimensions, senses, affections, passions? Fed* with the same *food, hurt* with the same *weapons, subject* to the same *diseases, healed* by the same *means, warmed* and *cooled* by the same *winter* and *summer* as a *Christian* is? If you *prick* us, do we not *bleed?* If you *tickle* us, do we not *laugh?* If you *poison* us, do we not *die?* And if you *wrong* us, shall we not *revenge?* If we are like you in the *rest,* we will resemble you in *that.*   (*Merchant of Venice,* III, i)

In the above lines of Shylock, the meaning is expressed almost entirely by nouns and verbs. In the last four lines, the key words are predominantly verbs. Other than nouns and verbs, there are only two italicized pronouns, "what" in line four and "that" in the last line. The predominant use of nouns and verbs to communicate the meaning, particularly with their strong sensory content, make this a direct and powerful speech. That other types of words, such as adjectives, adverbs, and pronouns, can be just as important in expressing meaning is evident in the following lines.

IAGO: Oh, sir, *content* you,
I *follow* him to *serve* my *turn* upon him.
We *cannot all* be *masters,* nor *all masters*
Cannot be *truly served.*   (*Othello,* I, i)

MIRANDA: *Why speaks* my father so *ungently? This*
Is the *third man* that e'er I *saw,* the *first*
That e'er I *sighed* for.   (*The Tempest,* I, ii)

CAMILLO: Good, my *lord,* be *cured*
Of this *diseased opinion,* and *betimes,*
For 'tis *most dangerous.*   (*Winter's Tale,* I, ii)

In the speech of Iago, the thrust of the meaning is clearly expressed by the nouns and verbs, but the clever use of "all," first as pronoun and then as adjective, and the adverb "truly" add a great deal to the meaning, particularly as they reflect the devious character of Iago.

In the speech of Miranda, the adverbs "why" and "ungently," the pronoun "this," and the adjectives "third" and "first" are equally as important in communicating the meaning as are the noun and three verbs. That Miranda can speak so directly to her father is a clear indication of their relationship.

In the speech of Camillo, the verb and two nouns once again tell us the subject and the action that Camillo feels should be followed in relation to that subject, but the meaning is made more emphatic by the key adjectives "diseased" and "dangerous" and the adverbs "betimes" and "most." And, once again, that Camillo feels free to speak so emphatically to his lord is an indication of their relationship.

Clearly, any type of word can be significant to the meaning. While we have been told that such words as adjectives and adverbs are modifiers, that they merely define, qualify, or supplement, and therefore should not be stressed, there is a more important rule for the speaker, however, and it is related to the sense, the import, and the significance. On the basis of this rule, we are required to stress important ideas, feelings, images, nuances, and actions, in whatever type of word they are contained. Such words must be clearly set apart and balanced with the subordinated context that supports them.

Bases for Stress

We have repeatedly stated that the reason for stressing is to clarify meaning. We need now to consider the word "meaning" and why we stress what we do. We need to understand why we stress a noun, verb, adjective or adverb, a pronoun, and sometimes even an article or conjunction. There are several bases of meaning.

The first basis of stressing for meaning, and probably the most common, is related to new information. In telling someone, "I went into the city yesterday morning, did some shopping, met a friend, had lunch, went to a concert, came home, had dinner, and read until bedtime," you are continually furnishing new bits of information. And, if you listen to conversations going on around you, this is the way the majority of them come off. "She did this," "We did that," "He said this," "I said that," and other such utterances make up the bulk of most people's conversation.

As Mrs. Page says to Mrs. Ford in *The Merry Wives of Windsor,* "Let's appoint him a meeting, give him a show of comfort in his suit, and lead him on with a fine-baited delay till he hath pawned his horses to mine host of the Garter." Or consider Petruchio's words to Kate, "Marry, so I mean, sweet Katherine, in thy bed. And therefore, setting all this chat aside, Thus in plain terms: Your father hath consented That you shall be my wife, your dowry 'greed on, And, will you, nill you, I will marry you." Or look again at the three speeches of Iago, Miranda, and Camillo.

In all instances, the meaning that is stressed is related to new ideas. The flow of sense is established as one thought follows another. There is only one exception to this principle and that is when Petruchio says first, "Marry, so I mean, sweet Katherine, in thy bed," and then concludes with "I will marry you." While the word "marry" is recognized as an Elizabethan oath, it is also a repetitive play on words in this instance.

This exception is classified as repetition, is not new information, and repetitions are generally not stressed. The only reason for stressing old information is if the speaker wants to emphasize an idea. I have heard the repetition "I will marry you" handled both ways. One actor gave only light stress to the opening idea, "Marry, so I mean, sweet Katherine, in thy bed," and gave heavy stress to the repetition, "I will marry you." The other actor completely reversed the stresses, emphasizing heavily the first statement of the idea and lightly tossing off the repetition. Unless it is for purposes of making an idea more emphatic, old information is not stressed, for the reason that stressing old information can fog the clarity of new information.

In the following speeches from *The Merchant of Venice,* Act V, sc. i, the principle of stressing new information can be demonstrated very clearly. Gratiano volunteers the information that "My lord Bassanio gave his ring away Unto the judge that begged it," to which Portia replies, "What ring gave you, my lord? Not that, I hope, which you received of me," and these speeches follow.

BASSANIO: Sweet Portia,
            If *you* did *know* to *whom* I gave the ring,
            If you did know *for* whom I gave the ring,
            And would conceive for *what* I gave the ring,
            And how *unwillingly* I *left* the ring,
            When *naught* would be *accepted but* the ring,
            You would *abate* the *strength* of your *displeasure.*

PORTIA: If *you* had *known* the *virtue* of the ring,
            Or *half her worthiness* that *gave* the ring,
            Or *your own honor* to *contain* the ring,
            You would *not* then have *parted* with the ring.

Since we already know that the object under discussion is a ring, and that Bassanio gave it to someone, these are both old information. The new ideas in Bassanio's speech are that if Portia knew the facts about the case she wouldn't be upset; and the facts include knowing:

• to *whom* (The ring was given to a specific person, and the tendency to stress the "to" must be resisted; this usually happens as a result of anticipating the "for" in the next line, but that is not the way people speak — ideas occur in the mind one at a time.)

• *for whom* (The ring was given to the judge for saving Bassanio's friend, Antonio, designated by the second *whom;* and the "for" is stressed, since it is not only new information, but is in contrast to the "to" in the first line.)

• *what* (The ring was given for a reason.)

• *how unwillingly* . . . *left* (The ring was parted with against his will, and *left* provides the new information that Bassanio was distressed by having to leave the ring behind.)

• *naught* . . . *accepted but* (Providing the new information that it was only the ring that was acceptable to the judge.)

• *abate* . . . *strength* . . . *displeasure* (If Portia knew all the foregoing facts she would calm down.)

In Portia's answer to Bassanio, the subject under discussion is still the ring that he gave away, and Portia's new ideas on the subject include:

• *you* . . . *known* . . . *virtue* ("You" has a double emphasis here. First of all, there is the connotation of "you talk about *my* not knowing, how about *you*"; and then there is the echoing of Bassanio's phrase "you . . . know," which has a mocking quality. Then we have the new information that the ring has virtue.)

• *half her worthiness* . . . *gave* (The "gave" is stressed here since it designates a different context and a different giver, and the giver introduces the new idea that she is not properly appreciated.)

• *your own honor* . . . *contain* (New idea being that Bassanio's own honor should have made him keep the ring.)

• *not . . . parted* (And the obvious point of all Portia's thoughts, that the virtue of the ring, her worthiness, and Bassanio's honor, should have prevented him from giving the ring away.)

Study these speeches for purposes of stressing new information and subordinating old information. The speeches also further indicate that pronouns, prepositions, and adverbs, generally not considered to be stress words, may indeed provide new information that must be emphasized.

A second basis of stressing for meaning is related to *cause and effect*. If this happens — then that will happen. If she does that — then I will do this. One action can trigger the occurrence of another. We have one example of the cause and effect stressing in the speech of Shylock, when he says:

If you *prick* us, do we not *bleed?* If you *tickle* us, do we not *laugh?* If you *poison* us, do we not *die?* And if you *wrong* us shall we not *revenge?*

Another speech that illustrates this type of stressing to project the meaning of cause and effect, is that of Petruchio, when he says of Kate:

> Say that she rail; why, then I'll tell her plain
> She sings as sweetly as a nightingale.
> Say that she frown; I'll say she looks as clear
> As morning roses newly washed with dew.
> Say she be mute and will not speak a word;
> Then I'll commend her volubility
> And say she uttereth piercing eloquence.
> If she do bid me pack, I'll give her thanks
> As though she bid me stay by her a week.
> If she deny to wed, I'll crave the day
> When I shall ask the banns and when be married.   (II, i)

Stressing such cause and effect phrases is an interesting cause and effect phenomenon in itself, for the act of stressing in this instance tends to impose its own rhythm. This is particularly true when the sequence of ideas is set down as parallel structures, as in the speech of Shylock. Particular care has to be taken with such structures so that they aren't delivered in repetitive singsong patterns. These singsong patterns can become very monotonous and can call attention to themselves instead of reinforcing the sense of the words.

This problem of repetitive structures is skillfully avoided in the Petruchio speech. The cause and effect sequences have the variety of the structure of the first two lines being repeated only once in the second two lines. The third cause and effect structure is longer, using three lines; and the fourth structure is varied again, in that the initial "If she" statement uses three metered feet in contrast to the two metered feet of the "say that" statements. Also, the fourth structure is repeated only once.

A third basis of stressing for meaning that must be considered is that of *contrast*. To stress contrasts is to point out differences when a person or thing is compared with another. We find such a contrast in Marc Antony's words, "Not Caesar's valor hath o'erthrown Antony, But Antony's hath triumphed on itself." Or consider the following two lines from *Hamlet:*

HORATIO: My lord, I come to see your father's funeral.
HAMLET: I pray thee do not mock me, fellow student. I think it was to
           see my mother's wedding.

A speech that is filled with provocative contrasting ideas is the following of Angelo, from *Measure for Measure.*

What's this, what's this? Is this *her fault* or *mine?*
The *tempter* or the *tempted,* who sins most?
Ha!
Not *she,* nor doth she tempt. But it is *I*
That, lying by the violet in the sun,
Do as the *carrion* does, not as the *flower,*
Corrupt with virtuous season. Can it be
That *modesty* may more betray our sense
Than *woman's lightness?* Having *waste ground* enough,
Shall we desire to raze the *sanctuary,*
And pitch our evils there? Oh, fie, fie, fie!
What *dost* thou, or what *art* thou, Angelo?
Dost thou desire her *foully* for those things
That make her *good?* Oh, let her brother live.
Thieves for their robbery have authority
When *judges* steal themselves. What, do I love her,
That I desire to hear her speak again
And feast upon her eyes? What is't I dream on?
O cunning enemy, that to *catch* a saint
With saints dost *bait* thy hook! Most dangerous
Is that temptation that doth goad us on
To sin in loving virtue. Never could the *strumpet,*
With all her double vigor, art and nature,
Once stir my temper, but this *virtuous maid*
Subdues me quite. Ever till now,
When *men* were fond, *I* smiled, and wondered how.   (II, ii)

There are twelve contrasting concepts and images at work in this speech: her fault–mine, tempter–tempted, she–I, carrion–flower, modesty–woman's lightness, waste ground–sanctuary, dost–art, foully – good, thieves–judges, catch–bait, strumpet–virtuous maid, men–I.

This pattern of speaking in contrasting structures is, of course, supportive of Angelo's role as judge. It is also supportive of the theme of the play and is found in the speeches of other characters, notably Isabella. The pattern generally indicates an educated, logical mind, one who can objectively see both sides of an argument or an issue and weigh the evidence.

In the act of stressing contrasting structures there is a similarity to cause and effect stressing, in that both tend to impose their own rhythmic patterns. If these are handled skillfully, however, and the writing is good, as with both the Petruchio and Angelo speeches, the rhythms serve to reinforce the stress and, therefore, the sense.

How to Stress

In the preceding pages, we have discussed the importance of stressing individual sounds, syllables, words, and phrases. We have also discussed reasons for stressing: new information, repetition, cause and effect, and contrast. We need now to consider the means of stressing, the techniques of emphasizing and subordinating key words and ideas.

VOLUME AND INTENSITY

You will probably have noticed in reading aloud the preceding lines and speeches, that when you stressed a word or phrase you made it louder by increasing its force and intensity. You increased the volume, in other words. We have already discussed volume in the chapters on breathing and voice production and you are aware of its importance in acting. First and foremost, an actor must be heard. If words are inaudible, there is absolutely no point at all in stressing them or grouping them into phrases. Any and all techniques are wasted if the audience cannot hear what you are saying. Volume is essential to basic audibility.

Variations in volume are also essential to express the meaning of words. By using slight increases of volume, or what I prefer to call slight intensifications of mental, physical, and emotional energy, you were able to make key words more prominent. And while it was not volume alone that made the words more emphatic, we must discuss it in isolation to be certain that we understand it.

Adequate volume depends entirely on adequate breath support. For words to be heard and their sense expressed, the breathing process must be full, deep, and firmly under control. The fundamentals of good breath support should be reviewed at this point and integrated with your work on stressing. Full, deep breathing means that the lungs need room in which to fully and comfortably expand. This expansion is dependent on an upright posture and breathing muscles that are free of excess tension. Sustained audibility and intensifications of meaning need controlled exhalations. These exhalations are dependent on flexible, toned, properly trained muscles. In proper stressing it is breathing that does the work.

Words are not stressed by being struck over the head from above. Stressing must be thought of as getting under a word and lifting it, or as a slight swell of energy. In fact, if your director ever tells you that he can't hear you, don't think "louder," instead think "wider and deeper." Think of increasing the fullness and intensity of your words. It helps here to use the image of the iceberg, which, we are told, exposes only one-eighth of its content above the water, there being seven-eighths of the iceberg below the surface that we do not see. It is certainly psychologically sound to see your self as having great vocal power in reserve, and this image of the reserve power deep inside you helps to keep the breath full and deeply centered as well as keeping you organically connected to your words.

Part of the energy of stressing is also dependent on how fully the words are resonated. Before proceeding further, you should reread the chapters on breathing and voice production. You should make certain that the body and facial posture are allowing for a fully resonated voice, that the body muscles are supporting your breathing, and the facial and throat muscles are amplifying your resonated tone. To achieve a fully supported, fully resonated voice, redo some of the exercises until you experience your total self as voice, until your voice seems to be flowing from and through every part of your body.

And now combine the energy of the breathing, resonating voice with that of stressing. Use any of the individual lines or speeches from this chapter or others and consciously increase the volume of key words and key phrases. Consciously intensify the meaning of the thought and emotion of key words and phrases with slight pulses or swells of energy. Feel that all of you is involved in expressing the sense of what you are saying.

As a visible test of your ability to employ slight intensifications of meaning, as well as your ability to sustain entire phrases, hold a lighted candle in front of your mouth. And as you increase the volume of key words and phrases, watch the movement of the candle flame. The added intensity of stressing the important words and sense-groups will bend the flame much farther forward than the weaker stress of unimportant words and phrases.

You can also use the candle in increasing your skill in employing volume for stress by simply counting numbers, and emphasizing every third or fourth number as if it were a key word.

Rereading the polysyllabic words and sentences while holding the candle in front of your mouth is also helpful. You can actually see the volume being exerted on stressing primary and secondary stressed syllables.

As you do the exercises, remember that it is the variation of loudness that conveys meaning, by making key words stand out from their supporting context, and by focusing attention on key phrases and connecting the key phrases that communicate the main ideas.

Sound Duration

Volume does not, of course, work as an isolated factor in stressing words. In addition to increasing your volume on stressed words, you are probably also aware that you are giving these words more space by holding onto them longer than the unimportant words. Or, to be more specific, you are holding onto certain sounds within the words. After determining from the meaning the basic reason for stressing a word, it becomes necessary then to determine which sound or sounds can be held without distorting the word.

For instance, in a word like *complacent,* in which the second syllable is stressed, it is clearly the diphthong [eɪ] that is prolonged. None of the other sounds which precede or follow the [eɪ] could be held without distorting the word and possibly making it and its context unintelligible. In a word such as *hungry,* one would sustain the vowel [ʌ] and the nasal consonant [ŋ] that follows. In a word such as *wealthy,* one would sustain the vowel [ɛ] and the continuant consonant [l] that follows. The three nasal sounds [m-n-ŋ] and the [l] are all continuant consonants, sometimes called semivowels.

The sounds that are the easiest to sustain are the diphthongs [eɪ–aɪ– ɔɪ – oʊ – aʊ], the long vowels [u – ɔ – ɑ – i – æ – a], the nasal continuants [m–n–ŋ] and the glide [l]. Theoretically all vowel sounds are capable of being lengthened or shortened, but the short, neutral vowels [ʊ–ɒ–ʌ–ɝ–ɪ–ɛ] do not adapt to sustention as easily as do the long vowels and diphthongs. The plosives [p–b–t–d–k–g] and the affricates [tʃ–dʒ] cannot be sustained at all. The fricative consonants [f–v–θ– ð–s–z–ʃ–ʒ–h] can be prolonged — in fact they tend to resist rapid delivery — but are generally prolonged only to support a mood or intention, as when Hamlet condemns his mother's hasty marriage to his uncle in the line, "O, most wicked speed, to post With such dexterity to incestuous sheets!" Shakespeare has supplied Hamlet with ten fricative sounds and two affricate sounds in this line, to enable him to fully express his scathing appraisal. The two remaining glide sounds [j] and [w] are almost impossible to sustain; in fact, following the initial positioning for the two sounds, they do exactly as the name implies and glide immediately into a following vowel. The [r] behaves the same way except when it occurs in a final position. [w] and [j] never occur in a final position.

In stressing a word then, we not only use an increase in volume, we use duration of specific sounds. Lengthening sounds is another means of emphasizing the sense of the words. It is also a way of expressing emotional content, as in the above line of Hamlet. A sensitive actor is fully aware of the dramatic value of lengthening, and sometimes compressing, specific sounds, and he uses this technique to effectively express the emotional content of his subtext. A good writer, such as Shakespeare, uses words, not only for their value of meaning, but for the theatrical value of their sounds.

The proper use of sound duration should be developed and used. It is a skill that effectively stresses words by giving them dramatic values. It is a device that provides a channel for the audible expression of meaning and emotion. It is an art that is an integral part of the delivery technique of any first-rate actor.

As you continue working with your candle and speaking aloud some of the speeches in the book, or something of your own if you prefer, combine the two elements of volume and sound duration in stressing key words and phrases. Think of the stressing process more and more, however, as intensifications of intellectual meaning, as pulses of emotional energy. As you hold onto specific sounds let your self experience their resonances and vibrations, let your self feel and taste the sounds in your mouth. Make them yours.

Pitch

There is, of course, another important factor of stress and that is pitch. When you were concentrating on the factor of volume, you were probably aware that you were also elevating your pitch. As it happens, these two factors seem to swing into effect simultaneously. This effect can be perfectly fine for most purposes of stressing. For in raising the pitch of a key word we are also emphasizing its prominence of meaning.

There are, however, such instances as when a director says, "Louder. We can't hear you!" that a substantial increase in volume will elevate pitch to such a height that entire speeches become thin, shrill, and extremely unpleasant to listen to. Since this act is usually accompanied by excessive tension, they can also become unintelligible. So it greatly benefits an actor's delivery to practice the exercise of slowly increasing volume without increasing pitch. This exercise was discussed in the section on phonation, and should be restudied and practiced. There is neither beauty nor dramatic power in a strident, tense voice.

We are referring here to the slight elevations of pitch used in most stressing. The word "most" is used intentionally, because a word can also be emphasized by suddenly dropping it in pitch. These up and down pitch changes in speaking are known as *steps,* and could be compared to a pattern of notes in a piece of music. In point of fact, the singer, who has his melody pattern all set out for him has a much easier life than the actor, who has to find his pattern within the meaning.

Take, for example, the line, "It is the East and Juliet is the sun!" Different meanings expressed in differing melody patterns might be set down as follows.

```
                                                              sun.
                                 Juliet
                East                            is      the
           the               and
      is
It
                                                              sun.


                East            Juliet    is    the
It         the               and
      is


                East                            is    the
           the               Juliet
      is                  and
It                                                          sun.
```

English is an emphatic language and almost all intelligible speech uses slight changes in pitch to stress the key words. There is only one exception to this practice and that is the deliberate use of a monotonic pitch pat tern to reinforce a mood. One such example would be Ophelia's speech in the third act of *Hamlet*. This is generally delivered as a lament; the key words are set apart primarily by the factor of giving them more space than the subordinate words, and there are few, if any, pitch steps.

> Oh, what a noble mind is here o'erthrown!
> The courtier's, soldier's, scholar's, eye, tongue, sword —
> The expectancy and rose of the fair state,
> The glass of fashion and the mold of form,
> The observed of all observers — quite, quite down!
> And I, of ladies most deject and wretched,
> That sucked the honey of his music vows,
> Now see that noble and most sovereign reason,
> Like sweet bells jangled, out of tune and harsh,
> That unmatched form and feature of blown youth
> Blasted with ecstasy. Oh, woe is me,
> To have seen what I have seen, see what I see!   (III, ii)

This speech, as we say, is truly a lament. To deliver these words in great bursts of wide-ranging pitches would belie the deep grief of Ophelia in this scene. It is generally delivered as one long, sustained "wo-o-o-oe" and this mood is supported by long, sustained vowel sounds, nasals, and glides.

The speeches of Hamlet's father's ghost also are spoken with long, sustained sounds, using duration for stressing key words, and few pitch changes, to suggest the hollow, sepulchral voice from the grave. Also, the Macbeth speech, "Tomorrow, and tomorrow, and tomorrow," set down earlier in the chapter uses a more monotonic delivery to suggest the character's intense weariness and emotional drain. And, of course, some of the more hollow characters in modern plays, particularly those in the Theater of the Absurd, express their emptiness generally in a monotonic delivery.

These instances of using a monotonic pitch pattern, particularly among trained speakers, are uncommon. They are the exception rather than the rule, and are usually the result of a deliberate choice. Good, intelligible speech employs pitch changes.

These pitch changes, classified as steps, can also fall into a monotonic pattern if the speaker elevates every stress word to the same pitch level. Such patterns usually are the result of speaking lines just from the memory level, lines that are not actively recreated and experienced as they are being spoken. This type of delivery is sound without sense and can quickly lose an audience. The same principle applies to someone reading aloud from a prepared script, such as a news broadcaster. When the words go from the printed page to the mouth, completely by-passing the active thought process, they are dull indeed. We hear words, but no thoughts.

It is equally as detrimental to communication when a speaker deliberately employs a varied pitch pattern just for an effect. This calls attention to itself rather than to the ideas, and once again we are hearing sound without sense. Pitch variety must be based on meaning. A speaker should extend his pitch range and increase his familiarity with pitch patterns apart from meaning, much as a singer practices arpeggios and other musical intervals, and increasingly find inner justifications on which to base them.

The potential extent of an individual's pitch range is determined by the physical structure of the larynx, particularly by the length, thickness, and tension of the vocal folds. These same features also determine the habitual pitch level at which people speak. We are defining a person's habitual pitch level when we say, "She has a low voice," or "He has a high voice." In both of these instances what we might also be indicating is that the person's habitual pitch level is not the best one for him or her. A person's habitual pitch level may not be his optimum pitch level, which is generally defined as "the production of maximum voice for a minimum of effort." If, for instance, a woman has an unusually low voice, it may be that she is forcing it down unnaturally, and this effort can have a harmful effect on the vocal folds, causing inflammation and even tiny lesions that become nodules. Any such misuse of the vocal folds, be it forcing the pitch level down or pushing it up for extended periods of shouting, may be attempts to go above or below one's normal range, and the imposed strain on the vocal folds can be damaging.

For a man to have an unusually high voice, however, is probably due to a different cause. Since men generally don't want a high voice, we may assume that an unnaturally high voice in our hypothetical man may be due to one of the following reasons.

Since an individual's habitual pitch, like that of his pitch range, is primarily determined by the length, thickness, and tension of the vocal folds, it is possible that our hypothetical man has unnaturally short, thin vocal folds. A second reason might be due to the fact that an individual learns to speak by imitating the first voices he hears, and our man may have been born into a home where he heard nothing but women's voices. A third reason might be that our hypothetical man is a very tense individual, since pitch is also largely determined by an individual's attitudes and tensions.

There are methods by which a trained speech teacher can determine whether or not an individual is using his optimum pitch, but this text supports the position that if a vocal instrument is properly trained and freed of tension it will find its own best pitch level. This optimum conditioning requires daily application of the principles and exercises set down in this text, including those involving self-awareness, relaxation, proper breathing and voice production, and body and facial posture.

Assuming this conditioning, we may proceed with further understanding of pitch changes for purposes of emphasizing meaning. We have already defined these as *steps,* which describe the movement of the voice from one discreet pitch to another. Steps occur in going from word to word and from syllable to syllable, and must be distinguished from *inflections,* which are movements of the voice within words and syllables. One of the significant differences between these two factors is related to their usage.

The use and range of steps generally needs to be encouraged and developed. The use and range of inflections generally needs to be discouraged and limited. A speaker who inflects, or uses a gliding movement, on every stressed word creates problems for himself and for his listeners. He will not be able to clearly communicate what he is saying and his audience will not be able to understand him. *Gliding on words and syllables should be limited to the key word within each phrase and all other stressed words should be spoken on discreet pitches.* Trained British actors are best at this and your understanding of this particular factor of stage speech will be improved by listening to some of their recordings. American actors, especially those without a great deal of training, inflect far too many stressed words, sometimes all of them, and as a result are not nearly as intelligible as they could and should be. Inflections can best be understood by a more detailed discussion of intonation. You will remember that the category of intonation was introduced with the study of phrases, sometimes called intonation groups.

Intonation

Intonation is the overall melody pattern of speech and comprises both steps and inflections. In stressing key words and subordinating connecting words, the pitch of the voice is continually rising and falling in steps, much as it does in singing musical passages. These varying pitch changes produce melody contours that can be transcribed, not unlike our various examples of the line "It is the East, and Juliet is the sun!" Another example might be the commonly asked question, "Hello, how are you?" which could be transcribed:

•	✓	•	•	↖
Hel-lo		How	are	you

The above transcription also illustrates three of the basic intonations. The pitch curves upward on the second syllable of "hel-*lo*" in what is called a *rising intonation;* it curves downward on the word "you" in what is called a *fading intonation;* and it stays on one level tone on the first syllable of "*hel*-lo" and the words "how" and "are" in what is called a *level intonation*. Since the sustention of a level intonation for too long a time would become intoning or even singing, the speaking voice tends to inflect a long level intonation into a fourth intonation called the *circumflex intonation* (ʊ or Ω). As also indicated in our discussion of phrasing, every phrase, or intonation group, ends with a glide, or inflection, signifying whether the idea is complete or incomplete.

A rising intonation generally indicates that the speaker has not finished and that there is more to come. For example, in the sentence, "I'm going to New York, Pittsburgh, and Chicago" there would be a rising intonation on "York" and on the second syllable of "Pitts-*burgh*" since the idea is yet incomplete.

A falling intonation generally indicates completion of a thought and would therefore occur on the third syllable of "Chica-*go*" to end the sentence.

A level intonation also indicates continuation of a thought and would occur on the word "New," on the first syllable of the word "*Pitts*-burgh," and on the first two syllables of "*Chi-ca*-go." This intonation would also occur on all but the final word in a sequence of numbers, such as "1, 2, 3, 4, 5"; and on all but the final word in a list such as "bread, butter, milk, and eggs."

A circumflex intonation, as indicated above, also indicates that there is more to come. It is also used to lengthen a word or syllable when it is necessary to define a special meaning or a specific character trait. Sometimes there's more to meaning than just a straight statement of fact, and we may need to add subtlety, nuance, or innuendo with the circumflex. For example in the sentence, "No, I don't think so," a circumflex on the words "No" and "so" tells us something special about the speaker's feelings, suggesting possibly that the speaker is not quite certain about what he thinks.

Or consider Iago's words after acquiring Desdemona's handkerchief, "I will in Cassio's lodging lose this napkin, And let him [Othello] find it." A circumflex intonation on the word "lose" is most effective in expressing the devious nature of Iago, the subtle, cunning villain of *Othello*. Read the word aloud and let your self experience the innuendo of the circumflex intonation of the word "lose." Then read aloud some of Iago's speeches in which he plots his villainous actions and find other words to which you can apply this intonation of innuendo. Be aware, however, that this can be overdone. When used in this manner, the circumflex is effective only when used sparingly.

There is one more factor of these intonation glides at the end of phrases and sentences that should be considered and it relates to the often misconstrued use in questions. Not all questions end with a rising intonation. Those questions containing specific interrogative words generally end with a falling intonation, for example: How did you know? What is he doing? Why? Where is she? Other types of questions usually end with a rising intonation, for example: Has he gone? Did you get my letter? Would you like a drink? These are, of course, not rigid rules. They are general assumptions based on prevalent usage. Any one of the above questions might be spoken with the opposite final intonation from the one indicated, depending on the attitude or feelings of the person speaking. For instance, a calm, considerate person would probably say, "Will you close the door" with a rising intonation, and would probably also add the word "please." An authoritarian, uptight person might speak the same words with a falling intonation, making it more of a command. Intonation glides are an expression of the sense and emotion of meaning. This can be illustrated with variations of one word.

Say the word *well* in the following ways.

1. well (◞)–with a slight rising inflection, meaning "What do you want?"

2. well (◞)–with a wide rising inflection, meaning "Aren't you ever going to finish?"

3. well (◝)–with a slight falling inflection, meaning "The letter finally came."

4. well (◝)–with a wide falling inflection, meaning "I've inherited money!"

5. well (—)–with a level intonation, meaning "It's possible."

6. well (◡)–with a circumflex, meaning "I'm not really sure."

7. well (◠)–with a reverse circumflex, meaning "I got the leading role!"

Overall intonation, the melody patterns of speech, should sustain the rhythmic flow of the words and support their meaning. Pitch steps, inflections within words and syllables, and glides at the end of intonation groups should all be studied, understood, and appropriately used. The discreet shifts, gliding movements, and overall intonation patterns of the voice release the attitudes and emotions of the speaker and affect the feelings and understanding of the listeners. Together with volume and duration of sounds, they are the actor's tools for projecting the inner life of his words to the back row in the theater.

The actor must always keep in mind that projection involves a great many more factors than sheer loudness. Projection means degrees of volume certainly, but it also comprises the pitch and duration of stressed words, of meaningful intonation glides, of phrasing and pauses. An actor does not project by tensely forcing the voice out in a horizontal line of loud shouting. As Constantin Stanislavski writes in *Building a Character*,[8] "When you need power, pattern your voice and your inflection in a varied phonetic line from top to bottom, just the way you use chalk to draw all possible kinds of designs on a blackboard. When you need real power in your speech, forget about volume and remember your rising and falling inflections, and your pauses." These interpretive factors, together with resonance and articulation, can enable an actor to project a softly spoken line, even a stage whisper, so that it is heard and understood by everyone in the theater.

Projection is not only a multifaceted phenomenon, it is an intensified and enlarged phenomenon. Just as the actor must expand and concentrate his acting life, so must he expand and concentrate his audible expression of that acting life. Breathing, resonance, articulation, body and feeling life must be enlarged. Phrases, pauses, sound duration, volume, pitch, and intonation patterns must be enlarged and varied. And when all the various facets are working well and working together, the projected expression flows so easily and so generously that it becomes a voluptuous act of sensual gratification for both actor and audience. There is such a pleasurable feeling of luxury that the actor perceives himself as

---

[8]Stanislavski, *Building a Character*, pp. 140–41.

controlling and holding in, rather than pushing out. There is no perceivable effort in skillful projection. It is aesthetically satisfying to everyone in the theater and is the sum total of the actor's art.

Range

Another element of pitch that must be considered is range. Range is the full reach of pitches from high to low over which the voice moves, and is understood and effective. An actor with a well-trained voice will have a useful speaking range which approaches in some instances as much as two octaves. Speakers whose voices are considered to be especially effective will have a useful speaking range of an octave or more, and poor speakers whose voices are considered to be monotonous will confine their range within the limits of three or four, sometimes within the limits of two or three, pitch changes. An individual's optimum pitch, discussed earlier in this chapter, and defined as the pitch level at which a voice performs with optimum quality and power, is at the approximate midpoint of the lowest octave of the individual's total range — or about three or four pitch steps (whole notes) above the lowest pitch that can be comfortably sustained. You will know that you have gone below your bottom pitch limit if you produce a gravelly, gargling sound that is known as *vocal fry* or *glottal fry,* a name that derives from the fact that the sound also resembles the noise of something frying in a pan.

Average persons in everyday speaking use a limited range because it seems physically easier and because they have never been trained to do anything else. When such a speaker becomes enraged or otherwise impassioned, the voice is forced out horizontally and can be extremely harsh and unpleasant to hear. Instead of moving easily into a higher range, it becomes jammed within the speaker's limited range, and he tries to force it out with physical tension, particularly in the throat. The throat muscles, being constrictor muscles, usually contract and limit the range further. This unfortunate condition will never produce power; it can produce an uncomfortable muscular reaction.

A wider range is available that any professional speaker, and certainly an actor, must discover and be able to use. To do this, the voice must be physically and mentally freed, so that it will move easily over the full extent of the range. To be physically freed means that the movement of the voice is not inhibited by poor posture, unnecessary muscle tension, and improper breathing. This requires the practice of physical techniques and constant monitoring. To be mentally freed means that the movement of the voice is not limited by incorrect perceptions of what voice is and by limited expectations. This requires the practice of psychophysical techniques and imagination. The physical "how" of voice movement must be mastered, so that it is firmly imprinted and automatic, making it possible to forget the "how" and transcend it with the vocal imagination. Changing one's vocal perceptions and expectations is a process of discovery and expansion into the outer limits. Together these processes enable the actor to express the full range of emotions, the total humanity of any character.

Limited ranges, associated in the mind and ear with daily mundane feelings and events, are simply not adequate for heightened dramatic effects. The audible expression of intense rage, grief, or joy requires a fully developed range. Without a vocal range to equal and support emotional range, the tragic heroes and heroines of dramatic literature cannot be fully realized. King Lear, Othello, and Lady Macbeth are characters of wide-ranging emotions that can only be illuminated by resonant, wide-ranging voices.

The power of voice range must be opened up and extended and there is no better way to do this than by singing. The practice of proper singing techniques adds nothing but plus values to the speaking voice. First of all, these techniques are based on the same fundamental principles of: (1) the controlled, sustained flow of exhaled breath; (2) the full use of resonators, especially the head resonators, sometimes known as "filling the horn"; (3) the use of larger mouth and throat cavities; (4) the precise shaping of sounds and words with the articulators; (5) the use of a wide pitch range; (6) the variation of sound duration, which for the singer means holding whole notes longer than quarter or eighth notes, and for the speaker means sustaining key words longer than connecting words; (7) the variation of pitch steps in the melody pattern; (8) the linking of phrases and the use of pauses; and (9) the support and sustention of the "last words" in a phrase.

It is surprising that so few singers have applied these fundamentals to their speaking voices. This author has listened with pleasure to the rich, resonant voice of a singer and too often been amazed at hearing that same singer speak. All of the above techniques stopped with the song.

In the following exercises, we will employ the techniques in singing and then, the significant part of the exercises for the actor, carry them over into speaking. Keep constantly in mind that the speaking voice as

much as the singing voice requires a full, supported voice filling the resonators, shaped by the articulators, and patterned into pitch intervals and
intonation groups.

Before beginning work on extending the voice range, it is essential that
the voice be physically freed of inhibiting muscle tension and that it be
supported by proper body and facial posture, full breathing, and resonance. Do not neglect this preparation. Go back in the book and work
over exercises for muscle relaxation, total respiration, posture, phonation, and resonation. Do such physically freeing exercises as jogging
while letting vocal sounds bounce easily from the top of your head to your
lower belly and back again; and then chew an *m* and feel the vocal sound
move around in the head resonators. Once this preparatory conditioning has been done you can then proceed to work on mentally freeing
the voice.

It is helpful to begin your study by experiencing just how wide your
available range is. Starting at F below Middle C on the piano, sing *la-
la-la* going up the scale as high as you can comfortably sustain the notes.
Then beginning at this highest pitch, sing *la-la-la* down the scale as low
as you can comfortably sustain the notes. Be certain to support the movements with full, controlled breathing. This should give you an idea of the
pitch range capability of your vocal folds. If you do not have a piano, get
your self a pitch pipe at a music store, and if you don't know music, have
someone explain its use. But get your self to a piano if you possibly can
and learn to drum out musical melodies and intervals with one finger.
This will be especially helpful in the following exercise.

Get a copy of a simple rhythm song such as "Hey, Look Me Over."
This type of song is written for both male and female chorus voices in
musicals, and is, therefore, pitched within a comfortable range for most
people. And it is important that you have the sheet music to help you see
the pitch steps as you sing them. Your mental perceptions of pitch intervals and range will begin to change once you begin to see them in the
mind's eye.

Work on one short musical phrase at a time; the first phrase in this song
being the title phrase, "Hey, look me over." Since singing the intervals
must lead to the important phase of speaking them, start with the first two
words, "Hey look." First sing "Hey," then speak it on the same pitch.
Then sing "look," and speak it on the same pitch. And stay with these two
words, repeating them again and again, until you have achieved an approximate spoken pitch for each sung pitch. Adding one word at a time,

next sing and speak the word "me," and when your spoken pitch has approximated your sung pitch, sing and then speak the three words, "Hey look me." Proceed in this fashion, adding one word or syllable at a time. Next add "o" and then add "ver," first singing and speaking them in isolation and then adding them to the phrase, until you can easily sing, then speak with an approximate pitch melody, the entire phrase, "Hey, look me over."

This is slow work and requires patient application. One phrase is all you may be able to master at the beginning. But one phrase at a time is perfectly fine; it tends to be the norm for most students. In subsequent work sessions, you can continue with the second phrase, "lend me an ear," the third phrase, "fresh out of clover," and the fourth phrase, "mortgaged up to here," and so on. To be able to approximate the sung pitches while speaking just one phrase is of greater value in your training than doing two or three phrases incorrectly.

In between your work sessions with a piano, keep the practice going. An aid to reinforcing the visualization of voice pitch movement is to use your forefinger and trace the melody pattern of pitches in the air in front of your eyes. Point to the pitch as you sing and speak it, then move the finger up or down and point to the following pitches. This helps you to see what your voice is doing. This slow, precise work may seem tedious at first, but it is well worth the time and effort. And once you begin to master the technique it will move along much faster.

The next exercise is best when done with a piano, but can be done without one if there is none available. You will be working with a musical scale of eight notes, the "do-re-mi-fa-sol-la-ti-do" sequence that starts on the key note and moves up the scale one octave; also with the arpeggio, "do-mi-sol-do." These are set down in the following two illustrations.

I   don't   want   to   go   with   you   now.

I   won't   go   now.

Also set down are the words, "I don't want to go with you now," and "I won't go now." You may use any eight or four words of your own if you prefer. You can begin by first singing and then speaking on approximate pitches the do-re-mi scale and the do-mi-sol-do arpeggio.

You then begin to work with the words in the same manner as in the previous exercise. Sing, then speak on the approximate pitch, the word "I," then sing and speak "don't," then sing and speak them together. Adding one word at a time in this way, keep on until you can speak the entire sentence on approximate pitch levels.

Then work on the arpeggio intervals which encompass one octave. First sing "do-mi-sol-do," then on the same intervals sing, "I won't go now." Since arpeggio intervals are wider, you must always start with the beginning word "I." For instance, you sing, then speak, on the approximate pitch the single word "I." Then you sing and speak, "I won't"; then sing and speak "I won't go"; and finally sing and speak "I won't go now."

When these are mastered to your satisfaction, begin to experiment with some variations. On the pitches, sol-do-sol-mi-do, as set down below, sing then speak, "I won't go with you." Then try the second version, do-mi-sol-do-do. Then experiment with some of your own words and varying melody patterns.

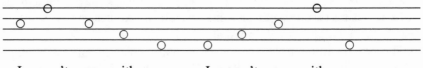

I won't go with you.   I won't go with you.

With the help of a piano, or by pointing out melody patterns with your forefinger, you can try out all sorts of intervals and pitch patterns. Try the techniques on phrases that you use everyday, such as, "Hello, how are you," "Let's get together," or "Why don't you call me." Experiment with pitch intervals and range on lines from a play: "To be, or not to be," "For Brutus is an honorable man," "O Romeo, Romeo, wherefore art thou Romeo?" or "And what's he then that says I play the villain?"

To put all of this in proper perspective, take one line such as, "To be, or not to be," and sing-speak it first in a complete monotone, on just one pitch level. Then sing-speak it in the widest possible range that you can. Then sing-speak it in what would be your interpretation if you were speaking it in a play. This gives you some idea of the two extremes that you don't want, at the same time speaking it in the widest possible range encourages you to do more in your natural reading. Experimenting in this manner with your lines is always helpful.

In fact, you should experiment in this manner with other factors of stress and movement for meaning. Be aware, first of all, of the necessity of making whole notes of your key words, of giving them more duration. Be aware also of sustaining vocal sound through the pauses between phrases; be aware of patterning the words into phrases and phrase groups. Do these kinds of things consciously both in singing and speaking until they become an integral part of your speech patterns. And keep uppermost in your mind that it is the mental pictures and perceptions of intonation patterns that you are trying to develop. Close your eyes if it helps you to see them, remembering always that your voice is your main channel of communication with your audience. Faces can communicate, but not necessarily all the way to the back row, particularly in a large theater. Movements, gestures, and facial expressions communicate a great deal, but don't reach an audience with the certainty that the voice will. That is, of course, if you develop and employ the techniques of projection.

Projection is neither a matter of using full volume, nor forcing the voice, nor insisting on speaking everything downstage. It is a matter of sensing in the mind and body that the voice has the quality and variations of meaningful stress that will carry. And to develop the variations of meaningful stress you must experiment. If a line is not working for you or not projecting, you will not put it right by just repeating it over and over again in the same way. You must jog your self out of your customary pattern of speaking it and experiment. Play with it. Toss the words around, up and down in pitch, slow and fast in rate, loud and soft in volume, and with variations of all these factors. Doing these things with your eyes closed helps you to focus on them. The following exercise will also help you to put it right.

You must constantly work at the visualization of melody patterns in speaking. You must learn to hear with your mind. When a trained musician looks at a musical phrase on a sheet of music he can hear mentally what that phrase will sound like when sung or played. He can hear the pitches and musical intervals, and he can feel the rhythm of long whole notes and shorter quarter and eighth notes. A speaker must develop this same facility. Select any line that comes to your mind or select one from this text, and after reading it silently, try to form a sound picture of what it will be when spoken. See the sound picture as a series of notes on a piece of music. Now write it down on a piece of paper. If you don't know how to designate whole notes for key words and quarter and eighth notes for subordinate words, then simply place the words up and down as if on different pitch levels and underline the key words that will be sustained the longest. Now read it aloud and see how near you can come to your anticipated transcription. If your reading didn't please you, try it again with a different transcription and reading.

This is a device that you should repeat many times until you no longer need to transcribe your sound picture on paper. Practiced often enough, you will soon, like the trained musician, be able to look at written phrases and hear in your mind what they will sound like when spoken. You will be able to both see and hear the pitch changes and the variations of sound duration. And you will also realize the value of this shorter, more direct approach to the problem of melody patterns in speaking. This technique should be applied to your first read-through of a new play.

In the initial read-through, and in the memorizing process, words are usually run together, one after the other. This is especially true when lines are memorized. Lines are run off rapidly, only the first couple of words in each line are stressed and the rest of the words drop off almost to a whisper. There is no attempt to imprint a meaningful pattern of stress, phrasing, or intonation, nor is there any association with breath support. Instead, these mechanical run-throughs are repeated over and over, imprinting the meaningless patterns deeper and deeper until they become so habitual that they are often impossible to overcome. They extend through rehearsal after rehearsal and often into opening night. How much more sense it would make and how much time could be saved for both actor and dialogue coach if the correct sound pictures were imprinted correctly at the very beginning.

The sing-speak technique that extends the range of the speaking voice and reinforces the factors of pitch and duration stress and the visualization technique which employs the sight and sound of mental intonation patterns are both very effective. Their continued use will free the voice, both mentally and physically. That the techniques are somewhat superficial is by design. That we isolate the techniques from inner content is for purposes of focusing on them. When the concentration is on meaning and subtext there is less awareness of vocal movement. So vocal movement must first be discovered from the outside, and then the extended range and intonation patterns must be applied to meaning.

In the following exercises, play with the relationship of meaning and vocal range and patterns. Think of the sounds and words as intellectual and emotional gestures. Begin by becoming quiet and experiencing the life-energy inside your body. Lying flat on your stomach with arms outstretched, experience energy inside and all around you without labeling it. Just feel it. Make no distinctions between the energy of the environment and your own internal energy, and make no distinctions between the combined internal and external energy and your response to it. Take each instant as it comes, and don't anticipate. Experience the rhythm of each full, deep breath as it involves you in total energy.

Now, easily vocalize on each exhaled breath, using sustained nasal sounds and open vowels. Forget the ego, and let your organism take over the direction of the movement. Let the stream of vocal energy flow easily into the upper and lower ranges.

Continue experiencing the energy and movement of sounds and let them bring you to a standing position. Now combine body movement with voice movement in slow, controlled patterns. Voice, body, arms and legs must engage simultaneously in rhythmic extensions of movement. Feel that all of you is making the sound and let that sound flow in the line of least resistance. Extend. Experiment. Discover. Let the voice go where it will. Let it flow easily from the deepest part of you to its outer limits. Experience an exhilarating sense of freedom that comes when you let all the rules and habits of your lifetime fall from you. Imagine that you are poised at the very core of life and can feel its heartbeat. *Live in your voice*. Continue with one of the following.

1. Look up and imagine that you see Death coming toward you from above. React to this event with voice and body movement, responding totally until you resolve the dilemma.

2. Imagine that an Unseen Force is moving over and around you, pushing and buffeting you from all sides. Resist the Force with voice and body movement. Let your feelings and your vocal response to them become a unity, until you resolve your dilemma.

3. Pick up some very strange object from the floor. Be aware that it neither looks nor feels like anything you've ever known. Study it and handle it and let your self react to it with body and voice movement. Be aware that it seems to be getting slowly larger and warmer in your hands. Respond to the increasing size and heat. Now imagine that it moves up your arms, encircles your shoulders and neck, and moves slowly down, encasing the trunk of your body and legs. Resolve the dilemma with body and voice movement.

4. Think of a secret desire or fantasy that is too intimate to tell. This could be an intense love or hate, a career fulfillment or disappointment, a hopeful or doomed feeling about mankind or the world. Let the secret desire be made evident through body movement and the vibratory power of vocal sound. Feel that you must communicate it to someone and let it out, very gradually decreasing the body movement and letting that energy flow into the movement of the voice, until you are standing still and communicating your desire solely with the movement of the voice.

All of these voice and movement experiences are full of emotion and meaning and only one of the four should be used at a time to follow the preparatory experience on the floor. They must be done freely and totally. They are a complete immersion into the meaning and emotion of voice sound and movement. If you think of life as a body of water, then you are not expected to merely move through its shallows. You must feel that you have been seized by the strong currents of the water and pushed into the deepest part. Test your endurance and your ability to be fully alive in your voice.

Or think of your voice as being like a kaleidoscope, in which one quick turn focuses all the little bits and pieces of colored glass into a different pattern; the vocal simile is that with a turn of emotion all the bits and pieces of color in the voice form a different pattern. Develop your vocal imagination and, as you listen to voices around you, think of them in terms of specific colors, or as patterns of color.

The only reason for possessing a wide vocal range is to express meaning and emotion; the only way to fully express meaning and emotion is to possess a wide vocal range. These rather bizarre experiences can help you to free both range and emotional meaning and, what is even more important, they can help you to unify them.

If these experiences are used in group sessions, then the group should be divided into a performing and a listening group. As with any other factor of the speaking voice, individuals learn about range and intonation patterns by listening to others. It is also of value to have short discussions in which performers tell what they experienced and listeners tell what they heard. Both performers and listeners benefit from these exchanges.

Within the framework of a wider vocal range and intonation patterns, of course, attitudes and emotions must be specific. They must be just as intense; and they must also be contained within less exaggerated body movement, much as we did at the end of the fourth experience.

In turn then, and if a group is working together, try the following exercise, although an individual may certainly practice this alone.

The entire group listens to one member who is given a cover line, such as: "I don't want to see you anymore." or "I never met anyone like you." The one cover line is then spoken by the individual with three different attitudes or emotions, such as:

- loving–affectionate–erotic
- frightened–cowardly–terrified
- self-assured–arrogant–insolent
- reserved–unfriendly–hostile
- angry–surly–exasperated

The person speaking, after telling his three choices, must change the order so that the listeners don't know what to expect, and have to, therefore, listen attentively. Each time before speaking, the performer should turn his back on his listeners and turn off all feelings to zero position. He will then assume the body condition for the emotion to be used. To assume the emotion, it helps to imagine oneself as polymorphous, and able to breathe in the emotion through the pores and nerve ends of the skin. This image has the added advantage of connecting the emotion to the breath and the body. After the performer is aware of the subtle inner motions of the feeling, he will turn and speak the line with the first selected meaning, and so forth, for the second and third readings.

The group is then asked to name in which order of meanings the three lines were spoken and to discuss with the performer the differing vocal ranges and patterns he used. This exercise is not easy for either performer or listeners, since the three emotions are of necessity within one general emotional area. However, the benefits are obvious: making emotions specific, distinguishing between closely related emotions, and getting away from using merely a generalized intensity that does not arise from the subtext and leaves meaning unclear.

The beginning part of this sequence of experiential activities is of great benefit in itself. Lying flat on your stomach with arms outstretched enables you to be more keenly aware of deep abdominal breathing and of the vocal vibrations in the body and against the floor. When the body is thus pressed against the floor's surface, you are also much more aware of the movement and intensity of the body's feeling life. All of these movements and feelings can be further experienced and intensified by extending the floor experience.

From the flat-out position on your stomach you can slowly stretch the entire body in a crawling movement across the floor, coordinated with either sustained sounds or lines. It must all be done in slow motion and with no physical strain reflected in the voice. You can include turning on your side or on your back, but it must all be done so slowly that each body movement is coordinated with a voice movement and with time to experience each vocal movement in the body. Here again, be certain to use a wide pitch range and variety of voice pitches in stressing key words. As you stretch open a sound, be aware of the accompanying release of body tension and allow time to experience that released energy in the body and voice, particularly on the key words. Feel the energy and substance of every key word in the body, slowly and luxuriously.

Two important factors are at work here. The first is that the exercise must not be done mindlessly. There must be complete involvement and concentration on the experiencing of the words. And second, the exercise should be immediately followed by a standing performance of the lines, experiencing the words in the same way. If you engage in this whole-heartedly, you will discover new textures in the words and new dimensions in the character who is speaking them.

Doing this exercise or any of the above with the eyes closed helps the focus and the intensity of the experience. Listening with the eyes closed can intensify the experience of the spoken word, whether you are listening to your self or to someone else. There is nothing that gives one so strong a sense of theater from the inside as the sound of invisible voices in action. The disembodied words, projected at an unseen mark and surrounded by an uncanny quiet and the sensations of a simmering expectancy, all combine to make a corporate life that seems to breathe and pulse, and give out a warmth which communicates itself. You have the glowing feeling of belonging to your art. In this euphoric state, suggestions can enter like those of a mesmerist, and that perfection of duality for which actors pray and which they so seldom achieve can fully invest you. You can be aware of both your self and the character you are playing. You will be able to guide your character and govern it by the obverse of other characters in the play. For these reasons, periods of closing the eyes, or complete blackout rehearsals are invaluable in scene and production work.

Quality

Quality is the voice factor resulting from resonance and overtone patterns. It is the factor that makes a voice immediately recognizable on the telephone. However, if you were asked to explain specifically what it was in a voice that was recognizable it would be difficult to explain. In explaining we frequently use such terms as "pleasant," "unpleasant," "weak," "breathy," "nasal," or "harsh." These terms do not really explain the factor of quality, they are merely our impressions of a voice. Voice quality is a difficult factor to explain and it is equally difficult to improve.

We do know that quality is, in part, determined by the inherited structure and surfaces of the resonators and by the overtones which can be produced by the physical make-up of the vocal folds. We also know that quality is determined by the way in which we can adjust the resonators and in the proper use of the vocal folds. Reviewing the sections on phonation and resonation will help to clarify this for you.

We are discussing quality here as it relates to the expression of meaning. Quality of vocal tone is important in communicating both meaning and beauty in the spoken word. It also makes for easy listening.

Differences in vocal quality express different attitudes and emotions. No other factor of voice can so subtly and effectively communicate meaning. It has been stated by experts on the subject that the quality of an individual speaking voice tells listeners how the speaker feels about himself, how he feels about his listeners, and how he feels about what he is saying. This is of prime importance for the actor to know. For a convincing performance, the attitude and emotion expressed by the quality of the voice must support the verbal text, unless, of course, the actor is intentionally saying one thing while meaning another—but this must be made clear as well.

Voice quality is also significant as the source of expressing the beauty of the language. The beauty of language can be completely dimmed by an unpleasant voice quality. A pleasing, dynamic voice quality can focus and delight a listening audience. To achieve voice quality that is pleasing, dynamic, and capable of expressing beauty rework the exercises on relaxing the throat and improving resonance. Increased resonance is necessary for a pleasant voice quality, as well as for power and projection.

The consideration of voice quality suggests another aspect: the opportunity the actor has to use different qualities of voice in his characterizations. While it is usually stated that such qualities as breathy, throaty, nasal, and the like are negative aspects of the purity of vocal tone, these qualities can also be used by the actor to communicate meaning. However, they must be used in moderation, so as not to injure the actor's voice nor make his speech unintelligible.

A slight breathy quality is often used to express anxiety or fear, such as in a character like Birdie in *The Little Foxes,* or to suggest intimacy, such as that between Romeo and Juliet. A slight harsh or throaty quality can be

used for the brutish Caliban in *The Tempest* or for a street character in
some of the modern, more realistic plays. A slight nasal twang can add
believability to rustics such as Corin and Silvius in *As You Like It,* and is,
in fact, an important factor in the dialect of a mountaineer or western
character. The hollow voice quality, without a great deal of nasal resonance can suggest the sepulchral tones of Hamlet's father's ghost or the
sententious character of Polonius. Variations of thin, high falsetto tones
have been successfully used by members of the group of rustics, Quince,
Snug, Bottom, Flute, Snout, and Starveling, in *A Midsummer Night's
Dream.* A slight tremulous or wavering quality can suggest advanced age;
a sharp, mechanical quality can suggest cunning; a full, rich quality can
suggest authority and confidence. It behooves an actor to discover and
employ factors of quality to support a characterization.

Characterizations can also be supported by various speech patterns. For
instance, a clipped precise speech can reinforce the qualities of arro-
gance, meticulousness, or the lack of desire to communicate; a more
liquid, freer type of speech can reinforce the qualities of friendliness,
eagerness, and even sensuality. These factors are all part and parcel of the
actor's tools and are well worth his consideration.

One other factor that occurs with enough frequency to make it worth
mentioning is related to why a character is speaking. In working with actors in the production of a play, it often happens that a director does not
have sufficient time to consult with everyone in a large cast as to the motivations for specific lines or speeches. In these instances, a better understanding of the psychology of speech can be helpful. Knowing some of
the basic reasons why people speak can provide a needed dynamic. For
instance, people speak to communicate a point of view, because they enjoy the act of speaking, or because they are substituting verbal contact for
physical contact, which could mean either a desire to caress someone or
to attack them. People speak as an oral gesture, because it is expected of
them; they speak to disarm hostility, to ease their anxiety, to manipulate
others, or because they cannot tolerate silence or need to assert themselves. A good book on the psychology of speech is well worth studying.

Concentration

Whatever your reasons for speaking, remember that words represent
the evocation of images. Words are not just sounds. "You must imagine
some basis for the words as a justification for saying them," Stanislavski
says, "not for the sake of realism, per se, but because it is necessary for

our own creative natures, our subconscious. For them we must have truth, if only the truth of imagination, in which they can believe, in which they can live" (p. 114). This involves the most important technique of all, that of concentration. No matter how effective the actor's use of interpretive techniques may be, he will not communicate truth unless he is living in the words. He must live through the physical feelings of the words and he must see their images as immediate mental events. The actor must live in the mind, by memory or imagination, the inherent and inseparable pictures that the words contain.

At some point you should rework the sections of this book on imagery, figurative language, and connotative and emotive meaning and apply the concentration of your mind and imagination to the literary passages therein contained, and then apply these faculties to selections of your own. Let the energy and intensity of your concentration brace and sustain the visual vibrations. Let the inner content of the words come to life in your mind.

The creative act of speaking lines involves the total energy of the body, the emotions, the breath, and the mind — but the mind must dominate. The mind must synthesize and synchronize all of the other energies of your performance. A good actor can do this. The mind should also be able to synchronize thoughts with the attention waves of the audience. Only a great actor can do this but the goal is well worth striving for.

Spoken words are the audible expression of thought vibrations, and these are occasioned by the infinite potency of the spirit. Words spoken without this force are so much emotional gibberish. To believe that one can impregnate listeners with them makes about as much sense as to believe that one can impregnate a concrete building by tossing sand at it.

To increase the energy and power of your performance, you must then intensify and concentrate the mind's vibratory rate. The following exercise can help you to do that. It is a yogic exercise that helps you to concentrate the mind by focusing it in the present.

Get a partner and stand about four feet apart, facing each other. Stand quietly and look into each other's eyes, or at the single yogic eye between the eyebrows. There must be absolute silence during this experience with no attempt at communication. The total concentration is on the present moment and in sharing the moment with another person. Clear your mind of everything but experiencing the immediate present with another presence. Concentrate totally on sharing the life of the immediate reality of energy.

Approximately five minutes is adequate for this experience. The benefits are enormous, if the exercise is done properly. Scenes between two people, when preceded by this experience, are astonishingly real and focused.

The mental concentration and imagination of entire groups can be intensified by sitting with closed eyes or in a blackout. It is then decided that the group will visit mentally one specific place, such as a beach, and each in turn will add a word that helps to create the scene in everyone's mind. Such words might be: sand, sea, sun, sky, clouds, bathers, umbrellas, or more abstract concepts such as: warm, happy, bright, colorful, relaxing, satisfying, good. These are done slowly, giving everyone enough time to softly echo and experience the images for themselves.

This experience can also be beneficial in concentrating the mental faculties of an entire cast on a play, as well as evoking the play's mood and atmosphere. For a play like *Othello* such spoken images might include: jealousy, ambition, trickery, blood, motion, levels, snobbery, deceit.

You can improve your individual concentration by employing such a device as counting backward from one hundred to zero, using conversational patterns of phrasing, pausing, and key word stress. You can also intensify your mind's vibratory rate by speaking extemporaneously for one minute without stopping about water, paper, lamps, clouds, cement, stairs, scissors, string, telephones, or some such subject.

Paraphrasing your lines is another way of focusing your mental energies. Rewording the thought and meaning of your lines also makes the thoughts yours and helps you to understand them. With some of the complex passages of Shakespeare this becomes a necessity.

There is another excellent exercise for intensifying mental energy and concentration that must be done with a partner. This is a variation of the "touching" experience recommended by Bernard Gunther in his book *Sense Relaxation*.[10] We recommend using it simultaneously with spoken sounds or words.

A sits in a straight chair with eyes closed and, with light head tones, repeats: *beam-beam-beam, bim-bim-bim, bem-bem-bem, bam-bam-bam, bomb-bomb-bomb, boom-boom-boom,* feeling the vibrations of the sounds in his head. They do not have to be done in that exact sequence. If you feel unusual vibrations on just one or two words, such as *beam* or

---

[10]Bernard Gunther, *Sense Relaxation* (Toronto: Collier-Macmillan Canada, Ltd., 1969).

bam, then stay with them. While *A* is thus engaged, *B* stands behind the chair and, with his finger tips, gently tap *A*'s head — all over.

After a minute or two of the above activity, *A* starts speaking some lines. And *B* stands on one side and places both hands on the upper half of *A*'s head, one hand and fingers curved around the back of the head and the other hand and fingers curved around the forehead, with the bottom edge of the hand just touching the bridge of *A*'s nose. *A* focuses on the mental energy and vibrations of the words, while *B* slowly increases and tightens the pressure of his hands. The maximum pressure should be held for about fifteen seconds, and then *B* should slowly decrease the hand pressure, leaving his hands lightly in place for a long moment after all the pressure is released.

B then drops his hands and relaxes his arms and hands for a moment, then moves once again in back of the chair and applies the head-press to the sides of *A*'s head. In this instance, the hands are placed just above the ears, with the fingers curving over the temples. It's a slow increase of pressure, a fifteen second hold of maximum pressure, and a slow decrease, leaving the hands lightly in place for a long moment before removing them. And all the while, *A* should be experiencing the things going on in his head, the images, sound pictures, sound vibrations, and the increased vibratory rate of the mind. When the exercise is completed, *A* and *B* should exchange places. The entire exercise for both partners should take no more than ten or twelve minutes.

The exercise is especially beneficial if the person doing the tapping and pressing is sensitive and relates to his subject. This, of course, helps his concentration too. And it helps the subject to more vividly experience the content of the words in his mind at the moment of utterance, to more intensely probe the dynamic of his mental responses.

Proper concentration is brought about by involving the mind in each idea, image, and feeling. Proper concentration can be helped by more intensely experiencing these factors. Effective communication can be helped by mentally reliving ideas, images, and feelings at the instant they are expressed.

Rhythm

As with all of the elements of the speaking voice, the interpretive factors and the vibratory rate of the mind are interdependent and interpenetrating and are related to the communication of meaning. They are also related to the more basic and universal factor of rhythm.

Rhythm, in speaking, is characterized by the regular recurrence of stressed and unstressed syllables in alternation, arranged in successive, interconnected metrical units or phrases, and pauses. Rhythm includes the overall rate of speaking, such as fast, moderately fast, or slow. Rhythm is the movement and flow of speech and indicates the ease with which the actor employs the interpretive factors in expressing the meaning. Rhythm is as basic and essential to speaking as it is to music and dancing.

Rhythm is basic to life itself. To live means to experience constant rhythmic changes. We live by the rhythm of the breath, of the heartbeat, of the nerve impulses, and by the peristaltic waves of the alimentary canal. We walk, dance, exercise, and shake hands in rhythm. We think, feel, speak, and eat in rhythm. We experience the external, environmental rhythms of day and night, the seasons, the winds, the tides, and those of atmospheric pressure.

To possess an awareness of this phenomenon is to possess truth. To possess awareness and control of one's own rhythm and a sensitivity to the rhythm of others is to possess power. To possess a sensitivity to the rhythms of nature is to possess expansive life, and the vital elements of spontaneity and creativity. For the actor there is no other way. As Boleslavsky states, "When you command and create your own Rhythm and that of others, it is perfection." To develop a sense of rhythm, Boleslavsky advises the actor to listen to music "where Rhythm is most pronounced," and further that the actor "give himself up freely and entirely to any Rhythm he happens to encounter in life . . . the waves of the sea, woods, field, rivers, the sky above, the city, small towns, your fellow men, absorbing their rhythms with the body, brain and soul . . . being sensitive to every change in the manifestation of their existence."[11]

A keenly developed sense of rhythm is essential for a first-rate actor, not only to clarify his own spoken words and emotional meaning, but also to allow him to fit in smoothly with the rest of the cast and with the director's overall concept. Not every character in the cast will speak in the same rhythm — unless the play is highly stylized. In real life individuals move, act, and speak in varying rhythms, which makes life interesting and certainly makes for a more exciting dramatic texture on the stage.

Individual rhythms, however, must serve to move forward the underlying objectives of the scenes, and each cast member must maintain an

---

[11]Richard Boleslavsky, *Acting: The First Six Lessons* (New York: Theatre Arts Books, 1965).

awareness of these objectives and of the relationship of the individual rhythms of each character, particularly his own, to the overall rhythms of the objectives.

A role in a play is not a solo performance. Being a cast member means being part of a combined effort. It is a situation comparable to being one member of an orchestra, in which all the musical voices combine to produce a total effect. And if every individual contribution blends smoothly into the whole the production will be worthwhile for everyone, certainly for the audience, which is the actor's reason for being.

Every living thing is a manifestation of energy and rhythm, and the performer who would command and hold attention must absorb and concentrate this fact. The ability to capture an audience and sweep them along is accomplished *only* when this awareness undergirds the performance. Appropriate rhythms not only clarify the words of the text that involves the minds of the audience, they also clarify the emotions of the text which involves the feeling and breathing life of the audience. "An all important acquisition for our psycho-technique," says Stanislavski, is to learn that "tempo-rhythm, whether mechanically, intuitively or consciously created, does act on our inner life, on our feelings, on our inner experiences."[12]

Appropriate rhythms also act as a control of emotion. For emotions not only need to be released and used, they also need to be governed. Displays of uncontrolled emotion can completely fog the clarity of the words and the communication of the ideas. Such displays can destroy the rhythm of a scene, can even bring the forward movement of the play to a standstill. For when a performer's emotional energy is chaotically whirling round and round and up and down it moves forward slowly, if at all. A well-developed sense of rhythm uses emotion, but keeps it controlled, and blends it with spoken thoughts into pulsing cadences of expressive meaning.

As with all of the interpretive factors, rhythms must vary to maintain interest. In orchestrating long speeches, the actor must employ variations in rhythm as well as variation of pitch, sound duration, and pauses. The opposite of variety is monotony, as is the case when long speeches or soliloquys are delivered in one rhythm. When this is combined with few variations of volume, pitch, and rate, the long speeches become extremely boring to an audience.

---

[12]Stanislavski, *Building a Character,* p. 237.

The attention span of any audience is limited and needs to be periodically recaptured with provocative variations. An appropriate comparison
would be to the type of musical composition that combines varying rhythmic movements, such as a symphony. Hypothetically, such a composition
might begin with full, sustained chords which command immediate attention; be followed by an *allegro,* which is a quick, lively movement; then
an *andante* movement, which is slow and peaceful, or perhaps a *largo*
movement, which is broad and stately; and the final movement might be a
fast *presto.* All of which makes for interesting variety and provokes attention in listeners. This is exactly what this writer finds missing in most
rock music. Everything is played at one tempo, at one volume (usually
deafeningly loud), and with limited variations of musical figures, and the
whole performance is monotonous and boring. Thought must always be
given to rhythmic variations in structuring parts of a long speech. Long
speeches must be orchestrated like a musical composition.

Rhythm for the actor means finding and using the human experience in
his role. It means knowing where your phrase is heading, much as you do
in playing golf, tennis, or baseball, when you know exactly where you're
aiming the ball. Rhythm has the same swing and focus that will project
your words forward.

To find the human experience in rhythm, study other actors, character
types, all sorts, conditions, and ages of people, and practice imitating
them. Think about the other characters in your play, and imitate their
rhythms. Think about what each of them expects of you and experiment
with these different rhythms. See yourself as a figure of authority, as a
daily worker, as an athlete; as a flyer, explorer, woodsman, farmer, bus
driver, policeman — and practice and feel their rhythms.

Observe the rhythms of different animals and decide which one most
closely approximates the rhythm of the character you're portraying —
which one most closely approximates the rhythms of the other characters
in the play.

Imagine that you are answering several telephone calls at one time and
speak first to your boss, then to a co-worker, then to a parent, to a close
friend, and to a child, and be aware of the different rhythms you use in
speaking to each person. Exaggerate the rhythms to increase your
awareness.

Do something with a marked rhythm and let your lines come through
it, like brushing your hair, pedaling a bicycle, walking briskly, jogging in
place, doing the simple gymnastic exercises in the earlier part of the text,
or clapping your hands.

Deliver one speech with different rhythms, slow, fast, and normal, and see if this doesn't tell you more about your character and about the way he speaks.

Sing songs in different rhythms, a waltz, a fox trot, a polka, and some Latin rhythm like a tango, and then speak your lines in these rhythms. Listen to Edith Sitwell's *Facade* on records, in which every poem is spoken in a different rhythm. And if there is a written script of the poems accompanying the record, as there should be, read along as you listen.

But whatever type of exercises or observations in rhythm that you engage in, let your self feel and absorb them. There are rhythms all around you, inside and out. Feel your pulse, experience your rhythmic breathing. There is rhythm in machinery, a large office, city traffic, a bus terminal, people walking, people either watching or taking part in athletic events. And the next time you go to the theater as a spectator, let part of your attention be involved in experiencing the rhythms of the individual characters, the rhythms of individual scenes, and the overall rhythm of the play.

To be able to understand the factor of rhythm in the life role of speaking, you must expose yourself to it, experience it, and consciously use it.

·8·

SELF-DISCIPLINE:
Warm-Ups and Maintenance

W ARM-UPS JUST PRIOR TO REHEARSALS and performances tend to be very much a series of personal choices. This is particularly true before performances. In the final period before curtain time, when the actor is plagued by the assault of nerves and excited by the stimulus of the theater, he does his "own thing" of last minute muscle-toning and "psyching-up." This is as it should be, and is part of the necessary and intensive preparation for the initial entrance when an actor must be possessed by the life he has created.

The type of warm-up outlined here is meant to be done much earlier, before costuming and making up, and should take the better part of an hour. If at all possible, the actor should find a quiet place to warm up where he can maintain an uninterrupted self-awareness and concentration.

A warm-up should begin with some physical activity to induce deeper breathing and to accelerate the body life. Jogging in place, bouncing up and down like a rubber ball, or imagining that you are a puppet that is being bounced up and down are fine. Another excellent warm-up activity is the shake-out. Stand straight with your arms hanging down. Shake the hands first, then the arms, then the trunk of the body; then drop the head forward and easily shake it. Finish by falling forward from the waist and bouncing the upper part of the body, head, and arms easily from side to side.

You should next stretch-and-yawn. Do this slowly, sensuously, and luxuriously. Stretch-and-yawn in all directions, straight up, bending backward, bending forward, bending to the sides, and bending down over each leg with the feet widely separated. Do this with your eyes closed and so slowly that you experience the release of excess tension with each stretch-and-yawn. Be aware also of your accelerated blood flow, full breathing and increased oxygen intake, and of your body and feeling life. The stretch-and-yawn is energizing, and when performed with total focus puts you in touch with your self.

Now lie on your back with your head elevated slightly and your eyes closed and experience your full, deep breathing. Begin with your knees pointed toward the ceiling so that you straighten your spine and back, and be aware of the breath flowing in and out as the result of the muscle activity in the deepest part of you. Let it just happen to you until you feel that all of you is breathing in and out, and then take over the slow control of the exhalations. Then let your head float you up to a vertical position and sit in a straight chair.

As you sit, let the head float up and out of the shoulder girdle, and the rib cage float up and away from the pelvic girdle. Imagine that you are breathing in and out through every pore of your skin.

Now easily rotate your shoulders, arms hanging down at the sides. Bring the shoulders forward and up, up, and over the top and down the back and around again. After rotating in this direction twice, rotate in the other direction twice, and then let the shoulders hang loosely down.

Now let the head fall forward onto the chest, and let the weight of the head and shoulders pull the trunk of the body down until you are lying on your own thighs. Breathe into the lower back twice, and then put your focus on your spine. Starting with the bottommost vertebra, stack up the vertebrae, one on top of another and let this pull you back into an upright position.

Now let your left ear fall toward your left shoulder and easily stretch the muscles in the right side of your neck. Bring the head back up, and let your right ear fall toward your right shoulder and easily stretch the muscles in the left side of your neck. Bring the head back up, and let it fall forward onto your chest. On full breaths, say [mi-mi]. Bring the head back up, and let it fall backward, and on full breaths, say [a-a]. Bring the head up straight, and on full breaths, say [u-u]. Leave your head floating upward and put it all together, [mi-a-u], like a cat.

With the head still floating upward, relax the muscles in the face and let the jaw drop. Now close your lips over your relaxed jaw and bounce your cheek muscles as you say "blubber-blubber" several times. Very gradually reduce the bounce, and as you do imagine that all the energy from the bounce is moving forward into the lips, and finish with "boo-boo." In all of these vocalizations, let the breath do the work, and experience the energy on the lips and the tip of the tongue.

Now put your focus on the slight tension spots in the hollows of your cheeks, as you keep repeating "boo-boo" a few more times. Then say "buy Bobby a peppy baby puppy" a few times. Remember that this uses only lip consonants, and bounce them out. Then say "The Canadian architect got hit in the head" a few times. Remember that this uses only tongue consonants and make them crisp. Then say "Coco got a cookie in the Congo" a few times. Remember that this exercises the soft palate and make the consonants sharp. Maintain full breath support for all of these exercises.

Sitting tall, with eyes closed, breathing deeply, rub your tummy until it feels nice and warm. Remember this is the center of the breath, the emotions, the sexual energy, the center of the balance — the power center. As you keep rubbing your tummy, feel the warmth spreading up through the body and onto the lips and facial muscles. Now chew an *m,* working it well forward and feel it tone up the facial muscles. Maintain light, soft tones as you hum-chew and use a wide range so that the tones will flow into the head resonators. Now say words like *bim, bam, bomb, boom — moonbeam — mean, mine, moan, moon* on a wide pitch range. Feel your voice flowing out of every pore and bouncing off the walls. Sing or speak any words that you like—a poem, or lines from your play—but give them pitch range and depth. Experience the resonances of the sounds and words in your body, and feel and taste them in your mouth, and on your tongue and lips. Wrap them round with music.

Now sit quietly and experience your inner self. Imagine that you are breathing in energy with each inhalation. Hold each inhalation at its peak, and imagine that all of the inhaled energy is being absorbed into your body, vitalizing every cell. And then breathe out your own energized breath. Do this five or six times or until you feel completely energized and in control.

Now stand and stretch your arms straight above your head and imagine that your fingers are touching the ceiling. Open your eyes for this, but look straight ahead and peripherally see yourself as filling all the space between the floor and ceiling. When this image is vivid for you, drop your arms and maintain this perception of floor-to-ceiling presence. Now stretch your arms straight out at shoulder height and imagine that your fingers are touching the walls. Make one slow turn, looking straight ahead, and peripherally see your self as filling all the space between the walls of the room. After a complete turn, drop your arms and maintain this perception of wall-to-wall presence. Repeat one more floor-to-ceiling stretch, drop your arms and see your self as filling the room, wall to wall, floor to ceiling.

This type of complete warm-up should be done before every rehearsal and before every performance. It would help to maintain the effectiveness of your speaking voice if you did it every day.

Maintenance of optimum conditioning of the speaking voice should be a daily ritual. It is very easy to fall back into bad habits. Left to its own devices, the speaking process will always take the line of least resistance and return to a less dynamic way of performing.

In addition, there should be daily periods of concentrated work on specific factors of the speaking voice. If you know that your breathing is not properly supporting your words, work on breathing. If you know yourself to be a tense person, work on the tension-relaxing exercises. If your throat is tight, work on phonation exercises. If you need resonance balance, work on this. If your articulation needs precision and flexibility, work on these. Work on such specifics as phrasing and pauses, stressing key words, pitch range and intonation. Work on whatever your instructor has told you is deficient. Or, on your own, make a plan to give special attention to a specific factor every day, with this special admonition — that you always conclude by consciously integrating the isolated factor with the whole. It is never a case of how well you breathe, articulate, resonate, or meaningfully interpret in themselves, but how well these factors blend in communicating your words.

An improved speaking voice requires the discipline of daily exercise and constant monitoring. Actors can howl all they want about structured discipline without meaning, but it is impossible to have meaning without structured discipline. Engage in the effort with concentration and enthusiasm, or it makes very little sense. Unearthly joys, like talent, are those that are given to us. Earthly joys, like acting and speaking well, are those we have to work at. Ugly actors and actresses can persuade an audience, with their voices, that they are handsome and beautiful. Old actors and actresses can persuade an audience, with their voices, that they are young. It's all in the mind, the spirit, and the preparation.

Above all remain open to new discoveries. Don't indulge in and be content with the repeated mannerisms and the technical box of tricks. Experiment. To restate the simple direction of Dylan Thomas, "Love the words!" As you speak your lines think of the continuous feel of the fabric in your mouth . . . . of the swift tonal punctuation . . . . of meshing the words and the emotion together like cogs in a wheel . . . . of conveying feeling through understatement and subtlety . . . . of blending the words with the musical pattern. Feel your self respond to the theatricality of individual sounds and sound combinations . . . . maintain affection and respect for the words and for your instrument . . . . let your inner discovery of word images become a work of art which you eagerly share . . . . play with sequences and transitions . . . . find an inner reason for sustaining key words . . . . trust your self to go where the places of meaning are . . . . let the words feed you . . . . sometimes let one word in a phrase do it all and think of syllables as a pathway to get you there . . . . feel your charm flowing through the words.

If you approach language with a probing mind and use it with skill and affection, you can become a speaker of uncommon ability. You can achieve eloquence and variety and be able to express your self in contemporary terms of warmth, flexibility, and humanism.

Index